Critical Issues in Football

Showcasing some of the most important current research in football studies, this book demonstrates the value of social theory and sociology in helping us to better understand the world's favourite sport.

This book sheds critical new light on key issues in contemporary football, with each chapter using a different theoretical lens, drawing on the work of key thinkers from Elias and Foucault to Hall and Maffesoli. It explores issues and topics central to the study of modern football, including homophobia, feminist-informed coaching practice, the racialised experiences of black professional footballers, the concussion crisis and the role of identity in online football communities. It also looks ahead at the issues that are likely to define the research agenda in football studies in years to come.

This is fascinating reading for any student or researcher with an interest in football, the sociology of sport, social theory or social issues in wider society.

Will Roberts is Senior Lecturer in Sport Development and Coaching in Te Huataki Waiora School of Health at the University of Waikato, New Zealand. Will's research interests cohere around pedagogical and socio-cultural aspects of sport, with a focus on the instrumentalism of coaching and youth sport. He is Series Editor for the *Routledge Studies in Constraints-Based Methodologies in Sport* series and continues to work in football in a coaching and consulting role, supporting coaches, professional clubs and national organisations regarding their focus on holistic development of young people in sport. Will tweets from @w_roberts6

Stuart Whigham is Senior Lecturer in Sport, Coaching and Physical Education in the Department of Sport, Health Sciences and Social Work at Oxford Brookes University, UK. His research interests in the sociology and politics of sport focus on national identity, nationalism and sport; the politics of sport and sporting events; the politics of the Commonwealth Games and the sociology and politics of Scottish sport. He has recently acted as Guest Editor for the *Sport in Society* journal for the 'Sport and Nationalism: Theoretical Perspectives' Special Issue. Stuart tweets from @StuartWhigham

Alex Culvin works in player relations at FIFPRO and is Senior Lecturer at Leeds Beckett University, UK. Alex's research interests lie in elite sport, business management, policy, work and gender. She has recently co-edited two books on professional women's sport and professional women's football respectively. Alex currently acts as Chair of the Football Collective, a global network of football scholars, as the knowledge and research exchange lead. Alex completed her PhD in 2019, in the first study to examine professional football as work for women in England. As a former Professional Footballer, Alex had unique access to professional footballers and maintains considerable networks within professional sport. Alex tweets from @alexculvin

Daniel Parnell is Associate Professor in Sport Business at the University of Liverpool Management School, UK. Dan's research interests lie in business management, policy, and social and economic networks in sport. He serves as Co-Editor-in-Chief of the journal *Managing Sport and Leisure* and is Co-Founder of The Football Collective, a global network of football scholars. He is also a Co-Editor of the Routledge book series *Critical Research in Football*. On top of this, Dan maintains extensive links within professional sport clubs, is Head of Football Research at Dundee United Football Club and is CEO of the Association of Sporting Directors. Daniel tweets from @parnell_daniel

Critical Research in Football

Series Editors:
Pete Millward, Liverpool John Moores University, UK
Jamie Cleland, University of Southern Australia
Dan Parnell, University of Liverpool, UK
Stacey Pope, Durham University, UK
Paul Widdop, Manchester Metropolitan University, UK

The *Critical Research in Football* book series was launched in 2017 to showcase the inter- and multi-disciplinary breadth of debate relating to 'football'. The series defines 'football' as broader than association football, with research on rugby, Gaelic and gridiron codes also featured. Including monographs, edited collections, short books and textbooks, books in the series are written and/or edited by leading experts in the field whilst consciously also affording space to emerging voices in the area, and are designed to appeal to students, postgraduate students and scholars who are interested in the range of disciplines in which critical research in football connects. The series is published in association with the *Football Collective*, @FB_Collective.

Available in this series:

Integrated Marketing Communications in Football
Argyro Elisavet Manoli

Football and Risk
Trends and Perspectives
Jan Andre Lee Ludvigsen

Diego Maradona
A Social-Cultural Study
Edited by Pablo Brescia and Mariano Paz

Critical Issues in Football
A Sociological Analysis of the Beautiful Game
Edited by Will Roberts, Stuart Whigham, Alex Culvin and Daniel Parnell

The UEFA European Football Championships
Politics, Media Spectacle and Social Change
Jan Andre Lee Ludvigsen and Renan Petersen-Wagner

https://www.routledge.com/Critical-Research-in-Football/book-series/CFSFC

Critical Issues in Football

A Sociological Analysis of the Beautiful Game

Edited by
Will Roberts, Stuart Whigham,
Alex Culvin and Daniel Parnell

LONDON AND NEW YORK

First published 2023
by Routledge
4 Park Square, Milton Park, Abingdon, Oxon OX14 4RN

and by Routledge
605 Third Avenue, New York, NY 10158

Routledge is an imprint of the Taylor & Francis Group, an informa business

© 2023 selection and editorial matter, Will Roberts, Stuart Whigham, Alex Culvin and Daniel Parnell; individual chapters, the contributors

The right of Will Roberts, Stuart Whigham, Alex Culvin and Daniel Parnell to be identified as the authors of the editorial material, and of the authors for their individual chapters, has been asserted in accordance with sections 77 and 78 of the Copyright, Designs and Patents Act 1988.

All rights reserved. No part of this book may be reprinted or reproduced or utilised in any form or by any electronic, mechanical, or other means, now known or hereafter invented, including photocopying and recording, or in any information storage or retrieval system, without permission in writing from the publishers.

Trademark notice: Product or corporate names may be trademarks or registered trademarks, and are used only for identification and explanation without intent to infringe.

British Library Cataloguing-in-Publication Data
A catalogue record for this book is available from the British Library

Library of Congress Cataloging-in-Publication Data
Names: Roberts, Will (William M.) editor. | Whigham, Stuart, editor. | Culvin, Alex, editor. | Parnell, Daniel, editor.
Title: Critical issues in football : a sociological analysis of the beautiful game / edited by Will Roberts, Stuart Whigham, Alex Culvin and Daniel Parnell.
Description: Abingdon, Oxon ; New York, NY : Routledge, 2023. | Series: Critical research in football | Includes bibliographical references and index. |
Identifiers: LCCN 2022039467 | ISBN 9781032183091 (hardback) | ISBN 9781032183114 (paperback) | ISBN 9781003253990 (ebook)
Subjects: LCSH: Soccer—Social aspects.
Classification: LCC GV943.9.S64 C757 2023 | DDC 76.33—dc23/eng/20220917
LC record available at https://lccn.loc.gov/2022039467

ISBN: 978-1-032-18309-1 (hbk)
ISBN: 978-1-032-18311-4 (pbk)
ISBN: 978-1-003-25399-0 (ebk)

DOI: 10.4324/9781003253990

Typeset in Goudy
by codeMantra

Contents

Preface	xi
Acknowledgements	xiii
List of contributors	xv

Introduction: Examining Critical Issues in Football Through Sociological Theory   1
STUART WHIGHAM, WILL ROBERTS, ALEX CULVIN
AND DANIEL PARNELL

PART I
Established Social Theories and Football   13

1 Tottenham Hotspur, Fan Identity and Figurational Sociology: 'Yid Army'   15
BONITA LUNN

2 How an Ethos of Amateurism Can Support the Integration of an Ecological Approach to Learning and Development in Football Academies: Too Much Too Early?   26
WILL ROBERTS, MARTYN ROTHWELL, HAYDN MORGAN, JAMES
VAUGHAN AND CARL WOODS

3 The McDonaldisation of Football's Formal Coach Education?: Creating the McCoach   38
ANTHONY BUSH AND SHAUN WILLIAMS

viii Contents

PART II
Emerging Social Theories and Football
51

4 Desire, Drive and the Melancholy of English Football: 'It's
(not) Coming Home'
53
JACK BLACK

5 An Alternative Lens for Grassroots Sport: De-schooling Football
66
ANDY PITCHFORD, BEN MORELAND,
DEBBIE SAYERS AND WILL ROBERTS

6 Negotiating Identity Conflict Through Football: Experiences
of People Living with Type 1 Diabetes
81
CHRISTOPHER BRIGHT AND GYŐZŐ MOLNÁR

7 Professional Knowledge Development in Performance
Pathways: A Futsal Case Study Through the Lens of Practice
Architectures
93
SIÔN KITSON, PETE VALLANCE AND SIMON PHELAN

PART III
Social Theories of Gender and Sexuality in Football
109

8 Experiences of Female Football Referees: Using the Lack of
Fit Model to Explore Gender Stereotypes in Football in England
111
LAURA GRUBB, TOM WEBB AND MIKE RAYNER

9 Critical Feminism and Football Pundits: Calm Down... It's
Just a Woman Talking Football
124
ALI BOWES, MOLLY MATTHEWS AND JESS LONG

10 Towards the Application of Feminist-Informed Pedagogical
Principles into Coaching Practice: Personal Narratives and
Implications for Football Coaches
137
ADI ADAMS, ALICE HUNTER AND ELLIE GENNINGS

Contents ix

11 English (Men's) Football, Masculinity and Homophobia:
    From Hegemonic to Inclusive Masculinity   149
    JAY WILLSON AND RORY MAGRATH

PART IV
Social Theories of 'Race' and Ethnicity in Football   163

12 The Racialised Construction of Black Professional
    Footballers in Engl(ish) Football: Love the Game, Hate the Player   165
    JASON ARDAY

13 Black Professional Football Players, Social Capital and Social
    Change: A Case Study of Marcus Rashford's Child Poverty
    Campaign   174
    KEON RICHARDSON

14 'Pogba x Stormzy' and the Politics of Race and
    Representation: An Introduction to Stuart Hall and British
    Cultural Studies   186
    MICHAEL HOBSON

    Index   197

Preface

This book showcases a range of contributions to the sociological study of football drawing upon contrasting theoretical approaches, facilitating a critical appraisal of the utility of sociological theory when applied to the specific topic of football. Furthermore, the collection offers a unique opportunity to showcase emerging scholars within the academic field. It has been a privilege to work alongside so many talented academics to produce a timely contribution to this field of study, with an eclectic range of theoretical approaches adopted within the book.

Each chapter draws upon a specific sociological theorist to explore a different issue or topic within the domain of football, offering an opportunity to critically reflect upon issues of identity, power, inequality, contestation and controversy within the global game. A range of classical and contemporary sociological theorists are used within each chapter, including theorists commonly used with the sociology of sport such as Elias and Foucault, as well as emergent theoretical approaches within the sociology of sport such as Žižek, Lacan and Illich, amongst others.

Acknowledgements

We would like to acknowledge the support, guidance and friendship from a number of colleagues in the academic community of whom many have provided the inspiration and motivation for embarking on this project. In this regard, particular thanks need to go to Jason Arday, Alan Bairner, Jack Black, Morph Bowes, Ant Bush, Michael Hobson, Győző Molnar, Haydn Morgan, Andrew Pitchford and Verity Postlethwaite – it's a pleasure to have contributions from a number of these colleagues and friends within this text.

Thank you to all our families, past and present, for the never-ending support and encouragement. Alan and Graham, we miss you!

To all the academic colleagues that have supported us and the students that have inspired us...this is dedicated to you.

Will, Stuart, Alex and Dan

List of Contributors

Adi Adams is Senior Lecturer in Sport, and former Programme Leader for BSc (Hons) Sport Coaching at Bournemouth University, UK. Adi's teaching, research and professional practice coalesce around the creation of more inclusive, equitable and diverse environments in sport, including a strong commitment to social responsibility and sustaining ethical sport coaching practices. Adi is a UEFA B (Level 3) qualified Association Football Coach with over 15 years' coaching experience, and ten years' experience working in professional football academies.

Jason Arday is Professor of Sociology of Education at the University of Glasgow, School of Education, College of Social Sciences. Previously, Professor Arday was Associate Professor in Sociology at Durham University in the Department of Sociology and the Deputy Executive Dean for People and Culture in the Faculty of Social Science and Health. He is a Visiting Professor at The Ohio State University in the Office of Diversity and Inclusion and an Honorary Professor at Durham University in the Department of Sociology. He holds other Visiting Professorships at Coventry University, London Metropolitan University and Nelson Mandela University. He is a Trustee of the Runnymede Trust, the UK's leading Race Equality Thinktank and the British Sociological Association (BSA). He sits on the Centre for Labour and Social Studies (CLASS) National Advisory Panel and the NHS Race and Health Observatory Academic Reference Group. He is a Fellow of the Royal Society of Arts (RSA).

Jack Black is Senior Lecturer at Sheffield Hallam University, UK and affiliated with the Centre for Culture, Media and Society, where he is Research Lead for the 'Anti-Racism Research Group'. An interdisciplinary Researcher, working within psychoanalysis, media and cultural studies, his current projects include examining the relationship between race/racism and psychosis as well as online hate during international sporting events (*Tackling Online Hate in Football* [AHRC/UKRI]).

Ali Bowes is Senior Lecturer in Sociology of Sport at Nottingham Trent University, UK. Ali is on the editorial boards of *Sociology of Sport Journal* and *Managing Sport and Leisure*, and is on the board of the Football Collective.

xvi Contributors

Christopher Bright is an Honorary Fellow at the University of Worcester and Welsh Futsal International, UK. His work involves exploring the impact of type 1 diabetes within the field of sport and exercise, with a particular interest in combining sport and peer support as a mechanism, to impact on healthcare outcomes for those with chronic health conditions. This has led to the formation of The Diabetes Football Community, a peer support community established in football, but focused on driving engagement with type 1 diabetes, which Chris founded in 2017.

Anthony Bush is Senior Lecturer (Associate Professor) in the Department for Health at the University of Bath, UK. He is a mixed-methods Researcher, and his research is driven by the power of sport to do good (and cause harm) at an individual level or at societal level. His work seeks to challenge taken-for-granted assumptions and utilises a diverse range of methods in order to provide evidence for alternate solutions to problems. He has produced reports for non-departmental public bodies (NDPBs), national governing bodies of sport (NGBs), private companies and professional sports clubs.

Ellie Gennings is Lecturer in Sports Coaching at Bournemouth University, UK. Ellie's research interests take a broad and holistic approach to sports coaching, where she is interested in social and environmental issues. In 2021, she completed a mixed-methods psychology-based PhD. Her research sought to understand adolescent wellbeing from the perspective of children, and develop and validate a psychometric measure of wellbeing, and enabled her to understand the role of the outdoors within physical activity intervention programmes. She is the Lead Collaborator between Bournemouth University and the Andrew Simpson Foundation where she has recently supported the launch of their most recent initiative #boatgen.

Laura Grubb is a PhD Researcher at the University of Portsmouth, UK. Her main research interest is exploring the professionalisation of women's football. She is also interested in researching the experiences of female football referees and the experiences of football coaches from different cultures.

Michael Hobson is Senior Lecturer in Physical Education, Sport and Youth Development in the Department of Psychology and Pedagogic Sciences at St Mary's University, Twickenham, UK. His research interests focus on the sociology of sport and education; social class in PE and sport; social class and higher education; inequalities in education; racial inequalities in PE and sport and sports interventions for young people at risk of becoming involved in the criminal justice system.

Alice Hunter is Lecturer in Sport Coaching at Bournemouth University, UK. Her research focuses on developing coaching pedagogies, and she completed her Doctorate in Sports Coaching at Cardiff Metropolitan in 2021, which focused on the use of phenomenologically informed explicitation style questioning to

Contributors xvii

develop understanding of players' decision-making in team sports. She was the U19 Wales Korfball Coach and is a current Player for the Wales Korfball Team and hopes to use her experiences as a Coach and Player to inform both her research and teaching practice as a Lecturer.

Siôn Kitson works as Talent Partnership Manager at the National Governing Body England Hockey, UK. Siôn has previously worked at Sport England and the Football Association in various coaching and sports development roles. Siôn is an ex-Wales International futsal player and has been coaching futsal for 15 years including leading and assisting senior and youth international teams with both England and Wales.

Jess Long completed her undergraduate sport science degree at Nottingham Trent University, UK, with her research project investigating women football pundits.

Bonita Lunn is a Doctoral Research Student at Oxford Brookes University, UK. Her current work examines antisemitism in British football while looking at effective anti-discrimination programmes that combat hatred in sports. In order to minimise antisemitism in society, and notably in British football, she is now developing an educational programme that may be utilised to inform people about the subject.

Rory Magrath is Associate Professor of Sociology at Solent University, Southampton, UK. His research focuses on declining levels of homophobia, with a particular focus on professional sport.

Molly Matthews works in sport and leisure, having completed a Master of Law in Sports Law and an undergraduate degree in Sport Science and Management at Nottingham Trent University, UK.

Győző Molnár is Professor of Sociology of Sport and Exercise at the University of Worcester, UK. Győző's current research focuses on politics, identity and marginalised populations.

Ben Moreland is Lecturer in Sport Development and Coaching and Doctoral Research Student at Plymouth Marjon University, UK. His research interests centre on the experiences of individuals in sport and particularly non-traditional activities. His current work examines the lived experience of mountain bikers, focusing on the embodied and sensory dimensions.

Haydn Morgan is Senior Lecturer (Associate Professor) in Sport Management in the Department for Health at the University of Bath, UK. His research coheres around the connection between participation in sport and physical activity and the enhancement of social inclusion and wellbeing in marginalised populations.

Simon Phelan is Senior Lecturer in Sport, Coaching and Physical Education at Oxford Brookes University, UK. His research revolves around the employment of ethnographic methodologies to investigate the development of professional coaching knowledge, questioning the role organisational culture plays in shaping learning communities. Beyond this, Simon is an active Coach Developer and Learning and Development Consultant for a number of sports organisations. In this role, he utilises his professional knowledge and current coaching role within England Athletics Youth Talent Programme to support practitioners' continued learning journeys.

Andy Pitchford is Head of the Centre for Education and Teaching Innovation at the University of Westminster, UK. In addition to his work on teaching and pedagogy, Andy has a long association with grass roots sport and The Football Association, which goes back to the early 2000s and his contribution to the team led by Professor Celia Brackenridge, focusing on safeguarding in football. He subsequently led evaluations of academy provision and the FA's Respect programme, and also contributed research to the FA's Youth Review in 2016. He has been active on the boards of community foundations at professional clubs and is currently a Trustee and Coach at his local grass roots club.

Mike Rayner is Associate Head at the University of Portsmouth, UK, with responsibility to provide academic leadership at strategic and operational levels for learning, teaching, assessment and Global Engagement. Mike is a Fellow of The Institute of Leadership and Management (ILM), Fellow of the Chartered Institute for Sports, Management and Physical Activity (CIMSPA), a Senior Fellow of the Higher Education Academy, and an Academic Member of the Chartered Institute of Personnel and Development (CIPD). Mike is also a Reader in the area of Global Sport Management.

Keon Richardson is Sport Development Officer at HR Sports Academy, UK. His research interests in the sociology of sport converge around capital accumulation, sport participation and youth from marginalised backgrounds. He completed his master's degree at the University of Tsukuba, Japan, with his thesis examining the sporting capital development of youth blind football players in Zimbabwe. Keon is also a UEFA B Futsal Licensed Coach and has grown blind football in Southern Africa, introducing the game in Zimbabwe, Zambia, Botswana and South Africa.

Martyn Rothwell is Senior Lecturer and Researcher in the Sport and Human Performance Research Group at Sheffield Hallam University, UK. He conducts field-based research that identifies key constraints on talent development. More recently this has included adopting ethnographic and case study research methods to explore how sociocultural constraints influence athlete development and preparation in applied settings.

Debbie Sayers is a Solicitor with a PhD in Human Rights Law. She is a published author on human rights matters. She founded Salisbury Rovers FC in April 2016. The club takes a player-led, human rights-based approach to football. She

Contributors xix

is a Member of the national Children's Coaching Collaborative, as well as a committee member of the National Children's Football Alliance.

Pete Vallance is Lecturer in Sport and Exercise at Coventry University, UK. His practice focuses on coach development through field-based research. Pete is an ex-England International Futsal Player and High-Performance Coach for the England U19 and U21 Futsal Squads. He is also an experienced Coach Educator and Coach Mentor for the FA. His research interests are in high performance cultures and elite behaviours in sport.

James Vaughan is Head of Football and Coaching Psychology and Research Coordinator at AIK in Stockholm, Sweden. His research views football as an emergent feature of the sociocultural ecology and proposes that sociocultural constraints influence playing style and player's creative development. James is an active Coach, Coach Developer and Researcher in football.

Tom Webb is Senior Lecturer in Sport Management at the University of Portsmouth, UK. He has published widely on the subject of sports officials at both elite and grassroots level. Tom works with officials and sporting organisations from around the world.

Shaun Williams is Senior Lecturer in the Department for Health at the University of Bath, UK. His research spans different pedagogical contexts from grassroots to elite and is indicative of his coaching background. Specific research areas would include critical work around the deployment of digital technologies in sport, applied coaching practice and exploring more collaborative ways to better understand and support coach learning.

Jay Willson holds a master's degree in Sport Development and Management from Solent University, Southampton, UK. He has conducted research on masculinities and sexualities in competitive team sport.

Carl Woods is Senior Research Fellow within the Institute for Health and Sport at Victoria University, Australia. His research interests reside at the intersection of ecological psychology, social anthropology and sport science, where he explores concepts of knowing, skill, learning and education. He has an extensive background in both academia and the industry, having held various positions within multiple Australian Universities and the Australian Football League.

Introduction

Examining Critical Issues in Football Through Sociological Theory

Stuart Whigham, Will Roberts, Alex Culvin and Daniel Parnell

Introduction

This book showcases a range of contributions to the sociological study of football, facilitating a critical appraisal of the utility of sociological theory when applied to the specific topic of football. Furthermore, the collection offers a unique opportunity to showcase emerging scholars within the academic field. It has been a privilege to work alongside so many talented academics and practitioners to produce a timely contribution to this field of study, with an eclectic range of approaches adopted within the book.

Each chapter offers a sociological exploration of a different issue or topic within the domain of football, offering an opportunity to critically reflect upon issues of identity, power, inequality, contestation and controversy within the global game. A range of classical and contemporary sociological theorists are used within each chapter, including theorists commonly used with the sociology of sport, such as Elias and Foucault, as well as emergent theoretical approaches within the sociology of sport such as Žižek, Lacan and Illich, amongst others.

This book is divided into four main sub-sections. The first sub-section entitled **'Established Social Theories and Football'** includes chapters which draw on Elias and Foucault – two of the most frequently cited theorists within the sociology of sport and football – as well as the widely cited work of Ritzer on 'McDonaldisation'. The second sub-section is entitled **'Emerging Social Theories and Football'** and showcases the application of theorists used comparatively rarely within the sociology of sport and football – namely, Lacan, Žižek, Illich and Maffesoli – as well as the concept of 'practice architectures' which draws upon numerous sociological perspectives. The third sub-section entitled **'Social Theories of Gender and Sexuality in Football'** draws together a theme of proposed chapters, with a specific emphasis on sociological theories relating to gender and sexuality, including contrasting schools of feminist thought and masculinity theories. The final sub-section entitled **'Social Theories of 'Race' and Ethnicity in Football'** also follows the themed approach of the previous sub-section, this time pulling together chapters focusing on issues of 'race', racism and ethnicity in football, informed by critical race theory and the theoretical approach of Hall.

DOI: 10.4324/9781003253990-1

2 Stuart Whigham et al.

This structure is therefore designed to provide an opportunity to chart the development of both well-established and innovative sociological analyses in football, whilst simultaneously showcasing some of the sub-disciplinary theoretical approaches in pertinent topics relating to entrenched social inequality in contemporary football such as gender, sexuality and ethnicity.

To this end, our introductory chapter will commence with a necessarily brief discussion of the benefits of sociological analysis for contemporary academic discussion of such issues within football, underlining the rationale for offering both theoretical and empirical analyses of trends, developments and controversies within the 'beautiful game'. The remainder of the editorial is then dedicated to introducing the various chapters which constitute the book, signposting the contrasting approaches and key findings from each contribution.

'Critical Issues in Football: A Sociological Analysis' – Genesis of the Project

The genesis of the idea for this book can be located almost a decade ago, from a module called 'Advanced Social Theory in Sport' at Oxford Brookes University on the BSc (Hons.) Sport, Coaching and Physical Education degree, upon which Will and Stuart taught together. The module content saw students lead seminars in the first four weeks on a chosen social theorist. We then explored those theorists with practical case studies of six or seven weeks, with students then asked to write about those issues using a particular social theorist.

Over time, we started to get essays that were innovative, critical and attacking some of the very urgent issues of the day (race, sexuality, athlete advocacy, governance, identity, fandom). What we noticed was that, given the right platform and a socio-cultural lens with which to view issues, student understanding of modern problems in sport and coaching could be extremely powerful. We also noticed that there were seldom any examples to offer to students other than some of the oft-cited sport scholars in the field.

So, in supporting each subsequent year, we put together a book of past student essays, anonymised but available as an iterative learning opportunity for each new year group. Not only has this generated an interesting and engaging undergraduate experience, but we have also seen emerging scholars go on to publish papers, book chapters and conference proceedings in socio-cultural analyses of sport.

The accessibility of the writing, and the inspiring moments that were created by each new year group, gave us the idea for this book. What if emerging scholars, writing about the problems of the day, using a socio-cultural lens to address those issues, got together and wrote a text that we could use for new students?

The subsequent realisation of this vision requires one final acknowledgement, and that is to The Football Collective, which is where Daniel and Alex come in as former and current Chairs of the Collective.[1] Whilst we were confident that we had a sound idea and could invest time in editing a collected series, what we

Introduction: Examining Critical Issues in Football   3

really wanted to do was create an edited text with four members of The Football Collective, with different areas of expertise in order to offer the best support and network for both emerging and established scholars in their field. Daniel and Alex's enthusiasm for the project and editorial involvement thus represented the final piece of the puzzle.

Therefore, what follows is the development of 14 chapters of scholarly, sociological critique of the 'beautiful game', almost all of which are written and co-produced by members of the Football Collective, students and/or emerging scholars in this field.

'Critical Issues in Football: A Sociological Analysis': An Overview

Without doubt, the toughest task in writing this introduction is attempting to do justice to the excellent scholarship and theoretical breadth evident within the various chapters incorporated within this text. Nonetheless, below follows a brief introduction to each article which signposts the contrasting theoretical approaches adopted by the authors of each article, as well as an explanation of their order of presentation within the issue.

Established Social Theories and Football

The first sub-section commences with Chapter 1 from Bonita Lunn, which draws upon the work of Norbert Elias to offer a figurational sociological account to explore the relationship between sport and religion, with specific reference to Tottenham Hotspur FC and their association with Jewish religious identity. Lunn's chapter commences with a necessarily concise introduction to Eliasian thought, rightly noting the plethora of past academic analyses within the sociology of sport which have been adopted figurational/process sociology as their theoretical influence, before turning her attention to the specific Eliasian concepts used primarily within her own analysis, namely, the 'established-outsiders' concept and the 'personal pronoun model'. Lunn provides a highly useful summary of each concept before highlighting the ways in which past scholars within the field have deployed these concepts to study sociological issues in sport. Attention then turns to the analytical utility of these concepts when applied to the analysis of the relationship between sport and religious identity through a case study of Tottenham Hotspur. For example, Lunn argues that the use of the phrase 'Yid' by both Tottenham fans (as a self-identifier) and their rivals (as an anti-Semitic slur) illustrates both concepts at play, contending that

> while some opposing teams may argue that their antisemitic chanting and use of the term Yid has no anti-Semitic content and is simply footballing 'banter,' their comments and chanting could have a significant impact on members of the Jewish community, making them feel like 'outsiders'.

4 Stuart Whigham et al.

However, Lunn notes that the self-identification of Tottenham fans with the phrase 'Yid' equally plays a role in this process, arguing that fans of the club portray 'a strong sense of group identity by utilising the term Yid in order to show strong group cohesion and solidarity with their fellow Jewish supporters'. To this end, Lunn concludes that Elias' theoretical approach has additional analytical utility for studying the relationship between football and religious identity, given that this specific aspect of Elias' work is relatively under-explored within the sociology of sport to date.

Chapter 2 from Will Roberts, Martyn Rothwell, Haydn Morgan, James Vaughan and Carl Woods draws upon an equally well-established theorist within the sociological study of work, Michel Foucault. The chapter draws upon Foucault's arguments regarding 'disciplinary power' to understand the potentially detrimental impact of (over)professionalisation in football academies, arguing that this process runs the risk of creating a culture of docility amongst players and coaches, alike. The chapter commences with an overview of the impacts of professionalisation within football academics, arguing that an 'increasing number of football organisations encourage, adopt, and foster a surveillance culture to acquire or maintain a competitive advantage over their opponents', this underlining the utility of Foucault's arguments in this regard. In this light, the authors argue that in 'the same way that Foucault suggested that the disciplinary regimes of workplace practices, schools, and social institutions marginalised personal development over power and control of individuals, academy programmes support the same systems of control to develop productive footballers'. Given their concerns about the malignance of this aspect of the culture of elite football academies, the authors dedicate the remainder of their chapter to a robust argument for recapturing elements of the ethos of amateurism in order to re-frame the culture of football academies and the aspirations of young footballers in terms of preparing for either a career in football or – more importantly – the likely scenario that they will pursue a career outside of the domain of football. They conclude that combining an amateur ethos with an ecological approach to the development of young footballers can thus buck the problematic trends of docility and surveillance evident in the status quo of football academy cultures.

The final chapter of the opening sub-section of the book – Chapter 3 by Anthony Bush and Shaun Williams – draws upon George Ritzer's concept of 'McDonaldisation' and its relevance for a sociological analysis of contemporary football coach education. Bush and Williams commence their chapter with a concise overview of the nature of football coach education in English football, highlighting the increasing institutionalised, hierarchical and commercialised nature of the coach accreditation system in England. For Bush and Williams, these developments lead to a number of concerns, contending that

> if the education of football coaching can be seen to be impacted by these McDonaldized structures, there are going to be perceptibly negative impacts on the quality of the formal coach education received by the developing

Introduction: Examining Critical Issues in Football 5

coaches and concomitantly on the quality of the coaching received by participants.

Attention turns to an insightful application of Ritzer's conceptualisation of the McDonaldisation process to the coach education system, illustrating the increasing focus on efficiency, calculability, predictability and control within this system, thus coming at the detriment of the autonomy and creativity of football coaches who navigate this educational system. To this end, Bush and Williams conclude the chapter by positing Ritzer's later work on 'Starbuckisation' as an alternative approach which should be embraced within the coach education system, arguing that this could facilitate a reframing of the 'output' of the system to 'a higher quality rather than quantity, [which] provides an environment where customers are enticed to stay, customer feedback is acted upon, employees are valued and respected, and there is a focus on ethical practice'.

Emerging Social Theories and Football

The second sub-section of the book moves away from the well-established theorists within the sociology of sport outlined above to illustrate the analytical utility of sociological theorists used comparatively rarely within the sociology of sport and football to date. This sub-section of the book is commenced in Chapter 4 with Jack Black's contribution which offers an engaging introduction to the benefits of adopting a psychoanalytic perspective for the sociological study of football, drawing upon a case study of the English men's national football team, the ubiquitous appearance of the phrase 'It's Coming Home' during major international tournaments and the expression of melancholy. Black commences his chapter with a discussion of the prominence of the 1996 song '*Three Lions (Football's Coming Home)*', performed by David Baddiel, Frank Skinner and The Lightning Seeds, from which the 'It's Coming Home' phraseology derived, outlining the symbolism of the phrase in relation to the expression of English national identity both within the context of football and a broader societal and historical context. To this end, Black argues that 'it is the contention of this chapter that the song – and specifically the chant, 'it's coming home' – does not exhibit a nostalgic significance, but, rather, points to the importance of adopting and promoting a melancholic outlook'. Black then draws upon the theoretical concepts of Slavoj Žižek and Jacques Lacan to critically examine the nature of melancholy with the expression of English national identity in football, offering an engaging analysis of this issue which skilfully interweaves theoretical discussion and insightful argument on this phenomenon. As Black concludes, this analysis allows him to move

> beyond common misconceptions that perceive psychoanalytic theory as concerned with unearthing our subjective depths for signs of malignance; as a method of behavioural alteration; or, as a path to recentring the 'ego', what psychoanalytic theory provides is a considered engagement with the

6 Stuart Whigham et al.

fundamental inconsistencies and contradictions that ontologically frame both 'reality' and the 'subject'.

The second chapter of this sub-section, Chapter 5 by Andrew Pitchford, Ben Moreland, Debbie Sayers and Will Roberts, draws upon the work of anarchist writer and philosopher Ivan Illich to offer an insightful argument on the potential benefits of 'de-schooling' in the domain of grass-roots football. The chapter commences with a concise summary of the central arguments of Illich's work, outlining his emphasis on the dehumanising nature of contemporary society and education, highlighting Illich's position that 'modern societies, particularly those in the capitalist form, have a series of dehumanising tendencies that make us, in various ways, lonely, alienated, unwell and disconnected from our fundamental capacities and purposes'. Attention then turns to the problematic impact of the formal education and schooling systems in contemporary society for young people, outlining Illich's critical stance on the malfeasant culture which he believes is symptomatic of modern education. For the authors, grass-roots football offers a potential example of what Illich would describe as a 'de-schooled' institution which can act as a bulwark against the impact of formal educational systems and 'enable and empower young people' and 'create convivial settings that foster creativity and association'. To this end, the authors draw upon a case study of Salisbury Rovers FC as an exemplar of how grass-roots football can resist the broader trends of contemporary society and its formal education systems, reinforcing the potential emancipatory and progressive power of football as a force for societal good.

Chapter 6 by Christopher Bright and Győző Molnár draws upon an alternative emergent sociological theorist within their analysis of empirical data on footballers with Type 1 diabetes, making use of Maffesoli's theoretical work on 'neo-tribes' to underpin their contribution to the book. As Bright and Molnár highlight, the concept of the 'neo-tribes' can 'offer an explanation of the sub-cultures which exist within our communities… [t]hey are said to demonstrate gatherings without organizational rigidity, whose members share a similar state of mind, that can be expressed through lifestyles or ritualistic behaviour', thus underlining the potential for using Maffesoli's work to overcome simplistic models of disability identity in their analysis of the lived experiences of footballers with Type 1 diabetes. The chapter provides a concise and insightful overview of comparative applications of Maffesoli's concepts in other studies of identity and culture in the context of sport before providing an in-depth reflection on original empirical data collated through the authors' 'netnographic' methodological approach focusing upon this specific population. The results demonstrate that the existence of a 'neo-tribe' for footballers with Type 1 diabetes allows its members to negotiate the social stigmas associated with disability in contemporary society, this reformulating more positive representations of identity and disability within football. To this end, Bright and Molnár conclude that this 'embodiment of a Neo-Tribe, utilising football, to positively link participants to their condition is one which future research and

Introduction: Examining Critical Issues in Football 7

healthcare professionals should consider when enhancing future treatment pathways for those living with chronic illness'.

The final chapter of this sub-section of the book – Chapter 7 from Siôn Kitson, Pete Vallance and Simon Phelan – outlines the potential utility of Mahon and colleagues' notion of 'practice architectures' to facilitate a sociologically informed account of professional knowledge development in futsal coaching. The chapter commences which a concise explanation of the concept of 'practice architectures', highlighting that this concept is a politicised practice theory, reflective of the work of Bourdieu, Giddens and Foucault, in its exploration of everyday interactions, using Reckwitz's argument that practices are situated, social and relational and that human behaviour is shaped by the historical and cultural conditions of a moment, time or location. These arguments are applied through an extended case study of the English U21 Futsal Performance Programme, wherein two of the authors (Kitson and Vallance) played an active role in implementation of applying the principles of 'practice architectures' through their coaching practice. This facilitates a reflection on the sociological tenets of 'practice architectures' in shaping the sub-culture within the Performance Programme, with discussion focusing on the 'cultural-discursive space', the 'material-economic space' and the 'social-political space' evident within this Programme.

Social Theories of Gender and Sexuality in Football

The third sub-section moves away from the eclectic range of theorists and topics towards a more focused emphasis on sociological theories relating to gender and sexuality within the context of football. Chapter 8 – the first chapter in this sub-section – from Laura Grubb and Tom Webb focuses on the experiences of female football referees through their use of Heilman's 'lack of fit' model. Grubb and Webb commence their chapter with a summary of the ongoing gendered inequities within contemporary football, highlighting the role of gender stereotypes in underpinning the experiences of discrimination and gender inequality experiences by female footballers, coaches and referees. Heilman's 'lack of fit' model is then concisely outlined to illustrate its potential utility for identifying strategies for challenging gender stereotypes within football. In particular, the model is argued to have two particular intervention strategies in relation to this problem, with the potential for 'firstly decreasing the lack of fit perceptions and secondly breaking the link between the expectations of incompetence that arise from lack of fit perceptions and the gender bias in evaluating performance it creates'. Drawing upon interviews with 12 female referees operating in English football, Grubb and Webb apply the 'lack of fit' model to identify a number of strategies for tackling experiences of discrimination for female referees, including enhanced education and training for male colleagues, enhancing female referee development and support networks, and modernisation of the Referees' Association to make a more inclusive environment for female referees. These findings thus illustrate the potential practical benefits of applying sociological theory within analyses of gender inequality in contemporary football.

In Chapter 9, attention turns to the experiences of female football 'pundits' in the contribution from Ali Bowes, Molly Matthews and Jess Long, with 'critical feminist' sociological theory used to drive their theoretical reflections on this issue. Bowes, Matthews and Long provide a comprehensive account of the increasing visibility of females within media coverage of football in recent decades, as female pundits have been able to challenge the dominance of males within this industry. However, as outlined by the authors, the successes of female pundits in redressing the ongoing inequality in this field have simultaneously 'pundits have provoked debates about the legitimacy of their involvement - discussions rooted in sexist discourse'. The chapter therefore offers a dual-pronged account of the ongoing issues faced for females in the football media through, firstly, an analysis of social media reactions to female football pundits and, secondly, a critique of the media's representation of female pundits, drawing upon critical feminist theory within this account. As Bowes et al. contend,

> [c]ritical feminist perspectives... begin with the assumption that society is organised in a patriarchal way, where gender is socially constructed and culturally defined to serve the needs and interests of powerful groups of society (in this way, men, and specifically white, middle-class men).

Their analysis thus sheds light on the double-edged sword of the increasing visibility of female pundits, highlighting that the opportunities for females in the media to push back against and reframe gendered stereotypes of their capabilities are simultaneously undermined by the continued perpetuation of sexism, misogyny and power imbalances within this domain.

The penultimate chapter of this sub-section, Chapter 10 from Adi Adams, Alice Hunter and Ellie Gennings, focuses its attention on the relevance of feminist theory for informing pedagogical practice in coaching practice, illustrating the importance of feminism as a form of praxis for ensuring that sociological theory is informing applied practice. Drawing upon reflective narratives from each author which capture their respective experiences coaching in football, the authors coax out various issues which hamper the achievement of gender equality within this traditionally masculinised domain. In particular, the chapter draws upon Connell's work on hegemonic masculinity to problematise the current status quo within football, contending that 'recent research in these masculinity-saturated spaces demonstrate that football coaches influence, and are influenced by, complexities of practice imbued with dominant masculine values and common beliefs, transmitting both explicit and "hidden" ideas about "acceptable masculine practice"'. To this end, the authors skilfully map out a number of practical suggestions for adopting a 'feminist-informed coaching pedagogy' to address problems within the world of football coaching, offering eight feminist-informed coaching

Introduction: Examining Critical Issues in Football 9

principles which can be used by coaches who are seeking practical meaning and workable strategies for tackling gender inequality in this domain.

In the final chapter of this sub-section, Chapter 11, the focus switches away from the female to the male experience in relation to gendered identities in football, with Jay Willson and Rory Magrath's work focusing upon the shifting nature of masculinities in contemporary football. Willson and Magrath draw upon Eric Anderson's 'inclusive masculinity' theory to argue that an inclusive form of masculinity has become the pre-dominant approach for conceptualising contemporary masculinities, thus challenging traditional theorisations such as Connell's work on 'hegemonic masculinity'. To this end, the chapter charts the shifting historical context with regard to the prevalent forms of masculinity within society and football as a microcosm of society, illustrating how attitudes towards sexual minorities and marginalised gender identities have gradually improved through time. Willson and Magrath therefore outline the contrasting theoretical stances of 'hegemonic masculinity theory' and 'inclusive masculinity theory' in terms of their respective utility for understanding these chronological developments, outlining the relative strengths and limitations of each approach. Whilst acknowledging that the culture of contemporary football still possesses significant issues in terms of achieving a truly inclusive culture in this regard, they conclude that Anderson's 'inclusive masculinity theory' has 'become a more dominant theory to underpin the changing nature of the game... [a]s homophobia continues to decline in Western society, and research continues to document positive attitudes in English football... IMT's dominant position is likely to remain'.

Social Theories of 'Race' and Ethnicity in Football

The final sub-section replicates the themed approach of the previous sub-section, this time pulling together chapters focusing upon issues of 'race', racism and ethnicity in football. The sub-section commences in Chapter 12 with Jason Arday's thought-provoking analysis of the racialised constructions of Black professional footballers in Britain and the media's role in sustaining enduring racialised ascriptions. Arday focuses his chapter on a reflection on the disgraceful racist abuse experienced by England players Marcus Rashford, Jadon Sancho and Bukayo Saka following their missed penalties in the final of the UEFA Euros 2020 versus Italy. Drawing upon a range of concepts and theoretical positions informed by critical race theory, Arday illustrates that this example acts as a case in point for demonstrating the dehumanisation and objectification of black British footballers within contemporary professional football. As Arday argues,

> this positions people of colour as a 'deviation' from that norm; an actress becomes a Black actress, a footballer becomes a Black footballer, and so on... [in] the context of racism it is often animalistic, not just mechanistic, dehumanisation that occurs.

10 Stuart Whigham et al.

Arday thus frames contemporary football as the 'new plantation' which is 'characterised by White-dominated leadership (i.e., club owners, football managers), and Black-dominated playing teams', providing an engaging and critical analysis of the ongoing manifestation of racism and racial inequality within contemporary English football.

Chapter 13 from Keon Richardson offers an extended application of the work of Robert Putnam on the concept of 'social capital' in an analysis of Manchester United and England footballer Marcus Rashford's campaign on childhood food poverty. Richardson commences his chapter with a useful articulation of Putnam's specific conceptualisation of 'social capital', illustrating the ways in which Putnam's work builds upon the work of Pierre Bourdieu by adding a further articulation of the importance of 'bonding' social capital and 'bridging' social capital. These particular forms of capital are illustrated by drawing upon his case study of Rashford's social activism on the topic of childhood food poverty, identifying Rashford's partnership with the charity 'FareShare' as an exemplar of 'bonding' social capital, before drawing upon Rashford's use of social media as a form of 'bridging' social capital. For Richardson, Rashford's success in his campaign lay in his ability to utilise both forms of social capital to effectively pressurise the British government to act on the matter to avoid a political embarrassment given the high-profile nature of the campaign. However, notwithstanding these successes, Richardson also concludes with a cautionary note about the 'dark side' of social capital for Rashford and other sporting activists, insightfully arguing that

> the 'dark side' of Rashford's bridging and linking capital efforts included the racist abuse he received from missing the aforementioned penalty in the Euro 2020 final, which suggests a rather performative relationship he has with the 'weak ties' he developed... his ability to bridge and link social capital could be temporary and at its peak while his physical capital as a professional footballer is deemed useful.

The final chapter of the sub-section – and the main body of the edited collection – witnesses an engaging application of the work of Stuart Hall in Chapter 12, authored by Michael Hobson. Hobson draws upon Hall's theoretical concepts to offer an extensive account of the representation of the 2016 transfer of Paul Pogba from Juventus to Manchester United for a world-record fee (at the time) of £89m. In particular, Hobson analyses the official announcement of Pogba's transfer which took the form of a viral social media video entitled 'Pogba x Stormzy' featuring Pogba and British grime artist 'Stormzy', using Hall's theories to illustrate the ways in which this event illustrated representations of Black youth culture, 'commodified Blackness', and the racial politics of football. Hobson commences his chapter with an overview of Hall's arguments in relation to decoding media representations and his work on the media and racism, providing a concise explanation of Hall's arguments as a sub-section of his overall theoretical canon. In particular, Hobson argues that Hall's arguments about the important of 'conjectural analysis' mean the 'Pogba x Stormzy' video 'needs to be read as product of this specific political and cultural moment, within the context of football, anti-racist activism, grime music, and politics more broadly'. Drawing upon Hall's work on conjectural analysis, hegemony, signs, semiotics, representation and discourse, Hobson skilfully articulates the nuanced ways in which the presentation of Pogba's transfer illustrates the hidden meanings and power imbalances in relation to race in contemporary football, providing a fitting conclusion to this sub-section of the book.

Conclusion

Drawing upon an eclectic range of theoretical approaches to the sociological study of the 'beautiful game', this edited collection showcases the theoretical diversity of contemporary scholarship on football. This theoretical diversity is evidenced in the range of conceptual and empirical approaches offered within each chapter, applied to a range of contrasting case studies to provide grounded analysis of contemporary football. Given this empirical and theoretical emphasis, coupled with the ongoing academic interest in the nature of the hegemonic position of football within the global context of the sports industry, this book acts as a timely reminder of the ongoing importance of theoretically informed analysis of the nexus between sociological theory and football. Whilst we acknowledge the relatively UK-centric nature of this text, it is clear that the ideas and cases discussed have merit for consideration in other cultures and parts of the globe where football is enjoyed – perhaps this will encourage other emerging scholars to commit their ideas to paper, just as our work with students encouraged us to assemble this. Indeed, this text does not serve to provide an all-encompassing answer and text but a starting point and foundation for others to build upon. We sincerely hope that this collection of chapters can act as a catalyst and inspiration for future sociological analyses of football, encouraging similar high-quality, theoretically informed accounts of the 'beautiful game'.

Note

1 Over 450 scholars form the Football Collective, offering critical debate in the study of Football https://football-collective.co.uk/

Part I

Established Social Theories and Football

Chapter 1

Tottenham Hotspur, Fan Identity and Figurational Sociology

'Yid Army'

Bonita Lunn

Introduction

Tottenham Hotspur Football Club, also known as Spurs, has been perceived to be a 'Jewish Club' for many years. This perceived identity has resulted from a range of factors; the most likely causes include the demographics of the fans, the religious identities of current and previous shareholders and the nickname that the fans identify with, 'Yid', which is a Jewish ethnonym (Poulton & Durell, 2016). As a result of this, it is evident that they have been targeted for antisemitic hate by opposing fans. This current issue of antisemitism at British football matches has sparked thoughts and discussion regarding what makes a club 'Jewish' or even religious and what bridges a football club to a certain religion.

This chapter will utilise a figurational sociological approach, pioneered by the work of Norbert Elias, as a theoretical framework to explore the relationship between sport and religion. Elias has been considered one of the greatest sociologists of the 20th century (Dunning & Mennell, 2003), whose work builds upon the work of Marx, Weber and Durkheim (O'Connor, Ashton & Smith, 2015). A figurational approach has been utilised to cover a wide range of subjects, including violence, ageing and death, art, gender, racism and, most importantly for this discussion, sport and leisure (Dunning & Mennell, 2003). Giulianotti (2004, p. 145) states how the figurational approach has 'acquired a very "established" position' within the field of sport sociology and leisure studies. In addition, his work has been utilised by a range of scholars including Maguire and Tuck (1998), Liston and Moreland (2009), and Liston and Maguire (2020) to explore identity, subsequently making it ideal for examining Spurs and their publicised 'Jewish' identity.

Figurational sociology has been derived from the concept of 'figurations', defined by Elias as 'generic concept for the pattern which interdependent human beings, as groups or as individuals, form with each other' (1987, p. 85). According to Elias (1978), groups/individuals are linked by 'chains of interdependence', through which they influence one another in both evident and indirect ways; in addition, these networks of interdependencies can be known to influence others not directly connected to them. This concept will be useful when examining the community of Spurs and their Jewish identity, given that this perceived identity

DOI: 10.4324/9781003253990-3

16   Bonita Lunn

has emerged as a result of 'chains of interdependence', in which some fans have adopted the religion and specific aspects (the use of Yid) due to the club's history and the demographics of other fans. It may be argued, however, according to Elias (1978), that this happened both directly and indirectly, which will be explored in greater depth within the later part of this chapter.

There are several components and key tenets embedded within the theory, with the 'most important sociological legacy' being his 1939 work 'The Civilising Process' (Giulianotti, 2004, p. 149). This work explored how individuals became more civilised (despite moments of decivilisation), through the shifting and changing of behaviour and psychological qualities of the people in the West, discussing examples of violence, manners and etiquette, including table manners and aggression. A variety of researchers, including Dunning (1992) and Maguire (2006), have employed the civilising process in which to examine the subject of sport. Maguire's (2006) work used the civilisation process to talk about folk games and how they have evolved into the sports we play now. This work has aided our knowledge of modern sport and the process of modern civilisation. Elsewhere, Dunning (1992) explored football hooliganism using the civilisation process to demonstrate, through football hooliganism, the potential for violence in today's more 'civilised' sports. Scholars have worked in the field of sport to apply an Eliasian viewpoint to the study of sport, with the civilisation process being the most commonly adopted owing to its prevalence and popularity in other academic fields.

Nevertheless, this chapter will focus on two key concepts, the 'established-outsiders' concept and the 'personal pronoun model'. Firstly, the 'established-outsiders' concept explores the figurations of interdependent groups and the shifting power relations between these groups (Mennell, 1994; Velija, 2012) and proves useful when examining the relationship between positive and negative community identities (Moore, 2010). Secondly, the 'personal pronoun model' examines how people are interrelated to one another in order to identify an individual's identity within a larger web of interconnected identities through the use of language (Moore, 2010). Within academia, the 'established and outsiders' concept has been addressed amongst a range of scholars in the field to investigate discrimination and migration (Loyal, 2011) and gender inequality (Liston, 2011; Velija, 2012). Despite the fact that there appears to be no prior literature using this model to investigate race or religion, the personal pronoun model has been used to investigate other identity factors including sexuality (Moore, 2010) and nationality (Moore, 2010; Leonardi, 2011). Thus, prior to the discussion of Spurs and their connection to the Jewish religion, some time will be dedicated to exploring previous literature using these two notions.

Elias' 'Established-Outsiders' Concept and Sport

The 'established-outsiders' notion explored how societies are split into two contrasting groups, the 'established' and 'outsiders' (Elias & Scotson, 1965). The more dominating group is the 'established' group, which has strong internal cohesiveness, social networks and a common background. Those who were the subordinates were called the 'outsiders', on the other hand, and are new and unfamiliar with one another, as well as having limited social networks, marginalised positions within society and lacking what is known as a 'we-identity' (Elias & Scotson, 1965). It became a source of worry to Elias and Scotson (1965) that members of dominant and strong groups saw themselves as superior to members of other interdependent groups, while outsiders were regarded as weaker and inferior.

Due to the evolving and dynamic nature of figurations, both the established and outsiders change status by contesting or becoming a part of the existing community (Elias & Scotson, 1965). The major concern, however, was how these group dynamics developed. In Elias and Scotson's (ibid) seminal work, the established group was composed of families who had lived on a housing estate for several generations, while the outsiders were comparatively newcomers. The established had formed a common identity, a set of rules and a hierarchical structure. Material and economic disparities, as well as social status and family history, are among the factors that contribute to these social figurations and the cohesion of these group interactions (Elias & Scotson, 1965; May, 2004). According to Elias (2008, p. 213), this model is a powerful tool in which to analyse issues regarding power, exclusion and inequality and with which academics 'can better come to grips with the similarities and differences of other cases'. Prejudice and culture, according to Elias and Scotson (1965), are insufficient explanations for power imbalances, which Petintseva (2015) criticises Elias and Scotson for, for additionally, failing to account for gender, ethnicity and colonial relations, all of which they believe could have a substantial impact. Petintseva (2015) states how the established-outsiders concept can also be used to talk about marginalisation and discriminatory behaviours, most specifically, when it comes to race, religion and ethnicity. Therefore, rather than using the 'established-outsiders' concept to explore neighbouring communities and the power between them, the main aim will regard exclusion and discrimination based upon religion in sport.

Maguire (2000), Black (2016) and Malcolm and Velija (2008) are amongst scholars who have used this notion to explore the field of sport. Maguire (2000) argues that 'Western' civilisations have used sport and other cultural practices to display status and superior social position in relation to the rest of the world. Westernised sporting taste and costumes subsequently became established and permeated throughout non-Westernised societies. This emphasises how within sport Western cultures have evolved into the equivalent of an established group through time, making those non-Westerns the 'outsiders' (Maguire, 2000). In addition, Black (2016) explored newspaper representations of athlete Mo Farah whilst drawing on this concept, alongside race. In terms of race, racist discourse construction entails the separation of established and outsider groups, with the former considering themselves superior to the latter (Kassimeris & Jackson, 2015). However, what Black (2016) explored was that the British press may mislead 'outsiders' groups and individuals. This study looked at how Mo Farah's 'outsider'

18 Bonita Lunn

position was handled and incorporated into the 'established' by the British press. It highlights how outsider individuals, including Farah, have become more accepted as an 'ethnic minority athlete' due to their sporting successes. Finally, through an Eliasian lens, Malcolm and Velija (2008) stated that female cricketers are considered the outsiders. Throughout the history of cricket, men have dominated the field and what Malcolm sees as 'oldness' has meant that they have greater cohesiveness than the 'outsiders' (Dunning, 1999). Nevertheless, as time develops and female cricketers become more 'mature', a more cohesive identity will be fostered (Malcolm & Velija, 2008). In addition, Malcolm and Velija (2008, p. 232) state that 'a shift towards equality is unlikely to occur until a more coherent 'we group' identity is formed by female cricketers'.

'Established-Outsiders', Religious Discrimination and Tottenham Hotspur

May (2004) discusses how 'established groups' practices of exclusion are particularly troubling. In addition to this, Petintseva (2015) states how the established-outsiders concept can be used to talk about marginalisation and discriminatory behaviours. Firstly, we can explore this notion by looking at Judaism within the United Kingdom. The UK has been considered a 'Christian country', with many individuals belonging to the faith; nevertheless, in more recent years, there has also been a rise in atheism. Therefore, when applying this notion, some may argue that Christianity and atheism are recognised as the 'established'. When Western European and Northern Jews migrated in the early 20th century, they were recognised as the newcomers and therefore considered as the outsiders. Using Elias' 'established and outsiders' notion, we can see that at Spurs the Jewish population, who in some contexts are regarded a minority by some and thus 'outsiders', have been absorbed into a group where they are deemed established members of a group with strong group cohesiveness regardless of religious affiliation. In the context of female cricket, Malcolm and Velija (2008) previously described how, over time, a more unified identity would be created, and therefore, they will become part of an 'established' group. When looking at Spurs, it is clear that this Jewish identity has been part of the club's overall character, which has been transferred to fans regardless of their religious background.

Next, this may be applied to this case study with the word 'Yid' in mind. The usage of the term Yid, which has sparked significant debate among football fans, the Jewish community and scholars (Poulton & Durell, 2016), has been investigated using an Eliasian approach. The term Yid, which was originally used by Ashkenazi Jews as a term of familiarity but was later exploited by Hitler and the Nazis as a derogatory name to attack the Jewish community, is a term used among the antisemitic abuse received by Spurs fans (Poulton, 2016). Firstly, we can acknowledge that when used by the Nazi regime, this term was used to diminish and belittle the Jewish community, subsequently making them thought of as 'outsiders'. When we discuss it in the context of contemporary football, while some opposing teams may argue that their antisemitic chanting and use of the term Yid has no antisemitic content and is simply footballing 'banter', their comments and chanting could have a significant impact on members of the Jewish community, making them feel like 'outsiders'.

Nonetheless, even though the name is frequently used in a pejorative manner toward the club, Spurs fans also utilise it to deflect attacks and unite with their club's Jewish members, according to a prior study by Poulton and Durell (2016). By integrating and supporting the attacked community, the phrase is used to deflect the attacks, reinforcing the Spurs' strong feeling of oneness. According to Elias and Scotson (1965), established groups are those that have evolved a shared identity. With this in mind, we can see how the term Yid, which is utilised by supporters as a form of 'identification', has strengthened their group's cohesiveness. The 'established' group, according to Elias and Scotson (1965), has high levels of cohesion, which is reflected within this case study, just by exploring the use of the term Yid.

Elias' 'Personal Pronoun' Model and Sport

According to Elias (1978), individuals are linked by 'chains of interdependence', via which they influence one another in both obvious and indirect ways; with this in mind, the above application of the 'established-outsiders' concept has reinforced that Spurs supporters have formed a Jewish identity in both obvious and subtle ways. Ethnic minorities are frequently excluded, but as Black (2016) discovered with Mo Farah, 'outsiders' may become part of the established 'us'. The Spurs case study demonstrates how certain outsiders might be discursively handled as members of the established, 'us'. The use of this pronoun can therefore be examined through the use of the 'personal pronoun' model, whereby language can be used as a method for illustrating how power dynamics between insiders and outsiders can make human interdependence and interconnectivity evident within groups (Nielsen & Thing, 2019). This argument is captured in Elias and Scotson (1965):

> ...how and why human beings perceive one another as belonging to the same group and include one another within the group boundaries which they establish when saying 'we' in their reciprocal communications, while at the same time excluding other human beings whom they perceive as belonging to another group and to whom they collectively refer as 'they'.
>
> (p.22)

This illustrates how the 'established-outsiders' concept is closely connected to the 'personal pronoun' model, as personal pronouns can also be used to investigate how group identities, such as 'we', relate to others and outsiders, such as 'they' (Crow & Laidlaw, 2019). This can have a powerful effect in generating feelings of inclusion and exclusion which enables people to recognise who are 'the established' and who are 'the outsiders' (Poulton, 2001).

The 'personal pronoun model' examines language and how people are interrelated to one another in order to identify an individual's identity within a larger web of interconnected identities (Moore, 2010). Individuals employ pronouns such as 'I', 'you', 'he', 'she', 'they' and 'us' to express social statuses and are thus utilised in social contexts (Moore, 2010). They enable us to express the interconnection of social life and, more significantly, they aid in the recognition of an individual's interdependencies and connections within communities (Smith, 2001). When a person speaks when the statement is about themselves, the pronoun 'I' is usually employed. The pronouns 'we' and 'us', on the other hand, denote a bond between individuals, emphasising a sense of belonging (Elias, 1969). Elias's (1991) work found that some individuals will prioritise their 'we-identity' over their 'I-identity', as a collective identity and group status can be deemed superior. It is important to note that subsequently the 'we-image' could overshadow a person's image as an individual, which is the reason why communities endure as vital components in people's lives. As individuals, we develop our own identities as well as our group identities, so it is important to note that personal pronouns can and do change (Moore, 2010); they are in 'constant flux and transformation, within interweaving processes of change occurring over different but interlocking time-frames' (Quilley & Loyal, 2004, p. 5).

In comparison to the 'established-outsiders' concept, the personal pronoun model has been used less frequently in the field of sport and leisure but has been used by scholars including Maguire and Tuck (1998) to address national identity and Nielsen and Thing (2019) to discuss students' experiences in physical education (PE) classes. Nielsen and Thing (2019) used the model to analyse students' personal experiences in PE classes. By applying this concept, they were able to examine the 'I', 'we' and 'they' identities in relation to PE classroom cultures in order to understand young people's interconnectedness within PE. They found that existing tensions and power dynamics were made apparent, demonstrating how individual relationships are both limiting and facilitating. Similarly, Maguire and Tuck (1998) believe that sport is a significant arena for the construction, maintenance and challenging of identities as well as a method of bringing individuals and local communities throughout the world together. When they looked at nationality in sport, they utilised the personal pronoun model to talk about how people saw themselves in different groups. When discussing national identity, they describe how rugby union offers one of the key sources of 'I/we' identity, where citizens regard rugby as more than simply a game. As a result of the game, individuals' we-identities might get stronger. In addition, Tuck (2003) used the concept in another study of national identity in sport, stating that people may become the embodiment of the nation by using pronouns in athletic settings, enhancing our understanding of what is known as 'national identity politics'. When established groups are faced by intruders, he claims that 'we-identity' and national habitus become stronger, cleaner and tighter.

'Personal Pronouns': Tottenham Hotspur's 'We-Identity'

A 'we-identity' has been argued to strengthen group dynamics (Elias & Scotson, 1965). This notion can be applied to the use of the term 'Yid' by Spurs fans, with the idea that the club has a strong sense of group identity by utilising the term Yid in order to show strong group cohesion and solidarity with their fellow Jewish supporters. Poulton and Durell's (2016) study looked at comments made by Spurs fans on the use of the name Yid on online fan forums. Questions such as 'how long have "we" used the term Yiddo as reference to Spurs fans?' and 'should and will "we" eventually be banned from chanting it?' were raised. Individuals used the phrase 'we' to explicitly emphasise that the term gives the club with a significant degree of team unity, as seen by some of the forum discussions and this conversation surrounding the term. Similarly, the pronoun 'we' continues to be used to express a strong feeling of belongingness in songs and chants related to the use of the name Yid, sung by Spurs supporters: 'We're Tottenham Hotspur! We'll sing what we want!', followed by their chant of 'Yid Army!' (Poulton & Durell, 2016, p. 16).

As discussed previously, Elias (1991) found that individuals may prioritise their 'we-identity' over their 'I-identity' as a collective identity and group status can be deemed superior. When exploring football fandom and religion, it is recognised how the collective pride in a sports team is deep-rooted. In addition to this, it can also be established that those who belong to a religious group also value their collective identity. It is also known that an individual's 'we-identity' can overshadow their individual identity. Elias (1991) noted that religious groupings tend to tilt more towards their 'we-identity'; likewise, in the case of football fandom, a person's fan identity can overshadow their individual image. One of the numerous parallels between sport and religion is the notion of having a strong 'we-image' as a fan or religious individual. Percy and Taylor (1997) emphasise the similarities between sport and religion, stating that for some individuals and groups, football functions as a faith and, in some ways, is a metaphor for religion:

> Football is like a religion to its devotees. It binds and divides, shapes, and delimits, providing a critical identity for a given group and individuals. The scarf, the ground, the songs and the ritual activity have a sacred quality about them; football is at least like a secular religion here.
>
> (p. 39)

Likewise, Wann, Melznick, Russell and Pease (2001, p. 198) said that 'similarities between sport fandom and organized religion are striking'. Individuals can be recognised by traits connected with their social grouping. 'We' and 'I' images are concepts that can shape an individual's and/or collective identity. Individuals may differentiate across groups using these 'we-images' (Rosenthal, 2016) and can be developed within these groups (Roseneil & Seymour, 1999). Despite being two different concepts, on closer examination sport and religion have similar 'we-images', making it possible to find similarities between the two. Sporting supporters wear merchandise with their favourite team's crest on it, and they are instantly connected with the club. Similarly, members of religious organisations wear garments, such as hijabs for Muslims and kippahs for Jews, and are therefore linked

22 Bonita Lunn

with their chosen faith. It is also acknowledged that fans and people of faith are dedicated to attending frequent gatherings in religious structures or sports stadiums, which for some are both seen as opulent temples (Wann et al., 2001). Words such as 'worship', 'dedication', 'sacrifice', 'commitment' and 'suffering' are used similarly by religious followers and sports fans (Wann et al., 2001). These 'we-images' reinforce the idea that although sport and religion are categorised as two separate entities, there are many structural similarities which make their resemblance difficult to ignore (Barber, 2009).

Conclusion

As highlighted within this chapter, there is relatively little study or writing in the field of sport that applies these two Eliasian notions of the 'established-outsiders' and 'personal pronoun' models to the relationship and interconnectedness of sport and religion. Sport fandom, like religion, is time-consuming, life-changing and revitalising and offers a social network for many (Murphy, Sheard & Waddington, 2000). Football fandom has been defined by Davis (2015, p. 423) as a form of leisure, whereby 'a person can pursue activities to gain feelings of joyfulness and belonging'. The football club that the fan belongs to becomes a fundamental part of the supporter's individual and social identity (Kossakowski, 2015; Maussier, 2017). Sport fandom provides a setting for developing identities; some identities are shared with others and some highlight differences and diversity (Malcolm & Mansfield, 2013). These concepts were thus deployed to investigate sport and religious identity in the case of Spurs and their Jewish associations to further examine this from an Eliasian theoretical stance. This chapter was motivated by a study on antisemitism in football, which is an area of research that demands further attention. However, this provoked debate, particularly as to whether Tottenham Hotspur is a Jewish club and, if so, what qualifies a club as having a religious identity.

According to Elias (1978), groups and people are linked by 'chains of interdependence', in which they exert influence on one another in both evident and indirect ways. The chain can be extended, and ties can be strained, tying groups and individuals together in unexpected ways, with unpredictable and undesirable effects. Figurations can have significant influence and impact upon others, including those not directly connected to them. This has been recognised through sport as many football fans transfer both their political and religious identities onto their teams, which has caused and still does cause issues at matches (Cronin, 2000). By exploring Tottenham Hotspur and their connection with Judaism, it can be recognised that in some ways directly but mainly indirectly, fans have become associated with the Jewish religion. Research found that fans identified with the Jewish religion not as a result of their religious upbringing but through supporting Spurs. Through football, Spurs fans have begun to share their identities with the club's perceived identity, alongside the religious identities of their fellow supporters. This reinforces Elias's beliefs that individuals are linked together by these 'chains of interdependence' or 'figurations', thus underlining the utility of this theoretical approach.

References

Barber, N. 2009. Is sport a religion? *Psychology Today*. Available at: https://www.psychologytoday.com/gb/blog/the-human-beast/200911/is-sport-religion

Black, J. 2016. As British as fish and chips': British newspaper representations of Mo Farah during the 2012 London Olympic Games. *Media, Culture & Society*, 38(7), 979–996.

Cronin, M. 2010. Playing away from home: Identity in Northern Ireland and the experience of Derry City Football Club. *National Identities*, 2(1), 65–79.

Crow, G., and Laidlaw, M. 2019. Norbert Elias's extended theory or community: From established/outsider relations to the gendered we-I balance. *The Sociological Review*, 67(3), 568–584.

Davis, L. 2015. Football fandom and authenticity: A critical discussion of historical and contemporary perspectives. *Soccer & Society*, 16(2–3), 422–436.

Dunning, E. 1992. 'Culture', 'civilization' and the sociology of sport. *Innovation: The European Journal of Social Science Research*, 5(4), 7–18.

Dunning, E. 1999. *Sport Matters: Sociological Studies of Sport, Violence, and Civilisation*. London: Routledge.

Dunning, E., and Mennell, S. 2003. *Norbert Elias*. London: Sage.

Elias, N. 1969. *The Court Society*. New York: Pantheon.

Elias, N. 1978. *What Is Sociology?* New York: Columbia University Press.

Elias, N. 1987. *Involvement and Detachment*. Oxford: Blackwell.

Elias, N. 1991. *The Society of Individuals*. Oxford: Basil Blackwell.

Elias, N. 2008. Further aspects of established-outsider relations: The Maycomb model. *The Established and the Outsiders, Collected Works*, Vol. 4, Dublin: UCD Press, 209–231.

Elias, N., and Scotson, J. L. 1965. *The Established and the Outsiders*. London: Sage.

Giulianotti, R. 2004. Civilizing games: Norbert Elias and the sociology of sport. In: R. Giulianotti, ed. *Sport and Modern Social Theorists*. London: Palgrave Macmillan, 145–160.

Kassimeris, G., and Jackson, L. 2015. The ideology and discourse of the English Defence League: 'Not racist, not violent, just no longer silent'. *The British Journal of Politics and International Relations*, 17(1), 171–188.

Kossakowski, R. 2015. Where are the hooligans? Dimensions of football fandom in Poland. *International Review for the Sociology of Sport*, 52(6), 693–711.

Leonardi, L. 2011. Changes in the We-I Balance and the formation of a European identity in the light of Norbert Elias's theories. *Cambio. Rivista sulle Trasformazioni Sociali*, 1(2), 168–175.

Liston, K. 2011. Sport and leisure. *Sociological Review*, 59(1), 160–180.

Liston, K., and Moreland, E. 2009. Hockey and habitus: Sport and national identity in Northern Ireland. *New Hibernia Review*, 13(4), 127–140.

Liston, K., and Maguire, J. 2020. The 'Great Game' and sport: Identity, contestation and Irish–British relations in the Olympic movement. *Journal of War & Culture Studies*, 15(1), 1–21.

Loyal, S., 2011. A land of a hundred thousand welcomes? Understanding established and outsiders relations in Ireland. *The Sociological Review*, 59, 181–201.

Maguire, J. 2000. Sport and globalization. In: J. Coakley and E. Dunning, eds. *Handbook of Sports Studies*. London: Sage, 356–369.

Maguire, J. 2006. Sport and globalization: Key issues, phases, and trends. In: A. Raney and J. Bryant, eds. *Handbook of Sports and Media*. Mahwah, NJ: Lawrence Erlbaum, 435–446.

Maguire, J. A., and Tuck, J. 1998. Global sports and patriot games: Rugby union and national identity in a united sporting kingdom since 1945. *Immigrants & Minorities*, 17, 103–126.

Malcolm, D., and Mansfield, L. 2013. The quest for exciting knowledge: Developments in figurational sociological research on sport and leisure. *Politica y Sociedad*, 50(2), 397–419.

Malcolm, D., and Velija, P. 2008. Females incursions into cricket's "male preserve". Tribal play: Subcultural journeys through sport. *Research in the Sociology of Sport*, 4, 217–234.

Maussier, B. 2017. The new ethical dimension of sports events: A reflection on the evolution from the ancient Greek Olympic sports festival to postmodern sports events. *Cultura, Ciencia y Deporte*, 12(34), 15–25.

May, D. M. 2004. The interplay of three established-outsider figurations in a deprived inner-city neighbourhood. *Urban Studies*, 41(11), 2159–2179.

Mennell, S. 1994. The formation of we-images: A process theory. In: C. Calhoun, ed. *Social Theory and the Politics of Identity*. Oxford: Routledge, 175–197.

Moore, A. 2010. 'I' and 'We' identities: An Eliasian perspective on Lesbian and Gay identities. *Sociological Research Online*, 15(4), 47–54.

Murphy, P., Sheard, K., and Waddington, I. 2000. Figurational sociology and its application to sport. In: J. Coakley and E. Dunning, eds. *Handbook of Sport Studies*. London: SAGE Publication, 92–105.

Nielsen, S. F., and Thing, L. F. 2019. Who is zooming who'? A study of young PE-students in their figurations. *Sport, Education and Society*, 24(5), 480–490.

O'Connor, H., Ashton, D., and Smith, D. R. 2015. Norbert Elias and social theory. *British Journal of Sociology of Education*, 36(3), 474–486.

Percy, M., and Taylor, R. 1997. Something for the weekend, sir? Leisure, Extasy and identity in football and contemporary religion. *Leisure Studies*, 16(1), 37–49.

Petintseva, O. 2015. Approaching new migration through Elias 'established' and 'outsiders' lens. *Human Figurations*, 4(3), 1–26.

Poulton, E. 2016. Towards understanding antisemitism and the contested uses and meanings of 'Yid' in English football. *Ethical and Racial Studies*, 39(11), 1981–2001.

Poulton, E., and Durell, O. 2016. Uses and meanings of 'Yid' in English football fandom: A case study of Tottenham Hotspur Football Club. *International Review for the Sociology of Sport*, 51(6), 1–20.

Poulton, E. K. 2001. *Media Construction and Representation of National Identities during the 1996 European Football Championships*. PhD Thesis, Loughborough University, UK.

Quilley, S., and Loyal, S. 2003. Towards a central theory: The scope and relevance of the sociology of Norbert Elias. In: S. Loyal and S. Quilley, eds. *The Sociology of Norbert Elias*. Cambridge: Cambridge University Press, 1–22.

Roseneil, S., and Seymour, J. 1999. *Practising Identities: Power and Resistance*. Hampshire: Palgrave MacMillan.

Rosenthal, G., 2016. *Established and Outsiders at the Same Time-Self-Images and We-Images of Palestinians in the West Bank and in Israel*. Universitätsverlag Göttingen.

Smith, D. 2001. *Nobert Elias & Modern Social Theory*. London: SAGE Publications.

Tuck, J. 2003. The men in white: Reflections on rugby union, the media and Englishness. *International Review for the Sociology of Sport*, 38(2), 177–199.

Velija, P. 2012. Nice girls don't play cricket: The theory of established and outsider relations and perceptions of sexuality and class amongst female cricketers. *Sport in Society*, 15(1), 28–43.

Wann, D. L., Melznick, M. J., Russell, G. W., and Pease, D. G. 2001. *Sport Fans: The Psychology and Social Impact of Spectators*. New York: Routledge.

Chapter 2

How an Ethos of Amateurism Can Support the Integration of an Ecological Approach to Learning and Development in Football Academies

Too Much Too Early?

Will Roberts, Martyn Rothwell, Haydn Morgan, James Vaughan and Carl Woods

Introduction

The pursuit of elite sporting success has been a common objective for governments across the globe and is reflected in much elite sport governance and policy design (Green, 2009). Uppermost in the policy discourse surrounding elite athlete development are two key principles: firstly, the implementation of a sophisticated and early identification system of sporting talent, and secondly, the institutionalisation of the development of elite sporting talent in highly professionalised specialist training centres (Houlihan, 2005). Accordingly, the notion of the professionalised 'sports academy' has become prevalent as the optimal method for developing elite sport performers. Typically, the focus of this approach is to indoctrinate young people into specialised ways of performing, with systematic talent development often commencing in childhood. Indeed, the current sporting landscape is focused towards early specialisation, with competitive structures for youth sport, extended training and playing seasons and funding incentives (among other factors) precluding engagement with healthy and diverse sport experiences (Abernethy, 2008). Consequently, the prevailing narrative for these young people encourages the single-minded pursuit of elite sport success, at the expense of other life aspirations and the health and wellbeing of future generations (Roetert et al., 2018).

In this chapter, we suggest that the over, or early, professionalisation of soccer academies is a threat to positive youth development practices (Vierimaa et al., 2018). In challenging the professionalisation of children's development, we argue that an *ethos of amateurism* should be the cornerstone of the sports academy, which can have merit in enabling the attainment of outcomes related to both performance preparation and personal development (e.g., Rothwell et al., 2022a). In professional work settings, the notion of amateurism is

DOI: 10.4324/9781003253990-4

How an Ethos of Amateurism Can Support the Integration   27

oft ridiculed by so called 'professionals', typically considered as being *experts* and *specialists* who perform to a set of prior established rules in order to achieve clear goals and targets (Woods et al., 2022). An amateur,[1] on the other hand, chooses to take part in a pastime for the sheer love of it, motivated by the simple joy of personal involvement, and is not concerned by goals or targets (Ingold, 2021). Within the context of a professionalised and highly disciplined football academy, we suggest that fostering an environment built on an *ethos of amateurism* can support an ecological approach to learning and development to better support the performance preparation of talented footballers (Renshaw et al., 2022).

Here, we present a theoretical argument that challenges professionalism, situating an *ethos of amateurism* at the forefront of performance preparation. In this sense, learning and development for performance are related to enrichment which concerns the 'perceptual, cognitive, psychological, emotional, and physical subsystems' that support the growth of young children's holistic capacities to strengthen their relationship with performance contexts (Ribeiro et al., 2021, p. 1116/1117). In presenting this argument, we draw on Ludwig Wittgenstein's (1953) concept of a *form of life* (e.g., behaviours, skills, capacities, attitudes, values, beliefs, practices and customs that shape how we live) and the relationship between learning and development possibilities in a football player's ecological niche (i.e., an academy setting) (Vaughan et al., 2021). In adopting an ecological approach, we suggest that specific forms of life in football that are entrenched in professionalisation can limit players' capacity to respond to the rich action possibilities available in their ecological niche. Denison et al.'s (2017) interpretation of Foucault's analysis of *disciplinary power* will be central to this argument, helping us make sense of what it means for football players to be normalised and rendered docile under specific regimes. Therefore, the specific aims of this chapter are to (i) explain what the issues are with professionalised approaches aimed at developing highly skilled footballers and (ii) provide a contemporary ecological account of how performance preparation and personal development based on an *ethos of amateurism* can co-exist in football academies to facilitate the development of healthy and skilful footballers.

Challenging Professionalism and Disciplined Practices in the Football Academy

An increasing number of football organisations encourage, adopt, and foster a surveillance culture to acquire or maintain a competitive advantage over their opponents. Fuelled by the pervasiveness of neoliberal governance structures (Silk & Andrews, 2011), the elite sport environment has become replete with disciplined practices that utilise extensive (predominantly quantitative) datasets to measure, monitor and predict performance outcomes (Williams & Manley, 2016). Within the development of young athletes, similar practices have become equally visible, where the measurement of such outcomes plays a key role within many 'academy' structures. However, there have been increasing calls for elite sport organisations to be attentive to their 'duty of care' of young athletes (see Cronin & Armour, 2018), particularly considering several high-profile examples of athletes who have experienced issues of burnout, compromised well-being and motivation, and mental health concerns. Further, the elite nature of professional sport has often seen promising athletes transitioning out of their sport careers at a relatively early age because of injury or deselection, with some left isolated and on the 'scrap heap'.

While the negative physical and mental well-being effects of overzealous developmental experiences have been well documented (e.g., Sothern & O'Gorman, 2021), another concern is how disciplined practices influence players' ability to skilfully respond to opportunities for action in competition. Drawing on a Foucauldian-inspired account of athlete development practices, Denison et al. (2017, p. 774) have suggested that the very nature of these normalised approaches serves as a form of power to make athletes more 'useful and productive'. Although coaches approach the challenge of developing football players with the best intentions, basing practice on a highly detailed and specific tactical and technical curriculum to create behaviours that align to a club's playing philosophy is problematic. In the same way that Foucault (1977) suggested that the disciplinary regimes of workplace practices, schools and social institutions marginalised personal development over power and control of individuals, academy programmes support the same systems of control to develop productive footballers. Evident in the wealth of recent academic work that has provided insight into the processes required to attain a competitive advantage in elite sport (e.g., Emery et al., 2005; Jones, 2019).

Another theme typically noted within 'professional academies' is the increased utilisation and acceptance of technology as a vital component in the training of (young) athletes (Starkes, 2008). Technology is an irrefutable element of modern football, where coaches provide players with video 'clips' of their performance to explore various tenets of their physical, psychological, technical and tactical performance. Whilst technological advancement has enabled coaches and performance directors to pinpoint where specific sport performance improvements can be made, a growing body of literature has noted how the introduction of technology creates an environment of surveillance (Woods et al., 2021a), where power can be exerted through such technology to discipline, normalise, judge and control athletic development (Manley et al., 2016).

Invoking the scholarship of Foucault (1977), such work has noted how the adoption of disciplined practices and modern technology (and the associated discourse that this technology generates) has shaped a culture of 'compliant athletes' (Lang, 2010). Further, such compliance leads to young athletes appearing to voluntarily surrender to the training regimens apparent within academies, whereby this docility may lead to individuals who are 'subjected, used, transformed, and improved' (Foucault, 1977, p.136). When used in concert with opportunities for social comparison, deploying normalised practices and technology to exert disciplinary power has the potential to create an environment that is highly regulated

How an Ethos of Amateurism Can Support the Integration   29

and exclusionary and concerned with classification, individualisation, totalisation and normalisation (Lang, 2010). While improving performance is core to football academy operations, the modern academy needs to be mindful of 'producing' footballers who fit a specific system or way of playing because as Denison and Avner (2011) have discussed in sport, this systematised development approach can serve to render athletes as compliant 'docile bodies'. Clearly, those involved in the development of young athletes have a responsibility to consider and understand how the environment that they create is likely to impact on the longer-term development (both performance and personal) of players.

To further unpack Denison's notion of docile athletes, Rothwell et al. (2022b) explored an alternative perspective on docility producing effects through the theoretical tenets of James Gibson's (1979) ecological psychology. Gibson's (1979) theory of *affordances* provides a suitable framework to understand an athlete's perception and action in sport. From this perspective, behaviours emerge from the continuous interactions in the athlete–environment system. Here, perception is of affordances, and action is the realisation of an affordance that emerges under the multitude of constraints that are placed on an athlete from moment to moment (Araújo et al., 2019). The contextual nature of affordances means that possibilities for action offered to players are always embedded in the relationship between deeply rooted socio-cultural-historical factors at the centre of a form of life and the specific athlete development practices in an econiche. From a Gibsonian perspective, docile athletes could be considered those who experience disciplined sociocultural practices that are 'manifest in the normative behaviours and customs' (Rietveld & Kiverstein, 2014, pp. 328, 329) of football academies, leaving them unresponsive to certain affordances. Vaughan et al.'s (2022) ethnography of the Stockholm-based AIK football club also illustrated these ideas – revealing how social and cultural constraints, deep in Stockholm's fabric, influenced the skill development and psychological wellbeing of young football players. More specifically, expressions of self-protection, manifest in aggression and controlling behaviours, were valued and termed 'balls over talent' (Vaughan et al., 2022, p. 13). What this led to is players, and teams, becoming responsive to a narrow range of affordances characterised as exhibiting *unskilled intentionality*. In the example of AIK, this meant that players were unresponsive to a wide landscape of affordances and were simultaneously docile and compliant to those specific to their curated form of life (e.g., being aggressive). It is this intertwined relationship between a form of life captured in an ecological niche which serves as a significant reference point for understanding how these practices can continually shape an athlete's intentional engagement with opportunities for highly skilled behaviour (Araújo et al., 2019).

An *Ethos of Amateurism* to Support an Ecological Approach to Player Development

Recently, Woods et al. (2022) presented an interesting perspective on the pitfalls associated with professionalism in the academy. These authors suggested that early career academics are often at risk of falling into strict 'disciplinary boundaries', working toward the establishment of pre-determined benchmarks that specify what it means to be 'productive' within the modern, neoliberal university. In this approach, the professional academic is oft-prevented from exploring the spaces in-between disciplinary boundaries, instead of being lulled into what the authors refer to as 'playing the academic game' – that is, confirming what it means 'to be' a *professional*. To us, this approach is synonymous with the developing academy footballer, who, like the professionalised academic, is trying to tick the necessary boxes to obtain the next contract or promotion. In these settings, the focus largely remains on the acquisition and retention of specific skills, and the reproduction of football knowledge to satisfy personal development plans that aim to produce a first team footballer. Consequently, these knowledge acquisition approaches decontextualise learning, treating skills as commodities that can be bought and sold on.

To alleviate these pressures within the modern university, Woods et al. (2022) proposed that early career academics could be encouraged to preserve their love of inquiry by embracing what they referred to as an *ethos of amateurism*. By this, the authors meant replacing the desire to 'play the academic game' with a genuine joy of inquiry – following their interests, not the conventions that specify what it means 'to be' (Woods et al., 2022, p. 4/5). Here, we follow these propositions, suggesting that an *ethos of amateurism* can provide an alternative view of how football academies can support young children's motivations to stay involved with sport, while developing the physical and mental capacities to excel at football. Shifting the focus from highly professionalised learning environments that focus on knowledge acquisition can have clear benefits to player development and personal motivation by supporting ongoing participation in contexts that consist of value (opportunities for action) and meaning (information). To help guide the integration of an *ethos of amateurism*, Rothwell et al. (2022a) proposed three characteristics, modified from Masschelein and Simons (2013), that National Football Associations and football academies could situate at their core. Here, we explain how these characteristics combine with an ecological view of learning to support player development.

Characteristic 1: An Amateur's Inquiry Is Not Bound by Disciplined Conventions or Paradigms, But by Their Love of 'It'

Adopting an *ethos of amateurism* can help coaches and players eschew conforming to pre-determined approaches to player learning and development that promote the idea of football knowledge and skills as something you must acquire to move to the next level (e.g., Bennett et al., 2018). This means that players are not hamstrung to reproduce specific talent development practices or methods but are encouraged to enjoy the experience, explore different skills without fear of criticism and collaborate with peers and coaches to design

How an Ethos of Amateurism Can Support the Integration   31

practice tasks. This approach can also reframe the idea of knowledge as situated, which is therefore an activity to be experienced in contextualised settings grown through interactions within the athlete–environment system (Barab & Duffy, 2000).

Characteristic 2: An Amateur Is Not as Concerned with Conforming to Desired Competencies or Professional Benchmarks

Research indicates that diversity of sporting experiences (i.e., playing a variety of sports) provides a stronger foundation for performance than specialising in one sport and that 'play activities' should be prioritised over more structured practice activities (Coutinho et al., 2016). This is an approach to engaging in sport that is considered to support intrinsic motivation and skill acquisition (Headrick et al., 2015). In practice, this position might be challenging considering the pressures on young children to specialise in one sport from an early age. However, if young children do specialise in one sport, coaches can provide practice opportunities that reject the rehearsal of specialised skills by fostering opportunities in which children continuously search and explore dynamic practice settings in their own unique way, through richly varied practice tasks. Through exploration, players can become selectively open to the perception of relevant affordances to guide skilled performance (Fajen, 2009). Thus, in such practice ecologies, players are encouraged to explore beyond conventionally established ways of being and doing in search for novel and highly adaptable solutions to a variety of movement problems.

Characteristic 3: An Amateur Does Not Work to 'Produce' and Is Not 'Demand Driven'

Designing player development environments that shift the focus from performance outcomes to developmental opportunities that support children's intrinsic motivation can have long-term performance and well-being benefits. This means that player development practices should focus on what motivates young children to start playing sport in the first place, such as feeling competent, having fun, experiencing enjoyment, learning new skills and social interaction (Bailey et al., 2013). However, many football academies do not align to or support children's motivations for playing and remaining in sport, rather focusing on repetitive and highly specialised practices that aim to control and regulate behaviour with the aim of satisfying competencies and benchmarks (for an example, see Premier League, 2011). In an ecological view of talent development, alleviating pressures such as accountability and performativity and focusing on individuals' intrinsic motivation can contribute towards strengthening the athlete–environment relationship.

32 Will Roberts et al.

Adopting an *Ethos of Amateurism* to Move Players from Docile to Dynamic: A Short Case Exemplar of AIK Football Club

In this final section, we provide a short case exemplar to highlight how a football academy can adopt an *ethos of amateurism* to support the development of more adaptable, dynamic and skilful footballers. Data are provided from an ethnographic study carried out by the fourth author. First, we describe the form of life that fosters professionalised approaches to the players' development, serving as a form of control across all levels of the football club. Exemplified by academy staff displaying a desire to be perceived as professional (organised and efficient) in the eyes of peers, parents and senior club staff. An emphasis on prestige, status and saving face (looking good in the eyes of others) was evident across the club and broader sociocultural context. Professionalism led to a fixation with box ticking, conforming to administrative procedures, and ensuring practice looked organised and was mistake-free. The quest for perfect practice conditions normally meant that coaches adopted controlling behaviours; consequently, a lack of player autonomy and a disregard for learning were evident across the academy. Second, we discuss how an *ethos of amateurism* can facilitate an ecological approach to the development of skilful footballers.

Professionalisation as a Form of Control

The desire to *control everything* was evident throughout all levels of performance at Allmänna Idrottsklubben (AIK). At the club, different system levels interacted with each other (i.e., first team and junior teams) and served to influence a specific form of life that could be categorised as controlling. A fans perspective profoundly highlights the issue of a controlling form of life, where comments on social media indicated a specific approach to performance:

> *The problem is that XXXX apparently tries to control the matches, keeping back the players offensive will...*
>
> *The primary thing about XXXX's football is about control. Not to let the game float away. Not to let our players have their own freedoms. Everything should be rigid and structured. As I see it, it's just the diametrical opposite of what AIK needs, to take the next step in its development...*

Academy coaches also felt that control was a common issue within AIK. At Forum Karlberg (coach education evenings) senior team coaching staff presented to partner clubs and academy coaches to provide insights into what happens in a first team environment. Reflecting on the presentation, a conversation between frustrated coaches went like this:

Coach 1: *We got a lecture in organisation.*
Coach 2: *Is it a professional organisation or a controlling organisation?*
Coach 3: *Controlling.*

How an Ethos of Amateurism Can Support the Integration   33

Coach 2: *It is the illusion of professionalism through control? That's how I'm experiencing it.*

Control was also evident in practice, with many Forum Karlbergs dedicated to discussing the defensive concept of 'shape' – a passive defensive tactic (a block) to prevent your opponent from advancing. Field notes from the third authors' experiences at Forum Karlberg highlight the focus on shape:

> *The forum started with XXX talking the coaches through the 3:5:2 formation and then asking each coach for a brief report on what they are working on... Although I missed a lot of the detail... I remember thinking that the academy teams were imitating the first team. A table was drawn up on the white board, a row for each academy team and one word was repeated at almost every row, 'shape'.*

As well as employing passive defensive tactics and focusing on 'shape', some academy coaches were attempting to adopt the principles of positional play or 'juego de posición'. In AIK, players were instructed to remain 'high and wide' when their team had the ball, a principle of play. During certain phases of the game, players would be instructed to stand as high and as wide as the pitch geography (side line) and rules of the game (offside) allowed. Coupled to the height of the halfway line and the width of the side line, the players complied to this principle to the point of docility, unresponsive to the dynamic movements of the ball, teammates and opposition, instead remaining steadfastly and safely anchored to the principle of high and wide. However, as the game progressed, coaches would become frustrated with the players' lack of engagement with the demands of the game, exemplified here by an academy coach, 'They don't move, they just stay there... they don't get involved in the game'. Away from game-based practice, it was also noted that other practice conditions did not facilitate perception, action and cognition for skilled behaviour. The third author commented:

> *I remember watching players waiting in lines and passing around cones (without opposition), in no way representative of football, this design is very easy for a coach to command, control, and look competent to those watching* (field notes).

In this specific sociocultural context, complying to controlling coach instructions became normalised and allowed players to remain free from the potential stigma of making a mistake and losing face (Vaughan et al., 2022). Exemplifying a football form of life characterised by unskilled intentionality, with docile players complying with decontextualised practice tasks. In this approach, players become decoupled from the rich in game information and responsive to only a narrow field of affordances permitted within the coaches' principles of play.

Moving Towards Dynamic Practice Environments

To move players from docile to dynamic, the AIK child and youth department has shifted the focus away from game models and principles of play towards skilled intentions that required players to direct their attention towards rich information *in* the game to guide skilled action (e.g., Vaughan et al., 2021, 2022). To facilitate skilled intentionality, the AIK research and development department aimed to embed a dynamic coaching pedagogy into academy coaching structures to support emerging practice designs from the bottom-up (player informed) as much as the top-down (coaching informed) (see O'Sullivan et al., 2021 for details). The aim of the co-design approach was to align player development practices with an *ethos of amateurism* discussed in the previous section. From a skill learning perspective, Woods et al. (2021b) have argued that the concept of 'representative co-design' can invite athletes to use action, perception and cognition, while engaging emotionally with a practice environment. Moreover, the less structured nature of practice that *does not conform to desired competencies* provides opportunities for individuals to self-organise while exploring the demands of football contexts in their own unique way without fear of criticism. As Vaughan et al. (2021) stated, the self-organisation of collective behaviours in football is optimised by methods that prioritise knowledge *of*, or direct attunement to, the local interactions of environmental properties in football (also see López-Felip et al., 2020; Ribeiro et al., 2021). Therefore, learning is prioritised through the continuous interactions of players, on the pitch and in the game, and not through the imposition of verbal instruction, game models or football concepts. We propose that shaping skilled intentions facilitates self-organisation in a local to global direction, amplifying bottom-up self-organisation and dampening top-down controlling coaching (Ribeiro et al., 2021). Moreover, such an approach situates exploration, love and ongoing participation at its core – features which clearly align to those of an *ethos of amateurism*.

Conclusion

A common thread in sport coaching and talent development settings is the influence of sociocultural factors on attitudes to learning and development approaches. The exposure of sociocultural factors on coaches and player development managers is manifest in issues of disciplinary practices that can render players docile, unable to respond to the many action possibilities available in practice and competition. Challenging and positively influencing these dominant forms of life may appear to be unrealistic due to the persuasive narrative that remains in many football academies. But here, we contended that moving towards an *ethos of amateurism* and focusing on players' motivations for taking part in sport in the first place could start to shift the balance and move away from highly disciplined practices. This conceptualisation needs further attention, and considerations need to be made within the messy, complex and dynamic context of player development settings. However, reframing player development as embedded in an *ethos of amateurism* can ensure that formal development practices are an extension of players' unstructured playing experiences. This can preserve the conditions that support intrinsic motivation, while strengthening the athlete–environment relationship – which is the basis of highly skilled behaviour when adopting an ecological perspective of football expertise.

Note

1 It is of note, that this word derives from the Latin verb *amare* which means 'to love'. Thus, an amateur is one who takes up with a pastime for the love of it.

References

Abernethy, B. (2008). Introduction: Developing expertise in sport – how research can inform practice. In: D. Farrow, J. Baker & C. MacMahon (eds). *Developing Sport Expertise* (pp. 1–14). London: Routledge.

Araújo, D., Hristovski, R., Seifert, L., Carvalho, J., & Davids, K. (2019). Ecological cognition: Expert decision-making behaviour in sport. *International Review of Sport and Exercise Psychology, 12*(1), 1–25.

Bailey, R., Cope, E. J., & Pearce, G. (2013). Why do children take part in, and remain involved in sport? A literature review and discussion of implications for sports coaches. *International Journal of Coaching Science, 7*(1), 56–75.

Barab, S. A., & Duffy, T. (2000). From practice fields to communities of practice. In: D. Jonassen & S. M. Land (eds). *Theoretical foundations of learning environments* (pp. 25–56). Mahwah, NJ: Lawrence Erlbaum Associates, Inc.

Bennett, K. J., Novak, A. R., Pluss, M. A., Stevens, C. J., Coutts, A. J., & Fransen, J. (2018). The use of small-sided games to assess skill proficiency in youth soccer players: A talent identification tool. *Science and Medicine in Football, 2*(3), 231–236.

Coutinho, P., Mesquita, I., & Fonseca, A. M. (2016). Talent development in sport: A critical review of pathways to expert performance. *International Journal of Sports Science & Coaching, 11*(2), 279–293.

Cronin, C. & Armour, K. (2018). *Care in sport coaching: Pedagogical cases.* London: Routledge.

Denison, J., & Avner, Z. (2011). Positive coaching: Ethical practices for athlete development. *Quest, 63*(2), 209–227.

Denison, J., Mills, J. P., & Konoval, T. (2017). Sports' disciplinary legacy and the challenge of 'coaching differently'. *Sport, Education and Society, 22*(6), 772–783.

Emery, C. A., Meeuwisse, W. H., & Hartmann, S. E. (2005). Evaluation of risk factors for injury in adolescent soccer: Implementation and validation of an injury surveillance system. *The American Journal of Sports Medicine, 33*(12), 1882–1891.

Fajen, B.R. (2009). Introduction to section on perception and action. In: D. Sternad (ed) *Progress in motor control. Advances in experimental medicine and biology,* vol 629. Boston, MA: Springer. https://doi.org/10.1007/978-0-387-77064-2_13

Foucault, M. (1977). *Discipline and punish: The birth of the prison.* London: Allen Lane.

Gibson, J. (1979). *The ecological approach to visual perception.* Lawrence Erlbaum Associates. Boston, MA: Houghton Mifflin.

Green, M. (2009). Podium or participation? Analysing policy priorities under changing modes of sport governance in the United Kingdom. *International Journal of Sport Policy and Politics, 1*(2), 121–144.

Headrick, J., Renshaw, I., Davids, K., Pinder, R. A., & Araújo, D. (2015). The dynamics of expertise acquisition in sport: The role of affective learning design. *Psychology of Sport and Exercise, 16*, 83–90.

Houlihan, B. (2005). Public sector sport policy: developing a framework for analysis. *International Review for the Sociology of Sport, 40*(2), 163–185.

Ingold, T. (2021). In praise of amateurs. *Ethnos, 86*(1), 153–172.

Jones, L. (2019). Wearable GPS devices in a British elite soccer academy setting: A Foucauldian disciplinary analysis of player development and experience. *Journal of Athlete Development and Experience, 1*(1), 4.

Lang, M. (2010). Surveillance and conformity in competitive youth swimming. *Sport, Education and Society, 15*(1), 19–37.

López-Felip, M. A., & Harrison, H. S. (2020). The touch & go dribbling model. *Chaos, Solitons & Fractals, 140*, 110186.

Manley, A., Roderick, M. & Parker, A. (2016). Disciplinary mechanism and the discourse of identity: The creation of 'silence' in an elite sports academy. *Culture and Organisation, 22*(3), 221–244.

Masschelein, J., & Simons, M. (2013). *Defence of the school: A public issue.* Education, Culture & Society Publishers.

O' Sullivan, M., Woods, C. T., Vaughan, J., & Davids, K. (2021). Towards a contemporary player learning in development framework for sports practitioners. *International Journal of Sports Science & Coaching, 16*(5), 1214–1222.

Premier League. (2011). *Elite Player Performance Plan.* Premier League Elite Player Performance Plan - EPPP.

Renshaw, I., Davids, K., O'Sullivan, M., Maloney, M. A., Crowther, R., & McCosker, C. (2022). An ecological dynamics approach to motor learning in practice: Reframing the learning and performing relationship in high performance sport. *Asian Journal of Sport and Exercise Psychology, 2*(1), 18–26.

Ribeiro, J., Davids, K., Silva, P., Coutinho, P., Barreira, D., & Garganta, J. (2021). Talent development in sport requires athlete enrichment: Contemporary insights from a non-linear pedagogy and the athletic skills model. *Sports Medicine, 51*(6), 1115–1122.

Rietveld, E., & Kiverstein, J. (2014). A rich landscape of affordances. *Ecological Psychology, 26*(4), 325–352.

Roetert, E. P., Ellenbecker, T. S., & Kriellaars, D. (2018). Physical literacy: Why should we embrace this construct? *British Journal of Sports Medicine, 52*(20), 1291–1292.

Rothwell, M., Davids, K., Woods, C., Otte, F. W., Rudd, J., & Stone, J. (2022a). Principles to guide talent development practices in sport: The exemplar case of British Rugby League Football. *Journal of Expertise, 5*(1), 28–37.

Rothwell, M., Stone, J., & Davids, K. (2022b). Investigating the athlete-environment relationship in a form of life: An ethnographic study. *Sport, Education and Society, 27*(1), 113–128.

Silk, M. & Andrews, D. (ed). (2011). *Sport and neoliberalism: Politics, consumption, and culture.* Philadelphia: Temple University Press.

Sothern, N. A., & O'Gorman, J. (2021). Exploring the mental health and wellbeing of professional academy footballers in England. *Soccer & Society, 22*(6), 641–654.

Starkes, J. (2008). The past and future of applied sport expertise and practice. In: D. Farrow, J. Baker & C. MacMahon (eds). *Developing sport expertise* (pp. 193–206). London: Routledge.

Vaughan, J., Mallett, C. J., Potrac, P., López-felip, M. A., & Davids, K. (2021). Football, culture, skill development and sport coaching: Extending ecological approaches in athlete development using the skilled intentionality framework. *Frontiers in Psychology, 12*, 1–13.

Vaughan, J., Mallett, C. J., Potrac, P., Woods, C., Sullivan, M. O., & Kerr, R. (2022). Social and cultural constraints on football player development in stockholm : Influencing skill, learning, and wellbeing. *Frontiers in Sports and Active Living, 4*, 1–18.

Vierimaa, M., Bruner, M. W., & Côté, J. (2018). Positive youth development and observed athlete behavior in recreational sport. *PloS One, 13*(1), 1–14. https://doi.org/10.1371/journal.pone.0191936

Woods, C. T., Araújo, D., Davids, K. et al. (2021a). From a technology that replaces human perception–action to one that expands it: Some critiques of current technology use in sport. *Sports Med – Open, 7*, 76. https://doi.org/10.1186/s40798-021-00366-y

Woods, C. T., Araújo, D., McKeown, I., & Davids, K. (2022). Wayfinding through boundaries of knowing: Professional development of academic sport scientists and what we could learn from an ethos of amateurism. *Sport, Education and Society*, 1–12. https://doi.org/10.1080/13573322.2022.2071861

Woods, C. T., Rothwell, M., Rudd, J., Robertson, S., & Davids, K. (2021b). Representative co-design: Utilising a source of experiential knowledge for athlete development and performance preparation. *Psychology of Sport and Exercise, 52*, 101804.

Williams, S. & Manley, A. (2016). Elite coaching and the technocratic engineer: 'Thanking the boys at Microsoft!'. *Sport, Education and Society, 21*(6), 828–850.

Chapter 3

The McDonaldisation of Football's Formal Coach Education?

Creating the McCoach

Anthony Bush and Shaun Williams

Introduction

Within this chapter, we address how the formal education of football coaches has become shaped – McDonaldised – by the omnipresent market pressures associated with the advent of late capitalism. To do this, we mobilise George Ritzer's McDonaldisation thesis, a sociological theory which for almost 30 years has captured the attention of a broad range of professions, businesses and disciplines but to date has largely evaded the critical purview of both football and coaching scholars alike. It should be emphasised that this chapter is not about McDonald's in the objective sense of it being a fast-food restaurant but rather how the principles designed by the founders of McDonald's (Richard and Maurice McDonald) were harnessed by the businessman Ray Kroc in the creation of the McDonald's franchise and subsequently articulated by Ritzer (1993) in 'The McDonaldisation of Society' have pervaded into almost all sectors of contemporary society, including the formal education of football coaches.

Perhaps, with football fully embracing the riches afforded by the late capitalist era, there is a hesitance or reluctance within football to direct a sociological lens which seeks to critically interrogate its impact on the sport. The symbiotic relationship between market forces and football can readily be highlighted through multiple, widely reported metrics, such as the English Premier League (EPL) media rights being sold for under £50 million per season in 1992, then 25 years later over £2 billion (Storm and Solberg, 2018). Additionally, EPL clubs' revenues are projected to be approximately £5.5 billion in the 2021/2022 season (Deloitte, 2022), top players are now being paid in excess of £1 million per week, and high-profile coaches earn in excess of £20 million per year. It is not the purpose of this chapter to be overtly critical of the global football economy and associated industries, something which numerous scholars have engaged with; however, it is important to be mindful of this context when considering why football – and the microcosm or setting of the formal education of the football coaching workforce – has been so acquiescent and unchallenging of the impact of market forces.

DOI: 10.4324/9781003253990-5

What Is Meant by *Formal* Coach Education and What Are the Problems With It?

This chapter focuses specific attention on what is commonly identified as 'coach education', namely, the *formal* education of football coaches. According to Barber (2008, cited in Watts and Cushion, 2017), the origins of The Football Association (FA)[1] educating football coaches can be traced back to the 1930s. Sport coaching has long been identified as a key component of sport provision at all points of the 'participation continuum' (Lyle, 2008; Lyle and Cushion, 2016), and academic attention has been levelled at processes that enhance the learning of coaches for almost as long as George Ritzer's McDonaldisation thesis has been in existence (see Cushion et al., 2003; Cassidy et al., 2006; Trudel and Gilbert, 2006) and continues to the present day (see Williams et al., 2015; Williams and Bush, 2019; Chapman et al., 2020; Dempsey et al., 2021a, 2021b). It is important to note that 'coach learning' can occur as a result of learning experiences in a range of contexts (Mallet et al., 2009; Cushion et al., 2010) with only one of which defined as 'formal'. We mobilise the typology of coach learning settings proposed by Nelson et al. (2006), who holistically conceptualised coach learning as formal, non-formal or informal.

Formal coach education is institutionalised and leads to certification and ultimately accreditation as a competent coach at a particular level in a hierarchically structured system (Coombs and Ahmed, 1974; Piggott, 2012). Typically, formal coach education is commonly referred to as certified 'training' courses, 'getting the badge', or National Governing Body (NGB) coaching qualifications. In the setting of football coach education, the coaching journey for aspiring coaches in England is prescribed by The FA and commences with the new 'The FA: Introduction to Coaching Football' course (which has replaced the 'FA Level 1 in Coaching Football' qualification), which can be accessed after completion of the free 'EE Playmaker by England Football' course. Following these courses, aspiring coaches can then undertake the 'UEFA C Licence', 'UEFA B Licence', 'UEFA A in Coaching Football', 'The FA Advanced Youth Award' and, at the pinnacle, the 'FA Level 5 (UEFA Pro) in Coaching Football' (The FA, 2022). There are additional formal courses provided by The FA targeting volunteering in football, disability coaching, medical courses (e.g., first aid, emergency first aid, managing trauma), talent identification (Levels 1–5), coaching goalkeepers (Levels 1–4), coaching futsal (Levels 1–3), online and face-to-face continuing professional development for physical education teachers and safeguarding children and adults. With the core coaching journey, the initial qualifications can be completed within a month, online at a cost of £160, with the time commitment and cost rising as the duration and immersion in the coaching journey progresses. A UEFA C licence will take 16–20 weeks at a cost of £500, a UEFA B licence will take 9–12 months at a cost of £960 and the UEFA Pro Licence will take 18 months at a cost of £9,890 (The FA, 2022). For context, since the turn of the millennium through to the end of 2017, over 360,000 learners have gained Level 1 certification with The FA, and during this timeframe, approximately 54,000 certifications were achieved at Level 2 (1st4sport, 2022). This indicates that for every 20 Level 1 candidates, only 3 go on to acquire Level 2 certification. Emphasising this drop off from those seeking the more advanced qualifications, a snapshot of coach certification in 2017 indicates that there were 1,796 UEFA A or UEFA Pro licence holders in England.[2] Extrapolating from these data, then there is only 1 UEFA A or UEFA Pro licence holder in England for in excess of 30 Level 2 candidates (The Guardian, 2022). Of course, cost is an important factor related to progression through the levels. For example, the cost of the UEFA Pro licence in Spain is £1,070, whereas in England, the cost is £9890 (The FA, 2022; The Guardian 2022). It is simplistic to assume that reducing the cost would increase the number of coaches holding the highest level of qualification; it cannot be overlooked that it is important that the qualification undertaken is fit for purpose and valued by those undertaking it.

Coach development and learning is a complex process, and in addition to the formal component, there is a necessity for individualised and ad-hoc learning pathways (Nelson and Cushion, 2006). Nelson et al. (2006) conceptualisation of non-formal coach learning is that it is something which takes place outside of the formal framework and is organised, mediated, systematic and targeted at subgroups of the population. In the setting of football coach education, this would include coaching conferences, coaching clinics, workshops and seminars which target a particular subgroup (e.g., community coaches, coaches of children or high-performance coaches) with content that is on a specific topic of interest and delivered in a short timescale. There may be a record of attendance, but no certification of competence and no pass/fail assessment. Coombs and Ahmed's (1974) work on attacking rural poverty is repetitively appropriated by coach education scholars to differentiate between the typologies of 'coach' learning. They identify informal learning as 'the lifelong process by which every person acquires and accumulates knowledge, skills, attitudes and insights from daily experiences and exposure to the environment' (Coombs and Ahmed, 1974, p. 8). This learning takes place in myriad contexts and is most likely to occur 'in the field' without any form of external mediation (i.e., it is self-directed learning). In the setting of football coach education, previous playing experiences, being coached by others, being an assistant or volunteer coach, mentoring or being mentored, observations of coaching practice, reading resources and having conversations – either face-to-face or online – with other coaches and players are all examples of how informal coach learning can occur.

It is not the purpose of this chapter to explore in detail the illuminating scholarly work that has been undertaken about the inadequacies of formal coach education courses (see Mallett et al., 2009; Nash and Sproule, 2012; Piggott, 2012; Sawiuk et al., 2016; Chapman et al., 2020). However, it is important that some of the key arguments relating to the quality of the formal coach education product are highlighted to provide context for applying the principles of McDonaldisation

The McDonaldisation of Football's Formal Coach Education? 41

to the setting. Piggott (2012), using Coombs and Ahmed's (1974) sliding scale of effectiveness of formal learning, argues that most formal coach education courses could be categorised as occupying the 'less effective' portion of the scale. Right from the start with the pre-conceived expectations NGBs make about those attending their coaching qualifications, there have been concomitant issues with the coach education product provided. This is attributed by Piggott (2012) to a misunderstanding of the nature of coaches and coaching, with coaches being perceived as 'empty vessels' requiring them to be filled with specific, pre-determined information and then for this acquired information to be delivered by 'technicians' who are expected to display a model – the 'gold standard' – of accepted coaching actions (Abraham and Collins, 1998; Potrac et al., 2002; Cushion et al., 2003; Nelson and Cushion, 2006; Cushion et al., 2010). This display of accepted coaching actions has been likened to a form of indoctrination, resulting in robotic coaches knowing and doing the same thing (Jones et al., 2004). Consequently, the literature resulting from multiple investigations into formal coach education across many sports posits that although helpful in providing some sport-specific content, it has a limited impact on coaches (Nelson et al., 2013; Williams and Bush, 2019).

The reluctance of NGBs to enable those undertaking their qualifications to have input or influence over the design and delivery of the course is an obvious issue (Nelson et al., 2013), and we are reminded here of the top-down assumption by NGBs about aspiring coaches being 'empty vessels' that need to be filled with information. Indeed, the powerful findings of the research by Piggott (2012, p. 535), which included three football coaches in their wider sample, suggested that coaches undertaking formal (prescriptive and rigid) coach education courses found them 'useless'. The literature is unanimous in its assertion that the strongest motivating factor for coaches to undertake formal coach education courses is that there are strong regulatory and coercive pressures on practitioners relating to having to 'pass' the prescribed course, simply abide by the rules and secure the necessary certification. To do this, practitioners therefore display the behaviours consistent with what would meet with the approval of the coach educators delivering and assessing the course (Nelson et al., 2006).

The importance of articulating the constituent components of coach education and summarising the scholarly critique of the formal component is crucial to ensure that the context is provided for the application of Ritzer's McDonaldisation thesis to the formal education of football coaches.

What Is McDonaldisation?

Ritzer's McDonaldisation thesis is an extension of the rationalisation process initially articulated by the German sociologist Max Weber's (1958) 'iron cage' of capitalism which captures:

> ...the increased organizational bureaucratization and productive rationalization of human existence within modernizing capitalist societies...this iron

cage traps individuals in highly complex and rule-based organizational structures (they are bureaucratized), in which evermore aspects of their existence become productivity and goal-oriented (they are rationalized).

(Andrews et al., 2013, p. 336)

The notion of individuals being trapped is perhaps more aptly understood by alternate terminology, not the metaphor of the vessels in which individuals are entombed as iron cages but as 'shells as hard as steel' (Ritzer, 2015, p. 64). This intimates that the rationalisation process in which individuals are enslaved is something that is very difficult to escape from. Ritzer (2015) points out that in some settings there are plenty of non-McDonaldised alternatives to select from and that consumers of a particular product or service are free to leave and make a different choice. For example, you have the choice to take your custom to another restaurant, buy your furniture from another store or attend a different university. Importantly, with the setting of educating football coaches, the freedom of choice is not available to those seeking the formally approved governing body certification of competence required by stakeholders and employers. So, thinking of the setting of football coach education as an island surrounded by the sea, what Ritzer (2015, p. 64) would identify as an 'island of the living dead' is one which is useful to keep in mind when forming and understanding of and critiquing the current coach education offering in football. Ritzer (2015, p. 64) asserts that it is the impact on the inhabitants of the island by the controlling structures of McDonaldisation which prescribe actions and behaviours akin to 'zombies' or the 'living dead'. The result of this is that

...if you were to watch both sides of a drive through window at a fast-food restaurant during a lunch or supper rush, you would observe a great deal of rote, scripted behavior (sic). The "zombies" who order are not required to think very hard about what they are ordering, and the "zombies" who serve them use the same few phrases and repeat the same few motions over and over again.

Thus, if the education of football coaching can be seen to be impacted by these McDonaldised structures, there are going to be perceptibly negative impacts on the quality of the formal coach education received by the developing coaches and concomitantly on the quality of the coaching received by participants (the players) who are the consumers of the coaching product.

It should be emphasised that – by design – this chapter seeks to offer a critical sociological reading of the formal education of football coaches and that we should be mindful that presenting the setting as either 'all good' or 'all bad' can be viewed as an unhelpful binary distinction. Even inhabitants of McDonaldised islands will be able to draw positive experiences:

The McDonaldisation of Football's Formal Coach Education? 43

> ...a lot of "life" takes place on McDonaldized islands as well. Most customers seem to not only enjoy the food but also to have a lot of fun while they consume it.
>
> (Ritzer, 2015, p. 64)

Therefore, although not the primary objective, we will ensure that an element of balance is offered in this chapter by highlighting where McDonaldised processes have brought about changes which could be interpreted by some stakeholders as having a positive influence on the formal education of football coaches.

We agree with the conviction of Appelrouth and Edles (2016) that when engaging with sociological theorists, then this should be with work authored by the theorist and not secondary textbooks which are interpretations or translations of the theorist's work into more easily digestible, simpler – perhaps modified or incorrect – versions of the original ideas. Thus, when articulating Ritzer's McDonaldisation thesis, we will draw directly upon the author's original terminology and authored works. Ritzer (1993) – and all subsequent iterations of McDonaldisation – deploys a framework comprising four dimensions as the basis for explaining the observable processes in a setting which has embraced McDonaldisation, namely, efficiency, calculability, predictability and control. Although initially presented as discrete dimensions, there is no question that there are certain elements of cross-over between the articulated dimensions and that in many cases they are intertwined. Indeed, Ritzer (2013) reorganised the latest iteration of 'The McDonaldisation of Society' by combining the dimensions of efficiency and calculability into a single chapter, and the same is true of predictability and control. This organisation of the dimensions will be used to frame the following discussion.

Efficiency and Calculability

There is relatively little ambiguity around the term 'efficiency' in that it signifies the meeting of an objective (the output) using the minimum – or optimum – number of inputs through the systematic elimination of superfluous energy, effort, money or time. According to Ritzer (2013, p. 54),

> Efficiency is generally a good thing. It is clearly advantageous to consumers, who are able to obtain what they need more quickly with less effort. Similarly, efficient workers are able to perform their tasks more rapidly and easily. Managers and owners gain because more work gets done, more customers are served, and greater profits are earned.

In the case of contextualising these sentiments to coach education, we need to be mindful that the 'consumers' are the coaches seeking accreditation, the 'workers' are the practising coaches and the 'managers' and 'owners' are The

FA. Efficiency is highlighted through numerous factors, such as through streamlining the definition and act of coaching as something which is undertaken to simply make participants better at playing football. This oversimplification of the ontological core of coaching has been critiqued by numerous scholars (see Bush and Silk, 2010; Bush et al., 2013) and is a complexity of understanding which is largely omitted from the design of formal coach education programmes. In doing this, the pathway to the output of certifying a competent coach at a particular level is made to be much more straightforward and eliminates many complications faced by practising coaches in the real world, enabling an 'optimum means to a given end' (Ritzer, 2013, p. 54) to be sought. The result of this is that certification can be acquired in a short period of time and delivered to many people. Indeed, the 'Introduction to Coaching Football' course is completed online (weekly webinars, e-learning, online resources and community support) over a four-week period, and at the end of this course, participants will be provided with the 'skills to coach players of all ages' (The FA, 2022, n.p.). To provide the training to the participants, The FA accredit 'expert' Coach Developers to deliver the curricula related to the specific level of award being undertaken. The compartmentalisation of content of the curricula and mode of delivery is analogous with Ritzer's (2013, p. 55) observations about streamlining the fast-food process:

> ...above all else, Ray Krok was impressed by the McDonald brothers' operation, as well as the enormous profit potential of such a system applied at a large number of restaurant sites. Here is how Krok described his initial reactions to the McDonald's system:
> I was fascinated by the simplicity and effectiveness of the system...Each step in producing the limited menu was stripped down to its essence and accomplished with a minimum of effort. They sold hamburgers and cheeseburgers only. The burgers were all fried the same way.

So, The FA offer a limited menu to their customers, comprising restricted content deemed core to achieving the necessary output of certification.

An interesting notion presented by Ritzer (2013) for increasing the efficiency is businesses putting customers subconsciously to work, what Ritzer terms 'prosumers' [customers who also produce (work)]. In the fast-food restaurant, this is characterised by customers ordering and paying at self-serve machines, standing in line or waiting in a parking bay to collect food, taking it to the tables or driving through and disposing of the waste in the appropriate receptacles. In relation to efficiencies in coach education, this can be seen by the self-directed nature of significant elements of the training and, as aspiring coaches work through their badges, the necessity to provide the coaching context for the qualification's learning to be embedded within.

McDonaldised systems are also characterised by calculability or the ability to count, calculate or quantify many things:

The McDonaldisation of Football's Formal Coach Education? 45

> ...Quantity tends to become a surrogate for quality. Numerical standards are set for both processes (production, for example) and end results (goods, for example). In terms of processes, the emphasis is on speed (usually high), whereas for end results, the focus is on the number of products produced and served or on their size (usually large).
>
> (Ritzer, 2013, p. 72)

Of course, the main impact of this on coach education is that there is an emphasis on the number of coaches that can secure accreditation in the shortest timeframe possible and that this becomes the primary concern rather than the quality (or competence) of the coaches in receipt of certification. There is no question that a McDonaldised coaching system can produce large numbers of coaches in a time- and cost-efficient manner. The Commission Report 2 (The FA, 2014, p. 38) explicitly stipulates that '...the England figures are inadequate and that the overall numbers of coaches holding B Licence level and above need to be increased substantially'. This call was supported by The FA (2014) setting a range of quantifiable measures or targets to increase numbers, for example, recruiting a further 25 full-time coach educators and increasing certified coaches at the different coaching qualification levels by up to 275% in some cases. To put the numbers into contemporary context, Dempsey et al. (2021a) estimate that approximately 30,000 coaches currently experience the FA coaching qualifications per annum, although most will be engaging with the introductory level qualifications. This is what Ritzer (2013) would identify as an example of the 'irrationality of rationality', where the drive for efficiency and calculability results in an inevitable negative impact on the quality of the coaching workforce.

Predictability and Control

Predictability is the dimension of McDonaldisation which purports to turn everything into a routinised activity. The positives to this are that there are no surprises and that workers, consumers and managers know what to expect. According to Ritzer (2013, p. 87),

> ...[people] want to know that when they order their Big Mac today, it will be identical to the one they ate yesterday and the one they will eat tomorrow. People would be upset if the special sauce was used one day but not the next or if it tasted differently from one day to the next. They want to know that the McDonald's franchise they visit in Des Moines, Los Angeles, Paris, or Beijing will appear and operate much the same as their local McDonald's. To achieve predictability, a rationalised society emphasizes discipline, order, systematization, formalization, routine, consistency, and methodological operation.

Much is the same for coach education and coaches. Aspiring coaches are trained by Coach Developers delivering the same curricula to all and assessed against the same standardised assessment matrices appropriate for each defined coaching level. Those undertaking the qualification possess the same formal qualifications as pre-requisites. They know what to expect, and they know which qualifications they need to select from the limited 'menu' in order to progress. For example, those wishing to undertake the UEFA B licence course must have completed – in addition to being able to effectively communicate in English and be actively coaching a team in a season-long competition – The FA Safeguarding Children Course, The FA Level 2 in Coaching Football course/1st4sport Level 2 Certificate in Coaching Football/UEFA C Licence and The FA Level 1 Introduction to First Aid in Football/The FA Emergency Aid in Football. The 'approved' way of delivering a coaching session is standardised, and to do this – and pass the assessment – the coaches perform in a routinised, perfunctory and seemingly scripted manner to achieve the pre-determined session objectives. Ritzer (2013) surmises that workers (coaches) in McDonaldised systems act and behave in predictable ways and that in many cases, what they do and what they say are very predictable.

The fourth and final dimension of McDonaldisation is control, specifically through the use of nonhuman technology. Ritzer (2013, p. 102) clearly articulates what is meant by the term 'technology':

> Technology includes not only machines and tools but also materials, skills, knowledge, rules, regulations, procedures, and techniques. Technologies thus encompass not only the obvious, such as robots and computers, but also the less obvious, such as the assembly line, bureaucratic rules, and manuals prescribing accepted procedures and techniques. A *human technology* (a screwdriver, for example) is controlled by people; a *nonhuman technology* (the order window at a drive-through, for instance) controls people.

For football coaches, in order to renew a coaching licence, there are several regulatory hurdles that need to be met, which emphasises the McDonaldised process. For example, re-licensing is performed through a personal online 'My Training' account where a coach needs to ensure that all pre-requisites set by The FA are met. These pre-requisites include an in-date FA first aid training, an in-date FA Safeguarding Children training, an FA Enhanced Criminal Record Check (CRC) Disclosure to work with under 18 players and 5 hours of documented continuing professional development (CPD) activities approved by The FA. This bureaucratic framework therefore controls – perhaps even dissuades – those wishing to make a positive contribution to football at all levels and leads to a coaching environment where innovation, risk and individuality are minimised. Again, some may see this as advantageous and would point to the fact that this bureaucracy should make the coaching environment safe for coaches and participants alike. However, despite these controlling measures, all we need to do is engage with the media to see that this is merely an illusion of safety and that despite the rules, the safety of participants cannot be guaranteed. Also, this level of bureaucracy has been identified

The McDonaldisation of Football's Formal Coach Education?   47

by The FA (2014) itself as presenting barriers to the inclusivity of the coaching profession, especially in the recruitment and retention of coaches from black, Asian and minority ethnic (BAME) backgrounds. The formal coach education system has also been identified as an aggravating factor for the underrepresentation of women coaches (Norman, 2008) and potentially other underrepresented groups – such as disabled sports coaches – in the coaching arena.

As a consequence of the formal coach education process, the enforced – predictable and controlled – routinised behaviour exhibited by some coaches, what we referred earlier to actions akin to 'zombies' or the 'living dead', has led to a de-skilling and dehumanising of the act of coaching. Coaches are 'trained to do a limited number of tasks in precisely the way they are told to do them' (Ritzer, 2013, p. 15). Although extreme, Ritzer's (2013, p. 135) example of how this plays out in a fast-food context is one which those with a critical focus on formal coach education will readily identify with:

> The main reason to think of McDonaldization as irrational, and ultimately unreasonable, is that it tends to be dehumanizing. For example, the fast-food industry offers its employees "McJobs". One "McTask" at McDonald's is known as HBO—"Hand Bag Out". As a Burger King worker has noted, "A moron could learn to do this job, it's so easy," and "Any trained monkey could do this job." Workers can use only a small portion of their skills and abilities. The minimal skill demands of the fast-food restaurant are irrational.

Good – effective and impactful – coaches recognise the limitations of the formal coach education process and would therefore challenge the irrationality of rationality presented to them in the way in which their coaching is moderated by McDonaldised processes. These coaches embrace informal learning experiences to enable them to be inspirational coaches in a variety of contexts but have the self-awareness to engage with formal coach education primarily to meet the demands of employers and governing bodies for licensing purposes.

Conclusion

We concede that many would embrace the rationalisation of The FA's coach education system as one which enables numerous aspiring and practicing coaches to acquire an initial validation of their coaching competence, take the next step up the coaching ladder, create a coaching landscape filled with educated coaches, provide a safe space for participants being coached and, when necessary, undertake the prescribed CPD and safety updates in order to re-license. However, this chapter has deliberately presented an alternate reading. By problematising The FA's formal coach education through the lens of George Ritzer's McDonaldisation thesis, this chapter has identified significant shortcomings of the system currently in place. We have argued that the McDonaldised system exhibits multiple irrationalities of rationality to the point where the formal coach education system no

48 Anthony Bush and Shaun Williams

longer provides the framework to improve the competence and effectiveness of the coaches that it is certifying and even in some cases is seen as a major barrier to making a step into the coaching arena.

We do agree with those who argue that the design and delivery of formal coach education are complex and challenging, are subject to economic and political influences and are socially constructed, constantly evolving and rarely uniform (Nelson et al., 2006, Griffiths et al., 2018; Chapman et al., 2020). Of course, the solution is easy on paper to write, simply de-McDonaldise the formal coach education system. Ritzer (2013) proposes 'Starbuckisation' as a potential antidote to rationalisation. Starbuckisation reframes the output to a higher quality rather than quantity, provides an environment where customers are enticed to stay, customer feedback is acted upon, employees are valued and respected and there is a focus on ethical practice. These five tenets of Starbuckisation, if applied to formal coach education systems, would permeate positive movement in provision. Formal coach education should provide an unobtrusive and inviting scaffold on which the informal learning, so crucial to the development of coaches (Christensen, 2014), can be moved to the centre stage. No longer should informal coaching experiences be seen as 'accidental' or 'ad-hoc'. Involving practising coaches in the rearticulation of formal coach education is crucial, and the practical suggestions posited by Watts and Cushion (2017) could be pivotal in beginning to de-McDonaldise the system, namely, more attention on flexible approaches around how to coach, increased prominence on communicating with participants, improving pedagogical awareness and the compulsory observation of different coaches. To eliminate or re-educate the McCoach, bridges need to be built across to the islands of the living dead, and to begin this process, organisations such as The FA need to concede that the financially rewarding, numerically advantageous, bureaucratic, rule-driven and highly regulated coach education system is simply not fit for purpose.

Notes

1 Although this chapter is contextualised in relation to The Football Association (FA) in England, in Great Britain, each of the Home Nations have a separate governing body responsible for organising all aspects of the game. In Scotland, the governing body is The Scottish Football Association (SFA), in Wales, The Football Association of Wales (FAW), and in Northern Ireland, The Irish Football Association (IFA). Although separate to The FA, there are commonalities with the approach to formal coach education in the SFA, FAW and IFA.
2 At the same time, Spain had in excess of 15,000 UEFA Pro or UEFA A licenced coaches (The Guardian, 2022).

References

1st4sport, 2022. *FA renews qualifications contract with 1st4sport qualifications* [online]. Available from: https://www.1st4sportqualifications.com/content-page/newsroom/2018-2/fa-renews-qualifications-contract-with-1st4sport-qualifications/ [Accessed July 14 2022].

The McDonaldisation of Football's Formal Coach Education? 49

Abraham, A. and Collins, D. (1998). Examining and extending research in coaching development. *Quest*, 50, 59–79.

Andrews, D.L., Silk, M.L., Francombe, J. and Bush, A.J., 2013. McKinesiology. *Review of Education, Pedagogy, and Cultural Studies*, 35(5), 335–356.

Appelrouth, S. and Edles, L.D., 2016. *Sociological theory in the contemporary era: text and readings*. Los Angeles: Sage.

Bush, A.J. and Silk, M.L., 2010. Towards and evolving critical consciousness in coaching research: the physical pedagogic bricolage. *International Journal of Sports Science and Coaching*, 5(4), 551–565.

Bush, A.J., Silk, M.L., Andrews, D. and Lauder, H., 2013. *Sports coaching research: context, consequences, and consciousness*. London: Routledge.

Cassidy, T.R., Potrac, P. and McKenzie, A., 2006. Evaluating and reflecting upon a coach education initiative: the CoDe of rugby. *The Sport Psychologist*, 20(2), 145–161.

Chapman, R., Richardson, D., Cope, E. and Cronin, C., 2020. Learning from the past; a Freirean analysis of FA coach education since 1967. *Sport, Education and Society*, 25(6), 681–697.

Christensen, M.K., 2014. Exploring biographical learning in elite soccer coaching. *Sport, Education and Society*, 19(2), 204–222.

Coombs, P. and Ahmed, M., 1974. *Attacking rural poverty: how non-formal education can help*. Baltimore: John Hopkins Press.

Cushion, C.J., Armour, K.M. and Jones, R.L., 2003. Coach education and continuing professional development: experience and learning to coach. *Quest*, 55, 215–230.

Cushion, C.J., Nelson, L., Armour, K.M., Lyle, J., Jones. R.L., Sandford, R. and O'Callaghan, C., 2010. *Coach learning and development: a review of literature* [online]. Available from: https:www.researchgate.net/publication/265566741_Coach_Learning_and_Development_A_Review_of_Literature [Accessed May 26 2022].

Deloitte, 2022. *Annual review of football finance: explore the data* [online]. Available from: https://www2.deloitte.com/uk/en/pages/sports-business-group/articles/annual-review-of-football-finance.html [Accessed April 4 2022].

Dempsey, N.M., Richardson, D.J., Cope, E. and Cronin, C.J., 2021a. Creating and disseminating coach education policy: a case of formal coach education in grassroots football. *Sport, Education and Society*, 26(8), 917–930.

Dempsey, N.M., Cope, E., Richardson, D.J., Littlewood, M.A. and Cronin, C.J., 2021b. Less may be more: how do coach developers reproduce "learner centred" policy in practice? *Sports Coaching Review*, 10(2), 203–224.

Griffiths, M., Armour, K. and Cushion, C., 2018. 'Trying to get our message across': successes and challenges in an evidenced based professional development programme for sports coaches. *Sport, Education and Society*, 23(3), 283–295.

Jones, R., Armour, K. and Potrac, P., 2004. *Sports coaching cultures: from practice to theory*. London: Routledge.

Lyle, J., 2008. Sports development and sports coaching. In: K. Hylton and P. Bramham (eds.), *Sports development, policy, process and practice* (2nd ed.). London: Routledge, 214–235.

Lyle, J. and Cushion, C., 2016. *Sport coaching concepts: a framework for coaching practice* (2nd ed.). London: Routledge.

Mallett, C., Trudel, P., Lyle, J. and Rynne, S., 2009. Formal vs. informal coach education. *International Journal of Sports Science and Coaching*, 4(3), 325–334.

Nash, C. and Sproule, J., 2012. Coaches perceptions of their coach education experiences. *International Journal of Sport Psychology*, 43, 33–52.

Nelson, L. and Cushion, C., 2006. Reflection in coach education: the case of the national governing body coaching certificate. *The Sport Psychologist*, 20, 174–183.

Nelson, L., Cushion, C. and Potrac, P., 2006. Formal, non-formal and informal coach learning: a holistic conceptualisation. *International Journal of Sports Science and Coaching*, 1(3), 247–259.

Nelson, L., Cushion, C. and Potrac, P., 2013. Enhancing the provision of coach education: the recommendations of UK coaching practitioners. *Physical Education and Sport Pedagogy*, 18(2), 204–218.

Norman, L., 2008. The UK system is failing women coaches. *International Journal of Sports Science and Coaching*, 3(4), 447–476.

Piggott, D., 2012. Coaches' experiences of formal coach education: a critical sociological investigation. *Sport, Education and Society*, 17(4), 535–554.

Potrac, P., Jones, R. and Armour, K., 2002. It's all about getting respect: the coaching behaviours of an expert English soccer coach. *Sport, Education and Society*, 7(2), 183–202.

Ritzer, G., 1993. *The McDonaldization of society: an investigation into the changing character of contemporary social life*: Thousand Oaks: Pine Forge Press.

Ritzer, G., 2013. *The McDonaldization of society* (7th ed.). Los Angeles: Sage.

Ritzer, G., 2015. *Introduction to sociology* (2nd ed.). Los Angeles: Sage.

Sawiuk, R., Taylor, W. and Groom, R., 2016. Exploring formalized elite coach mentoring programmes in the UK. *Sport, education and society*, 23(6), 619–631.

Storm, R.K. and Solberg, H.A., 2018. European club capitalism and FIFA redistribution models: an analysis of development patterns in globalized football. *Sport in Society*, 21(-11), 1850–1865.

The Football Association (FA), 2014. *The FA chairman's England commission report 2*. London: The FA.

The Football Association (FA), 2022. *Want to get into coaching? Your journey starts here* [online]. Available from: https://thebootroom.thefa.com/learning/qualifications [Accessed May 26 2022].

The Guardian, 2022. *Why I left England and moved to Spain to become a football coach* [online]. Available from: https://www.theguardian.com/football/2021/jan/28/why-i-left-england-and-moved-to-spain-to-become-a-football-coach [Accessed July 14 2022].

Trudel, P. and Gilbert, W., 2006. Coaching and coach education. In: D. Kirk, M. O'Sullivan and D. McDonald (eds.), *Handbook of physical education*. London: Sage, 516–539.

Watts, D.W. and Cushion, C.J., 2017. Coaching journeys: longitudinal experiences from professional football in Great Britain. *Sports Coaching Review*, 6(1), 76–93.

Weber, M., 1958. *The protestant ethic and the spirit of capitalism*. New York: Charles Scribner's Sons.

Williams, S.P., Alder, D. and Bush, A.J., 2015. A little less conversation; a little more (relational) action please. A fictional dialogue of integrating theory into coaching practice. *Sports Coaching Review*, 4(2), 115–138.

Williams, S.P. and Bush, A.J., 2019. Connecting knowledge(s) to practice: A Bernsteinian theorisation of a collaborative coach learning community project. *Sport, Education and Society*, 24(4), 375–389.

Part II

Emerging Social Theories and Football

Chapter 4

Desire, Drive and the Melancholy of English Football

'It's (not) Coming Home'

Jack Black

Introduction

In 2021, the men's English national football team reached their first final at a major international tournament since winning the World Cup in 1966.[1] This success followed their previous achievement of reaching the semi-finals (knocked out by Croatia) at the 2018 World Cup. True to form, the defeats proved unfalteringly English, with the 2021 final echoing previous tournament defeats, as England lost to Italy on penalties.[2] However, what resonated with the predictability of an English defeat was the accompanying chant, 'it's coming home'. A ubiquitous presence throughout the course of both tournaments – while chanted at England football matches, it was also repeated across social media, the press and commercial advertising – the chant originates from the 1996 single, *Three Lions (Football's Coming Home)*, performed by David Baddiel, Frank Skinner and The Lightning Seeds.

In what follows, critical attention will be given to examining how the song offers, what will be argued is, a melancholic outlook. By re-approaching examples of English nostalgia and hubris, this chapter will expose how illustrations of English melancholy offer the potential for promoting collective forms of expression, which, when contextualised alongside England's lack of footballing success (for the men's team, at least), can be offset against a melancholic mediation that is cognisant of the centrality of loss – for both the subject and our collective sporting endeavours.[3]

In meeting these aims, this chapter will ultimately seek to both introduce and apply a psychoanalytic perspective to sport, football and social theory. For psychoanalysis, any critical interpretation of our social practices requires us 'to question the specifics of desire' (Reynoso 2021, 593). Such questioning proves essential to the study of sport (and its enjoyment), for which the most puzzling aspect is the fact that while our relation to sport remains driven by attempts at 'victory', 'what the average fan will have to acknowledge, even begrudgingly, is that much of fandom involves tarrying with failure and loss' (Reynoso 2021, 593). It is in tarrying with this inherent 'loss' that a melancholic outlook can prove significant.

DOI: 10.4324/9781003253990-7

'Cause I remember…': England's National Nostalgia

The original release of Three Lions accompanied England's hosting of the 1996 European championship ('Euro '96').[4] Originally referring to the fact that 'Euro '96' was the first time that England had hosted a major football tournament since 1966 (when they hosted the World Cup), the phrase has come to certify a provocative English hubris, with the assumption that football was (or presumptuously is) returning home to 'England' – a nation who so often credits itself with 'inventing' the game of football. Since then, the line has undoubtedly become tied to the desire for an international trophy to 'come home'. This development was echoed by the fact that Italian fans provided their own resignification ('it's coming Rome') during the 2020 European Championship final.[5]

With criticisms suggesting that the lyrics help to perpetuate an arrogant English exceptionalism, alluding to certain national myths that evoke a sense of English entitlement, the chant can be perceived as a clear example of English nostalgia: a nostalgia which, in the case of football, is repeatedly associated with England's success in '66 as well as a post-war fascination tied to working-class grit and true English professionalism (Holt 1992). Although these themes underlie the song's lyrics, more broadly, they remain a reoccurring presence within accounts of English sporting culture as well as its nationalism and national identity (Black, Fletcher and Lake 2020). In fact, during the Euro '96 finals, Garland and Rowe (1999, 82) highlighted how 'Nostalgia for a lost era of football triumph and national self-certainty was a recurrent feature of the press coverage'. Equally, for Carrington (1998), the 'it's coming home' chant constituted a mantra for a nostalgic, culturally homogeneous and racially 'white' England. In so doing, both the chant and the Euro '96 tournament were neither representative nor inclusive but, instead, through the conjunction of sport and popular culture helped to perpetuate a pervasive cultural racism.

Certainly, while examples of British/English decline continue to be filtered through narratives that seek to frame this decline as set against Britain's former imperial dominance (Black 2016, 2019), to assert that the song offers nothing more than an ethnocentric account of England's control of the game, as well as an open resentment towards the apparent defects of uncontrolled immigration, is to play into the very hands of those who would seek to delimit what is 'good' about the nation and, thus, what must be 'dropped' and excluded. If anything, it downplays the extent to which such an 'impossible object' – in this case, the nation's 'essence' – is predicated on the fact that there is some assumed national essence that can be protected and shared amongst the included, while also critiqued and condemned on the grounds that it establishes exclusionary practices (Black 2021b). Whether one adopts a position of fervent nationalism (bolstered by a nostalgic 'desire' to return to the nation's past) or whether one justifiably critiques the very racial boundaries that delimit a sense of (false) national homogeneity, what both positions assert is a conception of the nation that bears no antagonism and which rests solely on the impossible demand that this 'nation' could ever be so clearly defined and so easily united.

Paradoxically, therefore, whether one remains favourable to promoting a nostalgic 'English' depiction or seeking its critique, both positions maintain a politically conservative social form, which either willingly relies upon or critically understates the importance of the 'nostalgic promise': a promise predicated on the fact that 'Nostalgia remains a useful political tool only insofar as one doesn't effectuate it' (McGowan 2013, 44). In other words, it is only in relation to a nostalgia that cannot ever return to 'the past' that its cultural and political effectiveness is maintained amongst both its proponents and its detractors. Indeed, it is the contention of this chapter that the song – and specifically the chant, 'it's coming home' – does not exhibit a nostalgic significance, but, rather, points to the importance of adopting and promoting a melancholic outlook.

'Everyone seems to know the score...': Melancholic Loss

We can differentiate between nostalgia and melancholy by noting that while both rely upon 'the past', it is melancholy which 'describes an outlook that looks less to re-living the past than to coping with the contemporary situation in which members of a particular linguistic and cultural community find themselves' (Resnick 2008, 790). This emphasis on 'coping' is echoed in a second differentiation that is identified in the distinction between mourning and melancholy, as detailed in the work of Sigmund Freud (2005).[6] In a clinical sense, mourning is often preferred to – even encouraged over – melancholy, so that while mourning refers to a painful working through of loss, from which the individual can then 'move past' (indeed, one works through the loss, eventually finding some manner in which to 'let go'); for the melancholic, there is no separation from loss, no 'moving beyond'. Thus, melancholy occurs when one can't let go of this loss, and, as a result, the subject ends up in a position of inertia, where, consumed by loss, they suffer psychological dysfunction. In examples of nationalism, instances of melancholy become apparent when a certain lamentation for a 'lost' national past is performed (Black 2016; Resnick 2008).

Nonetheless, Freud's differentiations between mourning and melancholy have come under criticism, especially when considered in relation to historical traumas and catastrophe. For example, does the preference for mourning simply absolve one of the loss of the past? What if one's relation to this very past is based upon their own perpetration of violence, or, in the case of former imperial states, the perpetuation of an abhorrent colonialism, for whom responsibility can, following Freud, simply be abdicated and, ultimately, forgotten. According to McIvor (2020, 37), 'Mourning, in this context, is perhaps only a means of reinforcing existing dynamics of power and powerlessness—calling on the (relatively) powerless to forgive and forget that which has not even been remembered'.

56 Jack Black

These contentions underscore Paul Gilroy's (2005) account of contemporary Britain as marked by a national malaise that remains tied to its imperial decline. Encapsulated in what he refers to as a 'postcolonial melancholia', for the UK, it is the effects of this melancholy that have resulted in 'a collective loss of memory that manifest[s] itself as an identity crisis and a neurotic preoccupation with heritage' (Dworkin 2009, 532). Such manifestation works to avoid

> the painful obligations to work through the grim details of imperial and colonial history and to transform paralyzing guilt into a more productive shame that would be conducive to the building of a multicultural nationality that is no longer phobic about the prospect of exposure to either strangers or otherness
>
> (Gilroy 2005, 99).

It is this obligation which is ambivalently managed by a postcolonial melancholia that works to disavow the very melancholy it relies upon. As Fisher (2014, 24) explains, 'The postcolonial melancholia doesn't (just) refuse to accept change; at some level, he refuses to accept that change has happened at all'.

However, what remains under-explored in Gilroy's (2005) account is the effects of this disavowal in elucidating upon the misrecognition it subsequently relies upon. However, for Gilroy, the loss of empire can be 'transformed' via a socially critical and politically engaged discussion of its legacies, what it neglects to recognise is the sense of 'loss' that mediates the melancholic's position and how our present relations to the past are grounded in but also maintained by this constitutive 'loss'. As a result, Gilroy's postcolonial melancholia never elucidates upon the very loss that pre-empts the melancholic's disavowal, ignoring the fact that it is this disavowal that works to 'protect' the melancholic subject, for whom the past as well as the present is always-already lost.

Indeed, the distinction between past and present in accounts of melancholy is given further consideration by Slavoj Žižek (2008, 14–15), who argues that 'when a certain historical moment is (mis)perceived as the moment of loss of some quality, upon closer inspection, it becomes clear that the lost quality only emerged at this very moment of its alleged loss'. Certainly, Žižek's remarks should not be viewed as a dismissal of historical loss but, rather, reconsidered on the basis that it is the (mis)perception of an 'alleged' loss which is fundamentally related to a lack that forever frames this loss. It is on this basis that Žižek's approach to melancholy offers a stark critique to that of Freud, drawing instead from the psychoanalyst, Jacques Lacan. Here, Žižek (2000, 658) notes,

> Against Freud, one should assert the conceptual and ethical primacy of melancholy. In the process of the loss, there is always a remainder that cannot be integrated through the work of mourning, and the ultimate fidelity is the fidelity to this remainder. Mourning is a kind of betrayal, the second killing

of the (lost) object, while the melancholic subject remains faithful to the lost object, refusing to renounce his or her attachment to it.

Elaborating upon this 'faithful' relation to the 'lost object', Žižek adds that 'A melancholic is somebody who has the object of desire but which has lost the desire itself. That is to say, you lose that which makes you desire the desired object' (Žižek and Daly 2004, 112–113). Indeed, what remains central to Žižek's (2000) account is the very way in which the melancholic relates to but also, more importantly, accepts 'loss'.

According to Lacan (2004), this sense of loss is, for the subject, a constitutive part of the subject's symbolic castration; that is, it occurs as part of the subject's entry into language. Here, language presents no fulfilment for the subject but rather cuts the subject – or, 'castrates' the subject – from a perceived prior fulfilment, now lost. The key to Lacan's (2004) account of loss, however, is that this loss is primarily imagined. The subject never had what it thinks it lost, and it is this constant searching for the lost object which preserves our desire. Where the subject's desire is founded in relation to some lost object, it is this 'impossible' object which, for Lacan (1991), constitutes the subject's lack. As a result, attempts to overcome loss are often fuelled by excessive efforts to overcome this inherent lack (which, nonetheless, remain lacking), with sport proving a notable example. Reynoso (2021, 594) emphasises that for both 'fans and many retired athletes ..., winning does not satisfy permanently but only perpetuates the quest for more'.

Consequently, it is not the case that when we receive the object we desire our desire disappears but that it is desire itself which must continually be perpetuated. As a result, 'Desire, ... is the desire for nothing nameable' (Lacan 1991, 223). Though we remain tied to objects of desire, what this desire rests upon is the very 'object-cause' (objet petit a) of desire itself, that which causes us to desire in the first place. If, as Lacan (1991, 223) asserts, 'Desire is a relation of being to lack', then it is this object-cause that is fuelled by the subject's lack.[7] In the case of melancholia, what we perceive is a 'subject who possesses the object but has lost his desire for it because the cause that made him desire this object has withdrawn, lost its efficiency' (Žižek 2000, 662, italics added). It is in this way that the lacking object takes on a certain positivisation for the melancholic: the 'presence' of the object is total, but the desire for it (the object-cause of desire) has been lost. In so doing, the 'deceitful translation of lack into loss enables us to assert our possession of the object; what we never possessed can also never be lost, so the melancholic, in his unconditional fixation on the lost object, in a way possesses it in its very loss' (Žižek 2000, 659–660).

To this extent, we can conceive how it is the melancholic who presents a transmutation of lack into loss. For example, in the case of a melancholic romance, it is often the lack of the very romantic relationship which in turn becomes melancholically transferred to one of loss. What is unique to this melancholic process is that the object of desire – the romantic relationship – never occurred and thus retroactively the lack of this relationship is conceived as already lost (before it even began). Subsequently, in contrast to any 'overcoming' or 'working through' of melancholy, what the melancholic position actively announces is the importance of loss and, as will be depicted in the case of 'it's coming home', the transferral of this loss into a shared symbolic frame of reference.

'Never stopped me dreaming': From Desire to Drive

Through the loss of desire, the melancholic stays clear of availing the desired object any exceptional status. What the melancholic provides, therefore, is the opportunity for an orientation that does not submit to the burdens of desire. In this sense, rather than succumbing to the ambivalence that constitutes one's disavowal of loss, as seen in Gilroy's (2005) postcolonial melancholia, the nation's past, its former glories and its sense of purpose are for the melancholic already pre-emptively lost, thus traversing desire by aligning the melancholic with the constitutive loss that structures both object and subject. This alternate experience of loss, separate from desire, steers towards Lacan's (2004) account of the drive.

Primarily, the distinction between desire and drive is one that can be articulated via the relation between the object-cause of desire and the location of its loss. For desire, the object-cause is always-already lost, resulting in the subject desiring a reprieve to this loss, so that desire 'emerges as lost' (Žižek 2006, 62). In the case of drive, however, the object-cause 'is ... loss itself', so that 'in the shift from desire to drive, we pass from the lost object to loss itself as an object' (Žižek 2006, 62). In sum, 'the weird movement called "drive" is not driven by the "impossible" quest for the lost object; it is a push to enact "loss" – the gap, cut, distance – itself directly' (Žižek 2006, 62).[8]

In examples of nationalism, we can observe the distinction between desire and drive as the void (or gap) which constitutes nationalism's 'lost object' (Black 2021b). Here, 'The mythic point of origin around which nationalism revolves is actually nothing but a gap or void that is positivized through the actions of believers' (Wood 2012, 37). This can be seen in Kenny's (2016, 300) claim that, for some, Englishness 'is ... a kind of void, an empty vessel'. This is echoed by Niven (2020), who highlights that 'One of the major problems with contemporary debates about "Englishness" is that England does not really exist as either a coherent idea or a concrete political reality'. The 'unsurprising' result of this is that 'England' very easily ends up 'as a receptacle for feelings of political disenfranchisement' (Niven 2020). As a receptacle to such disenfranchisement, we can link these examples to a constitutive void for which an apparent loss underlies a 'mythic point of origin' that structures the very object-cause of desire (Wood 2012, 37). That is, it is our desire to fill the void – in this case to fill the 'empty vessel' of nationalism with 'mythic origins' or 'feelings' of 'disenfranchisement' – that permits us to mask or veil our loss with an array of opposing and contradictory national myths, fantasmatic narratives and nostalgic lamentations.[9]

Desire, Drive and the Melancholy of English Football 59

Thus, in contrast to the metonymic process that underscores (nationalist) desire, we can, in accordance with the object-loss of drive, seek to locate a position which echoes that of the melancholic. We can, in other words, 'enjoy the experience of loss—the loss of the privileged object' (McGowan 2013, 70). This is clearly echoed in accounts of sport where so much of 'one's time [and enjoyment] as a fan is psychically spent avoiding loss, displacing loss, inflicting loss, minimizing loss, repairing loss and tolerating loss' (Reynoso 2021, 593). The effects of this form of enjoyment – predicated on drive and adherent to the melancholic position – is one that can both impede and reorientate the potentially debilitating effects of nationalism through examples of melancholy. I would go further here and argue that what melancholy provides – especially in accounts of nationalism – is the direct enactment of the presence of the lost object, from which a 'preoccupation with the past that often appears to be nostalgic [... can] contai[n] a strong element of critical reservation' (Purifoy 2010, 26). Such critical reservation is essential, not just for its aversion to a nostalgic promise of fulfilment but also for the fact that it prescribes a melancholic mediation that presupposes the very loss that endorses one's desire. It is this sense of melancholy that is best encapsulated in the 'it's coming home' chant.

'It's coming home...': The Melancholic Enjoyment of Loss

In interpretations of the 'it's coming home' chant, and the song itself, due attention has been given to the sense of 'irony' it evokes. Greene (2018) asserted that 'the chant-turned-phrase-turned-meme is a winking catch-all to evoke an ironic sense of hope that England could go all the way'. Indeed, the prevalence of such 'humour' was echoed by the current England manager, Gareth Southgate, who sought to link the song with well-known British comedies, such as Fawlty Towers, but who also suggested that such humour can very easily be misconstrued as a sense of English 'entitlement' (Mann-Bryans 2018).

Notably, examples of irony are, for the English, a formative part of what Easthope describes as a repetition of Empire. Here, examples of irony allow the English to recognise the 'inevitably' of empire's loss, while also mourning this loss itself. Easthope's appraisal bears a notable resemblance to the ambivalence that characterises Gilroy's (2005) postcolonial melancholia, an ambivalence evidenced in Malcolm's (2012, 163) concern that humour frequently serves to 'absolve the English from the negative connotations' associated with exclusionary forms of English identification. However, what each of these examples speak to is the very way in which irony serves to distance the comic defender from the social context, allowing them to humorously discount any cries of wrongdoing (Black 2021a). Accordingly, what examples of irony reveal is the very disavowal they contain and rely upon: expressed via a certain… 'I know this is racist, but I'm being ironic, let me have it (and have a laugh)'.

To this end, I argue that neither the chant nor the song depicts some form of 'ironic Englishness' but that any notion of comedy which may be perceived from the chant stems primarily from the comic subversion that it melancholically enacts (Žižek 2000). This subversion is encountered when examples of loss, perceived as a generative feature in the practice of sport as well as its spectatorship, are pinned to the subject's lack (Lacan 1991). This lack is exhibited when we consider the far more obvious assertion that, in 2021, for many attending the games, fan parks, bars, pubs or watching from home, the jubilation of England's success in '66 was a triumph that took place before they were born, and, as such, the essential narrative elements that comprise the lyrics have never been experienced. Equally, though these elements constitute a lack for those who did not experience England's World Cup success, such a lack is also apparent for those whose very lived experiences of '66 posit an absence that continually frames the England team's subsequent endeavours. As a result, the self-sustaining efficacy of this mythic moment, and the enjoyment it evokes, stems primarily, I argue, from the song's clear sense of defeatism. Note the following from Greene (2018):

> The intro features a recording of soccer commentator Alan Hansen complaining about how bad the national team is. 'We're not creative enough, and we're not positive enough,' he says. 'The song is aware of the negative aspects of being an England football fan,' songwriter Baddiel told The Independent in 1996. 'The fact the FA [Football Association] let us do it at all shows a lot of balls on their part.' The chorus mentions '30 years of hurt,' a reference to the 1966 World Cup in England, the last and only time the country has ever won a major tournament. Euro 96 gave fans reason to believe that England could once again 'bring football home,' and 'Three Lions' oscillates between fatalism and optimism for the team's chances.[10]

This defeatism can be identified in the melancholy that underscores the song's lyrics, whereupon 'the singers … rehearse a pain that will not be overcome', a pain emphasised by Young's (2007, 18, parenthesis removed) clarification that 'the Jules Rimet trophy that still gleams in the song was given to Brazil for winning it three times, and therefore can never be won again'. Young's comments are not mere pedantry but, instead, help to expose the lack of certainty and inevitable loss which echoes throughout the song:

> Everyone seems to know the score,
> They've seen it all before,
> They just know, they're so sure,
> That England's going to throw it away,
> Gonna blow it away

The repeated, 'it's coming home', stands, in this light, as a signifier of melancholic loss, indeed a loss which sits closer to the constitutive loss that characterises the Lacanian drive. As a mediation of melancholy – a nonetheless 'enjoyable' form (based, if only, on the fact that the popularity of the song posits a level of enjoyment on behalf of those singing it) – the song embodies loss and the enjoyment therein.

More importantly, this loss is not simply attributed to the fact that England remain, since '66, without an international trophy; instead, the song, the chant and the sense of loss that it portrays provide a unique possibility of procuring an alternative position to desire. It is by both outsourcing and, thus, evoking, our enjoyment through a collective mediation of loss, unreturned, that this position is averred. That is, while the heartbreak felt by English fans upon witnessing their team lose another penalty shootout can be devastating and though the possibility of footballing success would undoubtedly provide a clear sense of elation (for England fans, at least), what both responses ignore is the realisation that our 'enjoyment resides in the moment of the loss of the privileged object, not in the image of its return' (McGowan 2013, 220).[11] By accepting this loss at its very inception, we can assert the melancholic outlook that underlies 'it's coming home' as part of a collectively informed alienation (a universal lack) – one constituted through the inherent sociality of our shared sporting encounters (win or lose).

'It's (not) coming home...': Conclusion

This chapter has argued that an account of melancholy offers a unique response to English football and, specifically, to contemporary accounts of English nationalism. Theoretically, this significance draws primarily from a psychoanalytic (Lacanian/Zizekian) account of the subject and the potential that is afforded in applying Lacan's desire and drive to socio-cultural analyses of sport, football and society. Though this chapter has focused specifically on examples drawn from the English national football team, the adoption of a Lacanian-inspired and Zizekian-influenced account of desire, drive and melancholy offers a novel, yet important, avenue of inquiry into the critical study of sport and, specifically, football. Moving beyond common misconceptions that perceive psychoanalytic theory as concerned with unearthing our subjective depths for signs of malignance, as a method of behavioural alteration or as a path to recentring the 'ego', what psychoanalytic theory provides is a considered engagement with the fundamental inconsistencies and contradictions that ontologically frame both 'reality' and the 'subject' (Zupancic 2008).

In relation to the socio-symbolic field (the 'big Other'), sport plays a unique role in positing these very contradictions, from which 'Sports fandom offers psychoanalysis an unrivaled example of how subjectivity is not only rife with contradictions and conflicts but seeks them out' (Reynoso 2021, 592). Indeed, any relation that we may have with the world's 'beautiful game' is indelibly grounded in a host of social, political and cultural inequalities that are widely known and subsequently disavowed by football fans (as well as sports fans, in general). In fact, limited as much by its capacity to enthral as it is by its frequent frustrations, football's contradictions are marked not only by the well-known corruptions of a sports industrial complex (Maguire 2004) but also by an invented set of arbitrary injunctions, rules and regulations which constitute the game itself (Black 2021c). This is perpetuated in the very inequity that our unconscious sporting desires evoke. As a result, psychoanalytic theory allows us to explore how these contradictions rest upon the subject's unconscious subversion of desire and the enjoyment therein. Though often disavowed, it is here that sport serves to tie the subject to a range of social exclusions, which remain predicated on global systems of injustice that underscore sport's socio-political importance. Nowhere is this more apparent than in the game of football.

In this chapter, these sporting contradictions have been considered in relation to the melancholic significance of the English national football team and the constitutive loss and desire that such melancholy can evoke. Key here is the loss of desire that the melancholic position professes, one that does not succumb to a self-involved, narcissistic decline but which offers a far more critical account of the role of 'loss' for both the subject and society. By paying attention to examples of English melancholy as well as English sporting failure(s), we can observe how enjoyment occurs not at the accomplishment of what may seem impossible but in the realisation that enjoyment relies on the intersection of loss and its inception: a fundamentally melancholic perspective that underpins our sporting endeavours and the nationalism it undoubtedly evokes.

On this basis, both the song, Three Lions, and the accompanying chorus, 'It's coming home', encapsulate and exhibit a melancholic English nationalism that is perhaps best reflected in the current English national football team. Though the English may no longer have a tackle by Moore, a goal by Lineker, a Bobby to belt the ball or a Nobby dancing, there is the opportunity to break the cynicism and hubristic arrogance that so often follows accounts of English nationalism and, more importantly, remake and comically enjoy an unequivocally multicultural, heterogeneous England football team – an England team whose very Englishness is, if anything, certified with its (at present) lack of success. This lack does not desire loss but approaches it as a constitutive feature of English melancholy. A comic resource that always finds it home in 'our' very English failure.

Notes

1 For clarity, any further reference to the 'English national team' will refer explicitly to the men's team.
2 The initial idea for this chapter emerged after England's semi-final defeat at the 2018 World Cup. The relative success of the England team at the most recent international tournament (the 2021 European Championships) has meant that the following discussion will refer to both these tournaments.
3 Thankfully, on Sunday 31st July 2022, the England women's team won the Women's Euro 2022, beating Germany 2-1 in extra-time.
4 Since 1996, the song has received later releases and re-issues, with new version also recorded (Porter 2009). In this chapter, the original 1996 release will be referred to.

Desire, Drive and the Melancholy of English Football 63

5 Originally, the European Championship would have been hosted in 2020, but, due to COVID-19, was postponed until 2021. The 2020 final took place on 11th July 2021.
6 The original essay was titled '*Trauer und Melancholie* (Mourning and Melancholia)' and published in 1917. I have drawn from a later publication (Freud 2005).
7 Žižek elaborates: 'The object-cause of the desire would be that strange imperfection which disturbs the balance, but if you take it away the desire object itself no longer functions, i.e., it is no longer desire. It is a paradoxical obstacle which constitutes that towards which it is an obstacle' (Žižek and Daly 2004, 113).
8 A further way of differentiating between desire and drive is in McGowan's (2011) contention that desire is a means to an end, for drive, the means is the end.
9 In accounts of leftist melancholia, and in examples of nostalgia, it is a fantasy of loss which functions as a defence for the subject against the trauma of their enjoyment, but also the subtle—yet traumatic—realisation that one's loss is constitutive. Fantasy, melancholy, and nostalgia are, in these instances, defences against the subject's castration.
10 It is worth noting that Alan Hansen is a former Scottish footballer, playing for Partick Thistle, Liverpool, and the Scottish national team. His comments in the song's intro refer specifically to the 'English game'.
11 Here, Reynoso (2021, 12) emphasises, 'even when our favored athlete is triumphant and exposes the gap of vicarious relation, fans dwell in incompleteness'.

References

Black, J. 2016. "Celebrating British multiculturalism, lamenting England/Britain's past." *Nations and Nationalism* 22 (4): 786–802.
Black, J. 2019. "From mood to movement: English nationalism, the European Union and taking back control." *Innovation: The European Journal of Social Science Research* 32 (2): 191–210.
Black, J. 2021a. *Race, Racism and Political Correctness in Comedy – A Psychoanalytic Exploration*. Abingdon, UK: Routledge.
Black, J. 2021b. "Sport and the 'National Thing': Exploring sport's emotive significance." *Sport in Society: Cultures, Commerce, Media, Politics* 24 (11): 1956–1970.
Black, J. 2021c. "Football is 'the most important of the least important things': The Illusion of Sport and COVID-19." *Leisure Sciences* 43 (1–2): 97–103.
Black, J., T. Fletcher, and R.J. Lake. 2020. "'Success in Britain comes with an awful lot of small print': Greg Rusedski and the precarious performance of national identity." *Nations and Nationalism* 26 (4): 1104–1123.
Carrington, B. 1998. "'Football's coming home' But whose home? And do we want it?" In *Fanatics! Power, Identity and Fandom in Football*, edited by Adam Brown, 101–123. London, UK: Routledge.
Dworkin, D. 2009. "Paul Gilroy and the cultural politics of decline." *Rethinking History* 13(4): 521–539.
Easthope, A. 1999. *Englishness and National Culture*. London, UK: Routledge.
Fisher, M. 2014. *Ghosts of My Life: Writings on Depression, Hauntology and Lost Futures*. Alresford, UK: Zero Books.
Freud, S. 1917. "Trauer und Melancholie [Mourning and Melancholia]." *Internationale Zeitschrift für Ärztliche Psychoanalyse [International Journal for Medical Psychoanalysis]* 4 (6): 288–301.

Freud, S. 2005. *On Murder, Mourning and Melancholia*. Translated by Shaun Whiteside. London, UK: Penguin.

Garland, J. and M. Rowe. 1999. "War minus the shooting? Jingoism, the English Press, and Euro 96." *Journal of Sport & Social Issues* 23 (1): 80–95.

Gilroy, P. 2005. *Postcolonial Melancholia*. New York, NY: Columbia University Press.

Greene, N. 2018. "Why 'it's coming home' is the phrase that defines England's World Cup hopes." *Slate*, July 8. https://slate.com/culture/2018/07/three-lions-came-out-in-1996-but-its-coming-home-is-the-phrase-that-defines-englands-2018-world-cup-hopes.html

Holt, R. 1992. *Sport and the British: A Modern History*. Oxford, UK: Clarendon Press.

Kenny, M. 2016. "The 'Politicisation' of Englishness: Towards a framework for political analysis." *Political Studies Review* 14 (3): 325–334.

Lacan, J. 1991. *The Ego in Freud's Theory and in the Technique of Psychoanalysis, Book II*. Edited by Jacques-Alain Miller, translated by Sylvana Tomaselli. New York, NY: Norton.

Lacan, J. 2004. *The Four Fundamental Concepts of Pscyho-Analysis*. Edited by Jacques-Alain Miller, translated by Alan Sheridan. London, UK: Karnac.

Maguire, J. 2004. "Challenging the sports–industrial complex: Human sciences, advocacy and service." *European Physical Education Review* 10 (3): 299–322.

Malcolm, D. 2012. *Globalizing Cricket: Englishness, Empire and Identity*. London, UK: Bloomsbury.

Mann-Bryans, M. 2018. "Croatia missed the English humour in 'It's Coming Home' mantra during World Cup run, insists Gareth Southgate." *The Independent*, October 12. https://www.independent.co.uk/sport/football/international/croatia-vs-england-uefa-nations-league-what-time-where-live-stream-gareth-southgate-its-coming-home-world-cup-a8580126.html

McGowan, T. 2011. *Out of Time: Desire in Atemporal Cinema*. Minneapolis: University of Minnesota Press.

McGowan, T. 2013. *Enjoying What We Don't Have: The Political Project of Psychoanalysis*. Lincoln: University of Nebraska Press.

McIvor, D.W. 2020. "Clad in mourning: Psychoanalysis and race in contemporary America." *Journal of Psychosocial Studies* 13 (1): 35–48.

Niven, A. 2020. "Why it's time to stop talking about English identity." *The Guardian*, July 15. https://www.theguardian.com/commentisfree/2020/jul/15/english-identity-patriotism-england-independent

Porter, D. 2009. "Egg and chips with the Connellys: Remembering 1966." *Sport in History* 29 (3): 519–539.

Purifoy, C. 2010. "Melancholic patriotism and 'the waves'." *Twentieth Century Literature* 56 (1): 25–46.

Resnick, R. 2008. "Hubris and melancholy in multinational states." *Nations and Nationalism* 14 (4): 789–807.

Reynoso, J.S. 2021. "Boston sucks! A psychoanalysis of sports." *Psychoanalysis, Culture & Society* 26 (4): 591–607.

Wood, K. *Žižek: A Reader's Guide*. Malden, MA: Wiley-Blackwell.

Young, C. 2007. "Two world wars and one world cup: Humour, Trauma and the asymmetric relationship in Anglo-German Football." *Sport in History* 27 (1): 1–23.

Žižek, S. 2000. "Melancholy and the act." *Critical Inquiry* 26 (4): 657–681.
Žižek, S. 2006. *The Parallax View.* Cambridge, MA: The MIT Press.
Žižek, S. 2008. *The Plague of Fantasies.* London, UK: Verso.
Žižek, S. and G. Daly. 2004. *Conversations with Žižek.* Cambridge, UK: Polity.
Zupancic, A. 2008. *Why Psychoanalysis? Three Interventions.* Aarhus, DK: Aarhus University Press.

Chapter 5

An Alternative Lens for Grassroots Sport

De-schooling Football

Andy Pitchford, Ben Moreland, Debbie Sayers and Will Roberts

Introduction

For those of us whose livelihoods are supported by institutions and whose professional expertise lies in the realm of education or health, Ivan Illich's books can be an uncomfortable read. We proceed with our professional or vocational lives with great confidence in the basic assumption that education is a 'good thing' and that the more widely we share its benefits, the better place the world will become. We are also rarely prompted to question the value of professions themselves, those occupational communities which generously, charitably or altruistically choose to share their knowledge to help the (supposed) less fortunate – or the less educated or qualified. Many of the authors of this text lead quite agreeable and enjoyable lives on the basis of the intersection of schooling, professional expertise and institutional life. So, to encounter an author who so incisively questions the fundamental legitimacy and merit of these constructs in contemporary society can be quite disquieting and disarming. It certainly has been for us!

In a sense, Illich's willingness to critique otherwise unquestioned pillars of our society may be one reason for the fluctuation of interest in his ideas over the years. Initial excitement about his writing in the 1970s and 1980s faded as, arguably, the juggernaut of formal, accredited schooling which he so opposed continued its inexorable conquest of the globe. In the same period, Illich's work became unfairly associated with some reactionary movements in relation to the privatisation of education and the increasingly prominent questioning of the integrity of medical knowledge, which peaked during the Covid pandemic in 2020 and 2021. All the while, colleagues in higher education were also probably aware of his withering criticisms of universities themselves, which, far from being 'a liberated zone' for the contemplation of ideas 'old and new', were presented by Illich as indoctrination factories that supported the perpetuation of the very institutions and organisations of which he was so suspicious. It is perhaps hardly surprising that Illich's work rarely features in academic curricula and that his work has been effectively 'written out' of this world (Gabbard, 1993).

However, in many other contexts, the influence of Illich's work has become increasingly visible since the turn of the millennium. His views on the relationships

DOI: 10.4324/9781003253990-8

between industrialisation, consumption and the environment presaged contemporary debate over the climate crisis and possible community responses (see de Majo, 2016; Sajay, 1988); his critique of professional knowledge and his defence of community and tradition are a key influence in the rise of radical community development practices in the US (consider McKnight and Block, 2010) and associated movements in the UK and Republic of Ireland (Russell, 2020); and his quest for more humane forms of economy and association is increasingly referenced in texts that attempt to model new alternatives to capitalist structures and formulations (see for example Bregman, 2021).

We therefore present Ivan Illich to you as a heretical writer whose interpretation and articulation of our history and present offer us lenses through which to view our own lives differently and which may help us to imagine new ways of working, being and associating. Despite the disdain in which his work is often held, we consider his ideas to be provocative and enlivening and worthy of further consideration. The realm of grassroots football may appear to be a modest, inconsequential realm through which to explore his contemporary relevance, but we argue that its popularity and ubiquity afford us an opportunity to reflect on practices with which many will be familiar.

Exploring Ivan Illich: A History of Anarchism

Ivan Illich's work can be seen as part of a longer tradition of anarchist writing and activism that is fundamentally suspicious of the motives and tendencies of organisations and institutions. This suspicion is held in relation to the state and governments in particular but extends to all use of authority by individuals, communities and agencies. At the heart of this tradition is an interpretation of human nature that is essentially positive, which, contrary to mainstream Western liberal thought, perceives people as inherently good. Following this view, conflict, discord, unhappiness and misery are most likely to occur when, in various ways, we impose upon this goodwill through the often-illegitimate actions of institutions. This contrasts with the more familiar idea, to those of us living in the conditions of late capitalism at any rate, that human beings are, instead, selfish, 'egoist' and competitive at their core. Acknowledging and respecting such motives, according to contemporary wisdom, enable us to build societal structures and conditions that are most likely to support economic growth, entrepreneurial spirit and self-reliance.

Through his writing, Illich constructs a critique of capitalist society which is faithful to the anarchist tradition but which is searing in its intensity. He uses a historical lens to afford us refreshed interpretations of the role of major institutions in our society, questioning the legitimacy of those who hold power over us and unpacking how those groups or institutions came to claim authority in the first place. Illich's grasp of mediaeval history, in particular his understanding of religious institutions and how they were able to encourage and manage assent and

68 Andy Pitchford et al.

consent among populations, enabled him to generate a quite different reading of the purpose of many of our most familiar and reassuring institutions. Schools, for example, are so embedded in our imagination as a 'good and 'worthwhile' thing that Illich's critique of their fundamental purpose hits us like a train when we first encounter it. Illich is not interested in reforming schools or in finding ways to enable critical pedagogies to infiltrate the curriculum. Instead his argument is that the whole enterprise is pernicious and manipulative. For Illich, education serves only the interests of the powerful, and no amount of tinkering, review or adjustment addresses that essential fact.

An Austrian by birth, Illich studied in Italy but travelled extensively. His major works were written across the Atlantic, and he had a long association with Latin America. He spent his later years between Mexico, the USA and Germany and had a variety of 'visiting' associations with universities but never regarded higher education as his home ground. He died in 2002 aged 76. Illich associated with, and effectively mentored, several other writers from the left field of educational studies, including Paulo Freire, with whom he had a long friendship (Kahn and Kellner, 2007). With most of these relationships however, a point of departure was reached when it became clear that Illich's interpretation of the function of schooling was unwavering. He did not believe in reform or the notion that empowering approaches to learning might alter the nature of the curriculum and how it was experienced. Freire, in contrast, has inspired educators to embrace forms of pedagogy within, as well as beyond, formal institutions. Freire's work retains hope (see for example Freire, 2014) that, in broad terms, schooling can be reformed or that strands of the educative process can be liberatory for individuals and communities.

In his major works, Illich argues that modern societies, particularly those in the capitalist form, have a series of dehumanising tendencies that make us, in various ways, lonely, alienated, unwell and disconnected from our fundamental capacities and purposes. He considers society to be damaged by economic growth and that we as individuals are conditioned to accept our roles as contributors to a system that supports the powerful. Illich presents colonialism as a significant force in the process of domination and inequity, particularly the ways in which Western science has marginalised and undermined forms of knowledge that are grounded in community and tradition. His reading of the processes of exploitation and commodification led him to be fearful for our ecological future, and even in the 1970s, he foresaw many aspects of the current climate crisis.

Throughout his career, Illich's particular focus was on the role of institutions and professionals in perpetuating the dehumanising aspects of modern society. Increasingly, he argued, society is reliant on these agencies to support our 'obsession' with production and consumption. We need more and more institutions to manage this duality, and over time, their activity drowns out other aspects of our lives that might be more rewarding, collaborative or creative, for example, positive relationships at the community level. This process also diminishes our confidence as we learn to rely on institutions rather than having faith

An Alternative Lens for Grassroots Sport: De-schooling Football 69

in our own capabilities or those of our families or friends. However, in addition to the inexorable growth of institutions, there is also a contradiction in their function. Over time, they tend to move away from their original purpose and end up doing the opposite of what they were originally designed to do. For Illich, 'our major institutions have acquired the uncanny power to subvert the very purposes for which they were engineered and financed' (1978, p. 67). Hospitals, he argues, make us unwell; schools keep us docile and stupefied.

Within and between these institutions, groups of people who are designated as 'professionals' create and manage our needs in various subtle ways. These needs relate to interactions that in the past were the concern of communities but which now are the subject of services delivered to customers or clients. This is perhaps most easy to imagine in the realm of health and physical and mental wellbeing, but for Illich, it extends across great swathes of modern life. In Useful Unemployment, Illich argues that 'professions claim the power to prescribe. They not only advertise what is good, but ordain what is right' (1978, p. 41). They hold this power by 'concession' of an elite whose interests they serve and use professional discourse and language – their 'twisted jargon' – in order to communicate their status, presenting their knowledge as the truth, while simultaneously marginalising other forms of understanding. Needs are created by these professional groups, and we then fall into an 'illusory sense' of being a client who can be saved by experts, rather than a citizen with the strengths and capabilities to solve problems independently. Illich continues: 'Increasingly, needs are created by the advertising slogan and by purchases made by order from registrar, dietician, gynaecologist and dozens of other prescribing diagnosticists' (op cit, p. 59).

Professional power is further perpetuated by the maintenance of a series of myths about human nature and the ways in which societies and communities could and should work. Illich depicts us as being trapped in cycles of consumption and production, which we deem to be normal and natural but which are in fact the outcome of developments in Western capitalism over the centuries. We are 'prisoners to time-consuming acceleration, stupefying education and sick-making medicine' (op cit, 1978, p. 70) and are trained from birth to accept this as the natural order of things. At the centre of the system of acculturation and training that prepares us for these commodified, restricted lives, is the school.

Illich, the Institution of School and De-schooling Society

To make sense of Illich's interpretation of the school, we must take a moment to view everyday cynicism about education with renewed seriousness. 'Thought control', 'dark sarcasm' and children as 'bricks in the wall' are oft-cited lyrics reflecting an underlying distrust of mass education, but they are also notions that Illich wants us to consider more carefully. For Illich, schools are not institutions which are primarily focused on empowerment, creativity, fulfilment and solidarity. Instead, their role is to train us for submission to a system and to guide us towards acceptance of our future place in the production cycle and our position in the 'pecking order'. In some respects, this reads as the standard Marxist critique of schooling in capitalism, but Illich goes further, arguing that schooling subtly conditions participants to learn to need institutions and to rely on the expertise of professions.

> The existence of schools produces the demand for schooling. Once we have learned to need school, all our activities tend to take the shape of client relationships with other specialised institutions.
>
> (1970, p. 39)

Our lives, then, become shaped by these expectations. We will only progress in life if we accept the products on offer from institutions and the guidance available from professions. School sets these expectations through its formal curriculum, which serves as a 'creator and sustainer of social myth because of its structure as a ritual game of graded promotions' (op cit, p. 44), while what we would regard as the 'hidden curriculum' ... 'serves as a ritual of initiation into a growth-oriented consumer society for rich and poor alike' (op cit, p. 33).

The latent functions of school are, for Illich, custodial care, (de)selection and indoctrination. Through these functions, we first learn the myth of meritocratic advance and the reality of rewards for submission to the system. Formal schooling imposes conditions upon us to secure these forms of understanding. These conditions are so universal that we assume that they operate for the benefit of children, in the sense that they facilitate personal growth, learning and joy. Illich argues that in contrast, these impositions are intended to quash creativity, destroy intrinsic motivation and enforce dependence.

These conditions include grouping in age cohorts; the imposition of a daily timetable and submission to the bell or whistle; an obligatory curriculum with defined learning outcomes; the prioritisation of assessment, sorting and sifting; and reward structures including streaming and awards. All of this is underscored by two particular features – the compulsory nature of formal schooling and the centrality of the teacher. Schooling revolves around the teacher and their ability to instruct, but Illich questions this very notion:

> School is an institution built on the axiom that learning is the result of teaching. And institutionalised wisdom continues to accept this axiom, despite overwhelming evidence to the contrary.
>
> (op cit, p. 28)

> In fact, learning is the human activity which least needs manipulation by others ... Most learning is not the result of instruction. It is, rather, the result of unhampered participation in a meaningful setting.
>
> (p. 39)

An Alternative Lens for Grassroots Sport: De-schooling Football   71

The structures of the school shepherd us speedily to the conclusion that the teacher has 'sacred authority' as the custodian of rules, the master of ceremonies, the moralist (substituting for parents, 'god' or the state) and the therapist, legitimising their forays into the personal lives and choices of the student.

This reading of the school is difficult for us all to accept because we are all so acculturated to a more functional interpretation. Many of us are also heavily invested in the system, which brings us varied advantages and privileges. This acceptance is so deeply held that Illich does not consider reform to be a worthwhile pursuit. Instead, he argues, we should seek to 'de-school' society, abolish formal education and seek alternatives which recognise the conditions in which learners might find intrinsic motivation. This might include acknowledgement of other facets of life where learning can take place, perhaps leisure, the family, the workplace and other more 'convivial' settings. By convivial, Illich means relations between people that are characterised by autonomy, creativity and compassion. In later works (particularly Tools for Conviviality, 1973), Illich expounds this argument further and imagines new forms of institutional life that facilitate these forms of relationship.

Despite his dark reading of some of the most familiar and foundational aspects of our society, Illich does not lack hope. His vision of 'de-schooled' institutions may stretch our imagination and empathy, but this does give us a set of principles that enable us to reflect upon our current condition and upon how our lives could be if we were prepared to embrace alternative forms of organisation and association. In the next section, we outline the emergence of one such institution – grassroots football – to offer insight into the ways in which we might 'de-school' the beautiful game.

The Emergence of the Grassroots Game

Young people who participate in grassroots football[1] in England experience a version of the game that has undergone rapid transformation in the past 15 years. Safeguarding regulations and interventions aimed at mitigating poor practice have been accompanied by a series of modifications to the structures and laws of the sport, all of which were intended to advance the interests of young people (Howie and Allison, ibid). The Football Association National Game Strategies of 2008 and 2011 (The FA, 2008; 2011) cemented policies which adjusted space, equipment, team numbers, goal size and match-day management, apparently in favour of the participant. These processes reached their zenith with the publication of the 2012 Football Association Youth Development Review (The FA, 2012), which led to further refining of competition management, decision making and approaches to inclusion. The Review also initially included proposals to adjust age banding – so children would play in competitions organised by their year of birth, rather than their school year – in an attempt to counter the challenges of the relative age effect (Helsen et al., 2005; Cobley et al., 2009). However, this aspect was among the few that were eventually rejected by the governing body.

The nature of youth football has therefore arguably changed since the 1990s and early 2000s, when the sport was centred more overtly on adult control and values, with children of all ages playing on full-size pitches, with full-size goals, with full-size footballs and under the direction of largely unqualified and unregulated coaches. Junior teams, clubs and leagues had proliferated in this period, particularly after the withdrawal of Physical Education professionals from the extra-curricular sport realm in the 1980s and 1990s. The introduction of mini soccer, which followed the publication of The Football Association's Quarter for Quality in 1997, was intended as an attempt by the governing body to reassert control over this particular form of the sport. In essence however, mini soccer was appropriated by a newly active 'Dad's Army' of volunteer coaches, who adapted it to their own needs and interests (Pitchford, 2007, ibid), something that offers a rejoinder to Illich's argument regarding the way in which institutions serve those in power.

This version of football was organised under the auspices of voluntary sector clubs, leagues, and County Football Associations, who took responsibility for officiating and discipline. By the mid-2000s, the field had been subjected to attempts by Central Government to rationalise the voluntary sector to make its constituent organisations more 'business-like' and amenable to various government agendas (Lusted and Gorman, 2010). The Football Association's Charter Standard scheme, itself modelled on kitemarking schemes from other National Governing Bodies, was certainly successful in establishing a more accountable and sustainable model of club operations. It also cemented a particular interpretation of what it means to be a member of a club and what the purposes of that club might ultimately be. FA Charter Standard clubs, as they were known in the mid-2000s, are tied to competition sanctioned by the governing body; they are effectively vehicles for league entry. They create apparently safe and regulated environments, but they are not founded on democratic engagement or membership rights (see The Football Association, 2018). This is significant because it implies that FA Charter Standard clubs represent a quite different value set from many of the institutions that provided the foundation for football for adults and youths in the C20th. All of these help to demonstrate the view that propounded in Pitchford (2007) building on Gruneau (1983), that the football that young people experience is a constructed and contested domain. Its particular form is the outcome of the historical inter-play of agencies, the state and the market. As with all kinds of structured leisure activity, the football that we know is the product of the intersection of a range of variables. One of these is the practice of sport coaching.

The Practice of Coaching in Grassroots Football

Coaching in youth football is a significant social practice. According to data from The Football Association, there are over 300,000 qualified coaches in England, 200,000 of whom first qualified in the period since 2010. They are associated with 64,000 youth teams, which in turn compete within 1,200 leagues, supporting 460,000 young people who play affiliated football (The Football Association 2015, 2018). This is a separate realm from the form of football that significant proportions of young people experience in school as part of the national curriculum or associated provisions, which is overseen in the main by the teaching profession but, as we will see, also relies on coaching provision regulated by The Football Association and related bodies, such as The FA Premier League and the Professional Footballers Association. It is also distinct from coaching provision for elite forms of the sport, now predominantly managed under the banner of The FA Premier League's Elite Player Performance Plan (EPPP) (Premier League, 2012).

Coaching in the voluntary sector, or grass roots, youth football, has only recently developed as a distinctive social practice. Up until the late 1950s and 1960s and the emergence of the FA Youth Cup, which encouraged professional clubs to begin the process of developing specific provision for players under 18, the instruction of children in football was essentially the preserve of the teaching profession under the auspices of the English Schools Football Association (Kerrigan, 2004). In the first half of the C20th, the concept of coaching was conflated with leadership, management and training within the professional game. Many professional clubs persisted with the 'trainer', with the implicit focus on physical preparation and fitness, in preference to the more effete 'coach', well into the 1960s. However, as Taylor and Garrett (2010) demonstrate, the term gradually gained favour due to the success of migrant English ex-professionals to Europe from the 1920s onwards, who were able to translate technical and tactical knowledge for new audiences with a great impact. In the same period, the idea of the coach was becoming more widespread and accepted across a range of sports as traditions of amateurism began to wane, and science became more applied to support performance (Day and Carpenter, 2017).

On this basis, it is possible to see how the various components of grassroots football have been constructed and then reproduced by those actors with a particular stake in the process. Voluntary sector coaching has been professionalised through accreditation and licensing, with a protected and legitimised group now responsible for leadership and management in club settings. In turn, these settings are constructed in a particular form, one which essentially serves the purposes of affiliation and entry into competitions sanctioned by the governing body. The predominance of performance and competition in these settings, at the expense of inclusion and participation, can be explained in part by environmental factors. The sport is structured around inter-club competition, characterised by published results and league tables. We have argued elsewhere (Pitchford, 2007) that this supports the reproduction of coach-centred practices, where adults view the sport instrumentally and organise activities accordingly, selecting those players viewed most likely to be successful on the pitch regardless of age, maturity and other mitigating factors and then mimicking the 'bawl, bollock and bark' approaches that they perceive to be characteristic of the professional game or of coaching in their own younger days.

74 Andy Pitchford et al.

These factors coalesce in ways that remind us of some of Illich's fears about institutions. Rather than being settings where fun, enjoyment and celebration are paramount, grassroots football clubs are often highly pressurised environments, where outcome trumps process and where results on the pitch are more important than the experience of an individual. Illich would recognise the irony that a grassroots football club ought, in principle at least, to be a convivial institution. But conviviality frequently gives way to competitive instincts, and the bubble of joy is burst on the need to protect and enhance reputation. Viewed from this perspective, adult coaches are Illich's 'professionals', inventing the need for instruction and authority. Without coaches, the argument goes, children will not improve. Without improvement, they are unlikely to find success in the outcomes of matches or success in the quest to become a professional player. A narrative of production surrounds coaching in these settings, underlying the apparent need to develop or produce players for some other purpose. The authority of the coach, and the ability to condition the experience of the players, is legitimised by these largely unquestioned assumptions. So too is the dominance of white males in these settings, with the voices of women or ethnic minorities inevitably marginalised in a manner that reflects the long-standing values of the professional game.

We have demonstrated that it is possible to paint a picture of grassroots football that reflects Illich's fears about institutions and professionals. We have also been at pains to point out that the form of football that is currently predominant is a construction that has emerged as the outcome of particular historical events and processes. Other forms of the game, and the sport, can easily be imagined. Other forms of club principles and structures exist in other sectors, supporting other pursuits. We may infer discontent with grassroots football as it is currently experienced, but it is equally clear that other versions are possible. The question to ask now is whether other versions are available? To answer this, we turn to our case study to assess the extent to which clubs in the current climate can conceivably 'de-school' football and present an alternative to the dominant approach to leading and organising children's sport.

De-Schooling Football: The Case of Salisbury Rovers

According to Fred Bowen (2019) of the Washington Post in his review of a recent research publication on children's participation in sport from George Washington University, he noted, 'When it comes to organized sports, kids just want to have fun. Maybe everyone should listen to the kids'. This view of placing the child at the centre of sports practice is one not shared by many, yet one football club in Wiltshire, UK, Salisbury Rovers FC (SRFC), has been doing just that since 2016. This England accredited[2] football club in the heart of Salisbury has been working tirelessly to bring joy back into football for its participants. Spearheaded by Debbie Sayers, co-author of this chapter, a human rights lawyer, football coach and founder of SRFC, the club prioritises the power of community and is committed

An Alternative Lens for Grassroots Sport: De-schooling Football 75

to ensuring youth football is a children's game, passionately believing that it belongs to those who play it and not to adults that oversee it. Yet the problem for SRFC, and quite possibly football more broadly, is that the game is governed and organised in a way which allows young people little say or influence. How then has the club sought to challenge prevailing thinking?

In response to dominant football ideologies, SRFC have developed a philosophy (Salisbury Rovers, 2022) which underpins everything the clubs seeks to do. The first example of this can be seen in big red writing on their website:[3] 'ADULT WARNING! We are firm about our philosophy, and we want to encourage independence and autonomy in children, so if you are looking for coach-led/directed football, we are very happy to make recommendations for other clubs'. This clear commitment to empowering young people to exercise autonomy over their decision-making is accompanied by a set of eight rules and three pledges as follows:

SRFC Rules

1   We prioritise children's rights
2   Our child-centred goals mean we don't hold trials
3   We expect high standards from our coaches and promote continuing professional development
4   Our football is truly competitive
5   We organise equal pitch time for every child
6   We rotate positions
7   We do not direct play in matches
8   Kids' voices will always be louder than the adults. It is their game, let them play!

SRFC Pledges:

1   Provide the best quality environment
2   Allow kids to play with freedom
3   Develop the whole child

By communicating their values so clearly, SRFC are attempting to develop and preserve a consistent philosophy that can be shared by all stakeholders and to build a sense of belonging and purpose that guides the practice of all members. New members are made aware of these values right from their first interaction with the club, avoiding the confusion that parents frequently experience in mainstream clubs – will my child be picked? Is my child dispensable?

SRFC are also attempting to create a different form of relationship between members and the club. When parents take their first steps to 'sign up', they are encouraged to commit to voluntary activity and to making a contribution to the community, rather than viewing the club as a commercial service to be paid for. Children experience membership through a range of democratic devices and are empowered to lead, take decisions and take responsibility. SRFC is therefore not a

76 Andy Pitchford et al.

transactional setting, members are encouraged to participate in various ways and to play a part in the process. Here, we see the seeds of a new type of club, reflecting the rich democratic heritage of the British voluntary sector and eschewing the packaged, commodified experience so common elsewhere.

What can be seen in both the rules and pledges is that SRFC are indeed different: their philosophy, governance and approach to football at the grassroots level is uncommon. The long-term approach to youth sports is driven by a commitment to the rights of children, so it rejects a focus on short-term results, in favour of facilitating the holistic development of the young person. Although the club currently competes in standard FA-affiliated competitions, they consistently experiment with other formats. The competitive aspect is not the 'be all and end all', play is celebrated and facilitated in many different ways. Rather than characterise weekly sessions as 'training' and therefore as preparation for the ultimate goal of performance, SRFC use other terms to describe activity, always emphasising the value of play and participation. Whether SRFC continue to participate in mainstream inter-club competition remains to be seen; exponential growth in recent seasons may enable the club to host intra-club competition (on the Dutch or German model) and sustain itself without recourse to tournaments or leagues that may see them clash with other clubs or organisations.

The club places great emphasis on strength-based approaches to participation. Players are encouraged to co-create curricula and individual sessions, often working with leaders or mentors from older age groups. Adults are facilitators, finding ways to empower players while sharing responsibility for safety and overall structure. The club makes it clear that the football 'space' belongs to the child, openly stating that children should not play for adult entertainment, they should play for themselves and because they love football. Player ownership and a love of the game create self-motivated learners, driving individual development.

So, the example of SRFC is one of very few in football that seeks to push against the dominance of mainstream football, challenging the very premise of adults 'developing' players and more importantly people. The club openly proclaims the importance of community and social responsibility in club documents, asking everyone registering to play an active role if they can. Parallels can be drawn between the hallmarks of this philosophy and approach at SRFC and the work of Illich. It is here we now move for a closer examination.

De-Schooling Football: Repurposing the Beautiful Game

Ivan Illich has not been an influence on the development of Salisbury Rovers. The founders and members do not report any familiarity with his work, nor do they recognise his influence on other spheres. However, there do appear to be some accidental parallels between Illich's thinking about institutions and the principles that have informed the conception and growth of this unique football club.

An Alternative Lens for Grassroots Sport: De-schooling Football   77

Illich feared the growth of institutions. He saw them as disabling influences, often developing into parodies of their original intended purpose. Structures, bureaucracy and administration squeeze out the space for creativity, leaving behind nonsensical processes and arbitrary laws. In seeking a new version of football, supported by a new type of club, Salisbury Rovers are reflecting this fear – that mainstream organisations tend to close down fun, play and expression. They deem an alternative form to be necessary.

Illich was cynical about the motives and practices of professionals. These were groups who invented needs and convinced others of their unique ability to satisfy these requirements. In reality, individuals and communities have the capabilities and capacities to meet these needs – if they exist at all – but professionals insert themselves into the process and manipulate others to convince them of the legitimacy of their position. Salisbury Rovers share this cynicism, but for them, the 'professionals' are those coaches who prioritise their own need for status and productive activity over the expectations and hopes of the children involved. In most football settings, the coach is the central character, dominating goal setting and planning, organising time and activity and determining need and response. Coaches typically espouse a narrative of production, developing players for some external future need rather than focusing on the here and now. Salisbury Rovers are attempting to create a quite different conception of the coach as an individual who facilitates the requirements of the children and who listens, shares, supports and works in partnership.

Illich saw hope in the development of convivial organisations, mutual associations that prioritised creativity and collaboration. Typically, these organisations would be in the voluntary sphere, away from the constraining gaze of the state or corporate enterprises, unsullied by commercial motives or the broader commodifying tendencies of contemporary capitalism. Salisbury Rovers share this hope, railing against many grassroots clubs who pay scant attention to membership rights, democracy or creativity. They are searching instead for new forms of organisation that enable members to have greater say and that provide secure foundations that enable individuals to express themselves and to develop in ways that they chose, rather than have chosen for them.

Salisbury's attempt to 'de-school' football can probably be seen most clearly in their approach to player autonomy and decision making. SRFC's sessions are framed and designed to serve the interests of the players, asking and empowering them to make decisions. Sessions are co-created and can be delivered by players themselves in older age groups. In accordance with the United Nations Convention on the Rights of the Child (UNCRC), the club has developed principles based on Lundy's (2007) work for embedding the youth voice across its operations: tell, ask, listen and show. Adults tell children that their views are valued and have an impact. They ask children for their views and feedback, they actively listen to this feedback and they act upon it. The club's football sessions deliver on this by encouraging the young people to think for themselves, prioritising the internal motivation of the players. Further reading of the case

78   Andy Pitchford et al.

study also acknowledges another facet of Illich's thinking and is epitomised in the adult warning noted above. SRFC are committed to rejecting coach-led and adult-led philosophies in football, and this aligns well with Illich's rejection of structuring education, and we contest here the structuring of youth football. This manifests itself in the club's literature; for example, they have established 'Guiding Principles' which underpin practice and 'Who we are' documents sent to every prospective inquirer for a club place (both available on the 'Join Us' section of the club website). Their public commitments to no trials, equal game time and the lack of coach-directed play are not only bold (and some may say brave given the power of 'big football') but also a unique version of the de-schooling that Illich called for.

So, what SRFC provides is one response (if radical) in a footballing sense to the power and sell of big football and all the glories that ensue. SRFC will not be without its critics for its version of a de-schooled youth football, and there is a line of other examples that lay cast aside after trying to alter the foundations of youth football. Yet SRFC provides hope that football can be more than just a production line of potential talent that serves the powerful, a hope that football might just serve those who actually play the game, in a youth football context at least.

Conclusion

Though radical, and at times unpalatable, our reading of Illich has allowed us to explore some of the mechanisms and structures that are enacted upon individuals. The unhealthy control of young people in educational settings with 'their' best interests or good in mind is worthy of challenge. In our case study, we have found an example of a club who – however unwittingly – are trying to create 'de-schooled' environments. They are embracing some of the calls made by Illich to combat (de)selection, commodification, professional control and individualism. Embracing the community and connectedness might be an answer to some of the problems in grassroots sport. And perhaps more broadly in society as Illich contends. The trajectory away from an adult-centred, hyper-competitive culture that reinforces and reproduces various forms of domination and inequality, towards one that respects the rights of all participants, promotes their interests and fosters a positive and enriching environment which is enticing. And yet borrowing from Illich's ideas on schooling, conflict and tension still exist. It is evident that traditional approaches to coaching in grassroots football persist even if hidden under the auspices of growth and reinvention. Additionally, traditional values may still predominate and those who espouse child-centred or rights-based approaches may see themselves as 'alternative' or counter to the established norms of youth football. Perhaps Illich had a point; tinkering and adjusting the grassroots game may not be enough. Perhaps a more radical 'de-schooling' is required in order to truly place the child at the centre of their own experiences, an endeavour that should be educational, creative, liberating and engaging.

Notes

1 For the purposes of this paper, 'grass roots' youth football refers to affiliated forms of the sport – competitions, leagues and cups – run by voluntary sector agencies but regulated by the governing body, The Football Association.
2 England accredited has replaced the Chartered Standard approach to club accreditation https://www.englandfootball.com/run/leagues-and-clubs/england-football-accreditation
3 Salisbury Rovers FC website https://www.salisburyroversfc.co.uk/

References

Bowen, F. (2019) What makes sports fun? According to this study, winning isn't the most important thing. https://www.washingtonpost.com/lifestyle/kidspost/-what-makes-sports-fun-according-to-this-study-winning-isnt-the-most-important-thing/2019/11/27/63c52f06-0d8a-11ea-bd9d-c628fd48b3a0_story.html, accessed on 02/08/2022.

Bregman, R. (2021) *Humankind: A Hopeful History*. London: Bloomsbury.

Cobley, S., Baker, J., Wattie, N., and McKenna, J. (2009) Annual age-grouping and athlete development: A meta-analytical review of relative age effects in sport. *Sports Medicine (Auckland, N.Z.)*, Vol.39, 235–256.

Day, D., & Carpenter, T. (2017) *A History of Sports Coaching in Britain Overcoming Amateurism*. Routledge: Routledge Research in Sports Coaching.

de Majo, C. (2016) Ivan Illich's radical thought and the convivial solution to the ecological crisis. *The International Journal of Illich Studies*, Vol.5 (1). Available at https://journals.psu.edu/illichstudies/article/view/60126, accessed on 07/01/2022.

Freire, P. (2014) *Pedagogy of Hope: Reliving Pedagogy of the Oppressed*. London: Bloomsbury.

Gabbard, D.A. (1993) *Silencing Ivan Illich: A Foucauldian Analysis of Intellectual Exclusion*. Lanham, MD: Rowman & Littlefield.

Gruneau R. S. & Page C. H. (1983) *Class sports and Social Development*. Amherst: University of Massachusetts Press.

Helsen, W., Winckel, J., and Williams, A. (2005) The relative age effect in youth soccer across Europe. *Journal of Sports Sciences*, Vol.23, 629–636. doi:10.1080/02640410400021310.

Illich, I. (1970) *Deschooling Society*. London: Marion Boyers.

Illich, I. (1973) *Tools for Conviviality*. London: Marion Boyers.

Illich, I. (1978) *The Right to Useful Unemployment*. London: Marion Boyers.

Kahn, R. and Kellner, D. (2007) Paulo Freire and Ivan Illich: Technology, politics and the reconstruction of education. *Policy Futures in Education*, Vol.5 (4). doi:10.2304/pfie.2007.5.4.431.

Lundy, L. (2007). 'Voice' is not enough: Conceptualising Article 12 of the United Nations convention on the rights of the child. *British Educational Research Journal*, Vol.33 (6), 927–942.

Lusted, J., and O'Gorman, D. (2010) The impact of New Labour's modernisation agenda on the English grass-roots football workforce, *Managing Leisure*, Vol.15(1–2), 140–154. doi:10.1080/13606710903448236.

Kerrigan, C. (2004) *Teachers and Football: Schoolboy Association Football in England, 1885–1915* (1st ed.). Routledge. https://doi.org/10.4324/9780203006337

McKnight, J. and Block, P. (2010) *The Abundant Community: Awakening the Power of Families and Neighbourhoods*. San Francisco, CA: Berrett-Koehler.

Pitchford, A. (2007) Children and young people. In C. Brackenridge, A. Pitchford, K. Russell and G. Nutt (eds) *Child Welfare in Football*. London: Routledge, pp. 71–82.

Premier League (2012) *The Elite Player Performance Plan*. London.

Russell, C. (2020) *Rekindling Democracy: A Professional's Guide to Working in Citizen Space*. Eugene, Oregon: Cascade.

Sajay, S. (ed) (1988) *Beyond Economics and Ecology. The Radical Thought of Ivan Illich*. London: Marion Boyers.

Salisbury Rovers (2022) Available from https://www.salisburyroversfc.co.uk/ accessed on 22/07/2022.

Taylor, B. & Garratt, D. (2010) The professionalisation of sports coaching: relations of power, resistance and compliance, *Sport, Education and Society*, Vol.15(1), 121–139. doi:10.1080/13573320903461103.

The Football Association (2008) *The FA National Game Strategy (2008–2012)*. London: The Football Association.

The Football Association (2010) *The Future Game Grassroots – The FA Technical Guide to Young Player Development*. London: The Football Association.

The Football Association (2011) *The FA National Game Strategy (2011–2015)*. London: The Football Association.

The Football Association (2012) *Youth Development Review*. London: The Football Association.

The Football Association (2015) *The State of the Game: In Numbers*. London: The Football Association.

The Football Association (2018) *The FA Charter Standard: Club Criteria from 2018-2019*. London: The Football Association. Available at http://www.thefa.com/get-involved/player/the-fa-charter-standard/benefits-and-incentives, accessed on 27/4/ 2022.

Chapter 6

Negotiating Identity Conflict Through Football

Experiences of People Living with Type 1 Diabetes

Christopher Bright and Győző Molnár

Introduction

Diabetes mellitus is a medical condition that affects close to 4 million people in the UK alone, and the figure continues to rise (Diabetes UK, 2019). Despite the growing number of people affected by the condition and its social impact, research focus in sport has predominantly involved the management implications and physiological aspects of the condition (Jimenez et al., 2007). Although studies which investigate the social influence of diabetes within sport have recently emerged (Jaggers et al., 2016), research in this area is in its infancy. Given the scientific lacuna between diabetes and social sciences, there are multiple avenues to explore. Type 1 Diabetes (T1D) is classified as a hidden disability by UK law, but in relation to sport, the only participatory opportunity for people experiencing T1D comes in the form of mainstream sport (Equality Act, 2010). This contradiction is rare and further complicated by the distinction between Type 1 and Type 2 diabetes and that UK law designates very few cases of Type 2 Diabetes (T2D) as a disability (Diabetes UK, 2022).

Types 1 and 2 both fall under the umbrella term of diabetes, but there are key differences in the way they are managed and contracted (Diabetes UK, 2022). T1D is an autoimmune condition whereby the body attacks its own beta cells within the pancreas, which are responsible for producing insulin. Insulin is a vital hormone that moves glucose from the blood to cells to allow for the synthesis of glucose as a fuel when creating energy. There is no known cure for the condition or a clear understanding as to why it happens to certain people, but it leads to a life of exogenous insulin supplementation (Diabetes UK, 2022). T2D occurs when insulin is unable to work properly within the blood or not enough of it is produced to support the amount of glucose consumed or circulating. Often the treatment for the condition is improving diet and/or lifestyle as 50% of the cases relate to an unhealthy lifestyle or dietary choices (Diabetes UK, 2022). Therefore, the difference between Type 1 and Type 2 is that in some cases, Type 2 is avoidable and reversible. Society has a tendency to attach stigma to diabetes because of the links between unhealthy lifestyle choices and some T2D cases. This social generalisation, however, has created a fissure between the types of diabetes relating

DOI: 10.4324/9781003253990-9

to the identity of the community. Furthermore, given the dissonance between mainstream cultural narratives around diabetes and its sub-cultural perception, it is sensible to argue that identity formation associated with and within this community is a complex process which may influence the interaction of those living with diabetes with wider society (Cunnah, 2015; Carter, 2016).

The complexity of how the diabetes community's identity is constructed relates to broader issues around disability identity and classification for people with diabetes (Huang and Brittain, 2006; Fitzgerald, 2012). The medical model has been predominantly deployed to classify disabilities and designate the severity for conditions requiring the healthcare profession's support (Haegele and Hodge, 2016). This has given the medical profession the power to define what impairment and disability represent in society and sport, which has entrusted them with upholding legislative decisions that categorise health and illness (Howe, 2008; Kitchin and Howe, 2014). The health-illness binary narrative has created a unique scenario in relation to T1D and sport. To live with a disability that is not recognised in disability sport is an exceptional and, in many ways, challenging situation, for which the medical model's limitation is largely responsible. The narrow utility of the medical model regarding its practical and theoretical implications has been broadly recognised in academia, yet it remains the dominant paradigm in disability sports and adapted physical activity (Spencer & Molnár, 2022). The dominance of the medical model offers a possible explanation as to why there is still limited research around issues of disability identity for people with T1D and their complex identity formation in relation to football and sport more widely (Equality Act, 2010). Therefore, in this chapter, we explore how participants with T1D and passion for football have managed and negotiated their identity within the context of an online peer support community through Maffesoli's (1996) Neo-Tribe theory.

Neo-Tribe is an established sociological concept introduced in the past 25 years to offer an explanation of the sub-cultures which exist within our communities (Maffesoli, 1996). The concept was formulated by Maffesoli (1996) to theorise coherent sub-cultures that present themselves in different groups of people. They are said to demonstrate gatherings without organisational rigidity, whose members share a similar state of mind, that can be expressed through lifestyles or ritualistic behaviour (Kriwoken and Hardy, 2018). Importantly, Neo-Tribes do not link to traditional, permanent or tangible entities through which pre-existing communities have been established. The concept recognises that society has moved away from traditional frameworks and structures to an existence that is more fluid in its approach to social positioning, networks and values (Best, 2013). With emerging trends around online communities emanating as a result of traditional networks failing to fully encompass a community's need, the principles behind a Neo-Tribe may provide an explanation for the continued growth of the number and range of online communities such as online health communities, an example of which is discussed in this chapter.

The Neo-Tribe is an emerging concept within the field of sport studies as communities continue to adopt differing formats, gradually moving away from

Negotiating Identity Conflict Through Football 83

traditional physical communities, with reliance on omnipresent online connectedness that helps to provide foundations for expansion, as well as a fluidity, that underpins the existence of neo-tribes. The study from Asan et al. (2021) is an exploration of the concept's existence within cycling. Their work studied the online interactions of two cycling communities to ascertain whether the common characteristics of a neo-tribe continued to exist within a sporting environment. They present a view that demonstrates that the cycling communities continue to share values, concerns and a fluidity of identity that embody the main characteristics of a neo-tribe. This is congruent with Best's (2013) study; however, Asan et al. (2021) highlight the intensity of the 'feeling of us' which was a recurring reference to the togetherness seen within the community in their study. This feeling could be increased through exposure to sport, which encourages teamwork and can reinforce team culture and high levels of cohesion. Consequently, sport can heighten community cohesion striving towards those shared goals of sporting success and enjoyment. Given that shared concerns can enhance cohesion (Asan et al., 2021), it could be argued that the feeling of togetherness and the existence of neo-tribes in sport may be amplified when influenced by a medical condition such as diabetes. However, Asan et al.'s (2021) study has focused on cycling, an individualistic sport, which may have an impact on participants' desire to engage, as they are often less reliant on team connections. This does not appear to be the case in football that is a team sport, but the existence of neo-tribe-type cultures within and in relation to it is still under explored. Nevertheless, Asan et al.'s (2021) study is pertinent to this chapter as they suggested that a chronic illness would strengthen a Neo-Tribe's cohesion and increase interaction, which, in turn, may help contribute to the explanation for TDFC's (The Diabetes Football Community) success as an online sport and health community.

Yet, it is the choice between identification and non-identification with diabetes that seems to offer a stronger potential foundation for Neo-Tribe formation within the work of TDFC. The principles behind the Neo-Tribe concept may present an explanation for the creation of values that underpin TDFC (2022). Shared values and experiences, the fluidity of identity and the absence of a pre-existing community to identify with jointly replicate some of the key characteristics that a Neo-Tribe demonstrates (Best, 2013). When considering that TDFC (2022) presents a new formation of a community, created online, with members all living with the same chronic health condition, the potential for association with the Neo-Tribe concept becomes evident. Adding to the above list the temporary identification that online communities can offer, which may involve an infrequent post or a one-off engagement in a physical or online discussion, further connections can be detected (Hardy et al., 2012).

The ease of access to and flexibility of identification with the group's purpose may enable a transition to associate with T1D, a condition adversely framed by the medical model of disability (Haegele and Hodge, 2016). Consequently, pertinent questions to consider are whether TDFC (2022) is a Neo-Tribe? Does the potentially fluid identification with the community and stigma surrounding T1D make interaction in this instance easier than a traditional community? As members of the community can create distance between their condition and community engagement as a result of the intermittent nature of interaction in community activities, as well as an irregular identification with the values and purpose of TDFC (2022), the Neo-Tribe concept may help with our understanding as to why this online sport and health community has been successfully established. Therefore, it is possible to postulate that the concept of the Neo-Tribe in the TDFC context has utility in understanding the negotiation of identity in relation to diabetes, which has social stigma, through temporary, infrequent and self-determined interactions such as social media posts, reading blogs and engaging in online forum chats provided by TDFC. Furthermore, the Neo-Tribe concept may deepen our understanding of identity formation in this group concerning the interplay between their condition and community, which, in turn, may help ascertain future treatment pathways, thereby moving towards greater engagement with medical advice, such as the use of peer support communities.

Methods

To explore the experiences of the participants involved in TDFC and understand their motives and feelings, a qualitative approach was utilised (Huang and Brittain, 2006; Perrier et al., 2014). The study followed a multi-method approach involving a case-study design, which explored the community's interactions through semi-structured interviews and netnography (Cunnah, 2015).

To recruit participants, the process was similar to that of the work of Smith et al. (2016), whereby social media was utilised to communicate the research and need for participants who fit a number of inclusion criteria (Sparkes and Smith, 2014). Six male T1D football players were recruited for this study. Utilising an interview schedule devised to guide the process, each participant was interviewed once examining concepts including disability identity, community formation and peer support. To build upon the semi-structured interviews, a netnographic approach allowed for data collection from TDFC (2022) website, Facebook and Twitter pages, from which the project originates, to understand its establishment and continued development. The posts captured include the top five performing blog posts, top five Facebook page posts and top five tweets based upon views and likes, respectively (Zhang, 2016).

Online content and interview transcripts were put through thematic analysis (Wang, 2019). To do this, the raw themes were identified from the interviews and participants' posts expressed on TDFC media channels. Participants are represented by pseudonyms in the sections below.

Stigma – A Cause for Identity Conflict?

Goffman (1963) argued that deviating from dominant characteristics and qualities held throughout society creates a spoiled, undesirable identity. This leads to the ostracisation of non-conforming members and low perceived value of them within social hierarchies. Through the widespread adoption of social labelling, which reinforces cultural meanings associated with a term, self-identity can be impacted. This effect is particularly potent when a term acquires a negative connotation (Li and Moore, 2001). As T1D is classified as a hidden disability (Equality Act, 2010), the word disability suggests that the beholder has a lack of aptitude or skill which drives a negative perception of those associated with the condition (Zhuang et al., 2017). Consequently, it may be argued that disability is associated with low expectations and a perception of weakness around those who experience such conditions which can be seen by the accounts of participants (Zhuang et al., 2017). When asked about T1D-related negative social perceptions, many participants recalled instances and their feelings around stigma. David explained that

> I know society's perception of, not the condition diabetes, but the word diabetes, and what people relate it to. Then I just thought if someone looks upon me as a person, as a whole, as it was if I'd been for a job interview they could, possibly, see it as something that's a negative to me as a person.

Participants demonstrated their view of society's perception of T1D contributing to a feeling of shame derived from living with the condition. Society's interpretation of the word diabetes and its meaning is a real-life experience of stigma, a perception that the condition was self-inflicted and avoidable as well as highlighting the negative attitudes towards disability (Green, 2003). That is, even though this condition was not self-inflicted, participants have been labelled with an unfavourable association. Stigma impacting people with a health condition has been expressed in other works focusing on HIV/AIDS, mental health and T2D (Browne et al., 2017). In fact, one of the issues for participants was around the lack of understanding of diabetes and confusing T1D and T2D. Jordan explained:

> They [T1D and T2D] get grouped together by using the same word, and then just changing a number on the end. Yeah, I guess people have got their feelings on Type 2 that it's due to your unhealthy lifestyle and poor diet, because that's what society leads them to believe and that's the reason why someone would have Type 2... I think they're both conditions that you need help with, obviously, but it would make it much simpler if they were called different things.

As T2D equates to 90% of diabetes cases, most of society's understanding relates to this version, despite a significant number experiencing T1D (circa 400,000 people in the UK). T2D has been attributed a social stigma which is recognised by Browne et al. (2013). However, society's confusion around diabetes has seemingly led to a divide in the diabetes community within which people with T1D have grown frustrated as they are too associated with negative connotations that do not reflect their condition. The division has been reported by Browne et al.

86 Christopher Bright and Győző Molnár

(2014) but has not been recognised in a sporting setting, where weaknesses are frequently shunned as those may accentuate the potential for disassociation with and acceptance in sport (Brittain, 2004). Consequently, understanding how the conflation of T1D and T2D impacts on condition management, health and identity is vital in informing future treatment pathways.

Nevertheless, participants noted that they had adopted their own coping mechanism to manage social stigma associated with the conflation of T1D and T2D. David explains:

> I've hidden it for a good 20 odd years, as a feeling of being different to other people… Before I had the confidence to treat my diabetes in public, I'd go out for a meal where I should be injecting before, I'd leave right up until I got home to inject, which would then [make] my blood [sugar] go high and I'd have all the problems of that. So, it affected my own care for myself.

Highlighted is the impact that stigma has had on the decisions participants made about treating their diabetes to feel accepted in society, which meant hiding their identification with diabetes. Society continues to uphold stigma for disabilities which continue to demonstrate a difference to the majority (Goffman, 1963). Cunningham and Pickett (2018) showcased this through the stigma connected to bodyweight which is easily exercised via visible corporeal deviation from societal norms. However, T1D compares closely with mental health stigma through the invisibility of the conditions. Smith and Applegate (2018) showcase the enduring widespread stigma linked to mental health, which continues to impact on accessing help that furthers the likelihood of adopting secrecy to cope with the conditions. This is congruent with the work of Buttgieg et al. (2017), who suggested that the social stigma surrounding diabetes disrupted self-management whilst highlighting secrecy as a coping mechanism (see also Gredig and Bartelsen-Raemy, 2017). Rather than making choices that would mean better results and control for their T1D, participants expressed that they would rather behave in a way that conforms to society's expectations, despite the need to effectively manage their condition.

Identity – Disability – Diabetes

Interestingly, there is little literature referring to sports-specific T1D communities, the effect of elitism and its impact upon hiding perceived weakness by those living with a chronic illness (Trejo et al., 2017). There is also a low level of open diabetes identification amongst those living with T1D involved in elite football (Commissariat et al., 2016; Cunningham and Pickett, 2018). People with an athletic identity and T1D fear that by showing weakness they are assigned a stigma, which, in turn, could impact their athletic career and lead to limited self-management (Cosh et al., 2013; Commissariat et al., 2016). Coupled with the social expectation that athletes are supposed to embody health and peak performance, the fact that athletes experiencing T1D require exogenous insulin to survive yet compete within mainstream sport also troubles that image. To preserve the idea of corporeal health and peak performance, athletes may resort to hiding the condition (Fitzgerald, 2012). Liam explains:

> That stigma about male sport is a case of, it's alpha male. You have to be seen as untouchable and it's for your own self-worth and you know as well as I do, you walk out on that pitch and if you don't feel like you're untouchable and you're the best on that pitch then you're giving away an advantage. And if you think you'll be seen as that [having T1D] and that's given them an advantage then you do yourself... a disservice.

The need to show no weakness and appear 'untouchable' is unsurprising given that elitism is promoted within sport (Bailey et al., 2016; Buttgieg et al., 2017). However, it is evident from the narratives that having a hidden disability is emotive, personal and debated in the T1D community. As T1D is classified as a hidden disability under the Equality Act (2010), the medical model seems to be dominant as to how those living with the condition are perceived and treated (Fitzgerald, 2012). However, the perception of people living with T1D and their interpretations as to whether it is a disability differs from the identity prescribed by the medical model.

Members of the community demonstrate a divided view around T1D as a disability. Mark showcases these perceptions:

> I've had this question on questionnaires a few times. I would also tick no because I like to think that I can live without needing any particular, special support. Although, I do feel it would be good as a diabetic to know that you would have that support if you need it. There are times in case of an emergency where I think it definitely comes under the disability category.

This dualistic perception of T1D in relation to it being or not being a disability indicates a clash between the medical and social models of disability (Huang and Brittain, 2006; Cunnah, 2015). Both models suggest that the power to bestow disability identity upon someone is outside of the individual's control and is performed by either the medical profession or society. However, interviewees revealed that their own experiences of disability are complex and shifting, which demonstrates a closer link to the social-relational model. Importantly, as T1D is invisible, besides blood glucose monitoring and administering insulin, the hidden element allows the adoption of secrecy as a coping mechanism which provides greater autonomy around disability identification for this group. It is also seen through the participants' use of 'I think' and 'I perceive', which suggests that they hold some power in the way they view themselves in relation to disability, to which people experiencing other types of disability may not be able to relate. Therefore, the social-relational model and its focus on connecting lived

Neo-Tribe and the Football Community

experience with the impact of society and medical professionals are a closer representation of the disability identification process of those living with T1D and may also help underpin engagement levels with their condition and projects like TDFC (Campbell, 2018).

Neo-Tribe and the Football Community

Participants' views reveal that after becoming part of TDFC, they experienced a shift towards pride for living with T1D, an acknowledgement of support and shared experience as well as an ability to communicate and share through social media. By utilising social media, participants could remove geographic barriers, create aliases, participate when and however they preferred or even just 'lurk' (see Thomas et al., 2016). By having the opportunity to participate in TDFC (2022) and identify with it through the use of social media, the concept of the project portrays key characteristics of a Neo-Tribe (Kriwoken and Hardy, 2018). Jordan showcases those values in this account:

> I see on social media all the time people sharing positive stories of people with Type 1 diabetics, whether it's children, player of the match, or scored a goal, or people just having little wins. I just think it's so proud to be part of that community.

A Neo-Tribe is a type of sub-culture, where an organisational impact has not yet been felt and members share a similar state of mind which is also expressed through their behaviour (Best, 2013). The concept suggests that the dissolving of unity within existing societal structures has paved the way for more fluid movements of people, in which those associated will not label themselves with one particular identity but instead move between numerous groups (Dedman, 2011; O'Reilly, 2012). Its premise aligns closely with the foundations of TDFC (2022), and participants' accounts demonstrate a clear connection to its values and purpose. As society has moved away from traditional frameworks to social positioning, values and networks in favour of a more fluid approach, there has been a space afforded to online communities which, in this case, may present through the concept of Neo-Tribe (Best, 2013). As TDFC (2022) is connected to social media as a movement that embodies shared values, a new form of networking and a new approach to anything society had provided before for this population, it again stands to reason that a Neo-Tribe may provide the closest representation as to how this emerging community has come to exist. Hardy et al. (2012) explored a population within a sub-culture which experienced a fluid identity that shifted through their temporary experiences together and the multiple facets of the group's identity. As participants had been grappling with an identity linked to T1D which is stigmatised, the opportunity to temporarily access that identity to seek out positive experiences through TDFC seems conceivable. This helped participants gain T1D-related information, peer support and an acceptance of their condition, whilst utilising football, which embodies desirable social attributes, to support with their T1D whilst potentially avoiding some of the stigma attached to the condition (Snelgrove, 2015). By participating in TDFC in a temporary way, stigma could be avoided, identity towards their condition may be enhanced and, as Browne et al. (2013) suggest, this may also have a positive impact on their long-term self-management of T1D through greater levels of acceptance and adherence. Therefore, in establishing a movement through social media, TDFC has embodied the characteristics of a Neo-Tribe, which may have also aided with navigating a stigmatised identity for those with T1D through the use of an online peer support community (Hardy et al., 2013; Browne et al., 2014).

Conclusion

The form that TDFC has taken on is an emerging topic for academia to contemplate when addressing a stigmatised group of people living with a chronic illness. When considering the frustration at the social stigma that this T1D population feel, and subsequent reluctance to associate with the condition through fear of non-acceptance in an elitist masculine football culture, it would seem that the cohort would be destined, as referenced by the literature, to a lack of identification with their condition which leads to poorer self-management outcomes (Gredig and Bartelsen-Raemy, 2017). However, TDFC (2022) has brought about change for this population in how they view and interact with the condition, which demonstrates close links to the sociological concept of Neo-Tribe (Hardy et al., 2012). The temporary acknowledgement and identification with the condition allow the participants to engage with T1D on their own terms, without the pressure of traditional communities (Zhao et al., 2015). Nevertheless, the main reason for engagement with their condition in this population is because the community is built upon their interest first. Football as a sport with a widespread appeal is positively viewed across the world, and in this population, in particular, it is a large part of with what they self-identify. Football may have presented a problem for this community previously with its cultural perception of illness that those living with the condition found difficult to overcome. However, the sport through this project now links participants to their condition positively, which has aided identification with T1D that may never have occurred otherwise (Browne et al., 2014). Instead, through the adoption of a positively viewed sport, combined with the opportunity to temporarily identify with T1D through the use of social media, a group of people have found a way to meaningfully connect with their chronic condition. In providing a platform that has connected a population to their condition, potentially for the first time, greater health outcomes may be achieved (Browne et al., 2014). This embodiment of a Neo-Tribe, utilising football, to positively link participants to their condition is one which future research and healthcare professionals should consider when enhancing future treatment pathways for those living with chronic illness.

References

Asan, K., Chi, C. and Yolal, M. (2021) Cohesion in cycling neo-tribes: A netnographic approach. *Leisure Studies accessed at:* https://doi-org.apollo.worc.ac.uk/10.1080/02614367.2021.2006277

Bailey, A., Gammage, K. van Ingen, C. and Ditor, D. (2016) Managing the stigma: Exploring body image experiences and self-presentation among people with spinal cord injury. *Health Psychology Open* 3, 1–10.

Best, S. (2013) Liquid fandom: Neo-Tribe s and fandom in the context of liquid modernity. *Soccer & Society* 14, 80–92.

Brittain, I. (2004) Perceptions of disability and their impact upon involvement in sport for people with disabilities at all levels. *Journal of Sport and Social Issues* 28, 429–452.

Browne, J., Ventura, A., Mosely, K. and Speight, J. (2013) 'I call it the blame and shame disease': A qualitative study about perceptions of social stigma surrounding type 2 diabetes. *BMJ Open* 3, 1–10.

Browne, J., Ventura, A., Mosely, K. and Speight, J. (2014) 'I'm not a druggie, I'm just a diabetic': A qualitative study of stigma from the perspective of adults with type 1 diabetes. *BMJ Open* 4, e005625.

Browne, J., Ventura, A., Mosely, K. and Speight, J. (2017) Measuring Type 1 diabetes stigma: Development and validation of the Type 1 Diabetes Stigma Assessment Scale (DSAS-1). *Diabetic Medicine* 34, 1773–1782.

Buttgieg, N., Ersser, S. and Cowdell, F. (2017) The influence of social stigma on diabetes self management amongst Maltese individuals with diabetes. *European Journal of Public Health* 27, 30.

Campbell, N. (2018) Higher education experiences of elite student- para-athletes in the UK. *Journal of Further and Higher Education* 42, 769–783.

Carter, M. (2016) An autoethnographic analysis of sports identity change. *Sport in Society* 19, 1667–1689.

Commissariat, P., Kenowitz, J., Trast, J., Heptulla, R and Gonzalez, J. (2016) Developing a personal and social identity with Type 1 diabetes during adolescence: A hypothesis generative study. *Qualitative Health Research* 26, 672–684.

Cosh, S., Crabb, S. and LeCouteur, A. (2013) Elite athletes and retirement: Identity, choice, and agency. *Australian Journal of Psychology* 65, 89–97.

Cunnah, W. (2015) Disabled students: Identity, inclusion and work based placements. *Disability & Society* 30, 213–226.

Cunningham, G. and Pickett, A. (2018) Body weight stigma in physical activity settings. *American Journal of Health Studies* 33, 21–29.

Dedman, T. (2011) Agency in UK hip-hop and grime youth subcultures – Peripherals and purists. *Journal of Youth Studies* 14, 507–522.

Diabetes UK (2019) Available at: https://www.diabetes.org.uk/professionals/position-statements-reports/statistics/diabetes-prevalence-2019 (Accessed: 02/01/2021)

Diabetes UK (2022) Available at: https://www.diabetes.org.uk/guide-to-diabetes/life-with-diabetes/your-legal-rights (Accessed: 02/01/2022)

Equality Act2010, C.15. Available at: https://www.legislation.gov.uk/ukpga/2010/15/pdfs/ukpga_20100015_en.pdf (Accessed 22/11/2017)

Fitzgerald, H. (2012) Paralympic athletes and "knowing disability". *International Journal of Disability, Development and Education* 59, 243–255.

Goffman, E. (1963). *Stigma: Notes on the Management of Spoiled Identity*. New York: Simon & Schuster.

Gredig, D. and Bartelsen-Raemy, A. (2017) Diabetes-related stigma affects the quality of life of people living with diabetes mellitus in Switzerland: Implications for healthcare providers. *Health and Social Care in the Community* 25, 1620–1633.

Green, S. (2003) "What do you mean 'what's wrong with her?'": Stigma and the lives of families of children with disabilities. *Social Science & Medicine* 57, 1361–1374.

Haegele, A. and Hodge, S. (2016) Disability discourse: Overview and critiques of the medical and social models. *Quest* 68, 193–206.

Hardy, A., Gretzel, U. and Hanson, D. (2013) Travelling Neo-Tribe s: Conceptualising recreational vehicle users. *Journal of Tourism and Cultural Change* 11, 48–60.

Hardy, A., Hanson, D. and Gretzel, U. (2012) Online representations of RVing Neo-Tribe s in the USA and Australia. *Journal of Tourism and Cultural Change* 10, 219–232.

Howe, D. (2008) The tail is wagging the dog: Body culture, classification and the Paralympic movement. *Ethnography* 9, 499–517.

Huang, C. and Brittain, I. (2006) Negotiating identities through disability sport. *Sociology of Sport Journal* 23, 352–375.

Jaggers, J., Hynes, K. and Wintergerst, K. (2016) Exercise and sport participation for individuals with Type 1 diabetes: Safety considerations and the unknown. *ACSM's Health & Fitness Journal* 20, 40–44.

Jimenez, C., Corcoran, M., Crawley, J., Hornsby, G., Peer, K., Philbin, R. and Riddell, M. (2007) National athletic trainers' association position statement: Management of the athlete with Type 1 diabetes mellitus. *Journal of Athletic Training* 42, 536–545.

Kitchin, P. and Howe, D. (2014) The mainstreaming of disability cricket in England and Wales: Integration 'One Game' at a time. *Sport Management Review* 17, 65–77.

Kriwoken, L. and Hardy, A. (2018) Neo-Tribe s and Antarctic expedition cruise ship tourists. *Annals of Leisure Research* 21, 161–177.

Li, L. and Moore, D. (2001) Disability and illicit drug use: An application of labeling theory. *Deviant Behaviour* 22, 1–21.

Maffesoli, M. (1996) *The Time of the Tribes*. London: Sage.

O'Reilly, D. (2012) Maffesoli and consumer tribes: Developing the theoretical links. *Marketing Theory* 12, 341–347.

Perrier, M., Smith, B., Strachan, S. and Latimer-Cheung, A. (2014) Narratives of athletic identity after acquiring a permanent physical disability. *Adapted Physical Activity Quarterly* 31, 106–124.

Smith, R. and Applegate, A. (2018) Mental health stigma and communication and their intersections with education. *Communication Education* 67, 382–408.

Smith, B., Bundon, A. and Best, M. (2016). Disability sport and activist identities: A qualitative study of narratives of activism among elite athletes' with impairment. *Psychology of Sport and Exercise* 26, 139–148.

Snelgrove, R. (2015) Youth with chronic illness forming identities through leisure. *Journal of Leisure Research* 47, 154–173.

Sparkes, A. and Smith, B. (2014) *Qualitative Research Methods in Sport, Exercise and Health*. London and New York: Routledge.

Spencer, Nancy L. I. and Molnár, G. (2022) Whose knowledge counts? Examining paradigmatic trends in adapted physical activity research. *Quest* 74(1), 1–16.

TheDiabetesFootballCommunity(2022)Availableat:https://thediabetesfootballcommunity. com/ (Accessed 02/01/2022)

Thomas, J., McVey, N. and Twogood, R. (2016) Physiotalk – Understanding the reach of a socialmediacommunity. *Physiotherapy* 102, 140–141.

Trejo, F., Attali, M. and Magee, J. (2017) The experience of defeat: Applying Goffman to examine a football tournament for socially excluded homeless individuals. *International Review for the Sociology of Sport* 52, 615–630.

Wang, L. (2019) Perspectives of students with special needs on inclusion in general physical education: A social-relational model of disability. *Adapted Physical Activity Quarterly* 36, 242–263.

Zhang, Y. (2016) Understanding the use of online health communities from a self-determination perspective. *Journal of the Association for Information Science and Technology* 67, 2842–2857.

Zhao, J., Wang, T and Fan, X. (2015) Patient value co-creation in online health communities: Social identity effects on customer knowledge contributions and membership continuance intentions in online health communities. *Journal of Service Management* 26, 72–96.

Zhuang, X., Keung Wong, D., Cheng, C. and Pan, S. (2017) Mental health literacy, stigma and perception of causation of mental illness among Chinese people in Taiwan. *International Journal of Social Psychiatry* 63, 498–507.

Chapter 7

Professional Knowledge Development in Performance Pathways

A Futsal Case Study Through the Lens of Practice Architectures

Siôn Kitson, Pete Vallance and Simon Phelan

Introduction

Perhaps overly simplistically, the goal of professional sport coaching has at times been conceived as the simple passing of technical knowledge to athletes in a linear fashion to support their achievement of set performance targets (Werthner & Trudel, 2006). Whilst this means that levels of success can easily be measured, it negates consideration for the distinctive needs of different sports and undervalues the importance of preserving professional knowledge development through the cultivation of shared language, relationships and behaviours. Indeed, it has been argued that talented athletes only achieve their full potential when 'appropriate and stimulating' development opportunities are provided (Vaeyens et al., 2008, p. 709). There is a need, therefore, to evaluate the appropriateness of each practice environment, ensuring that coaches are continuing to progress in their understanding of the needs of athletes in order to be able to adapt accordingly.

Within academic discourse, sport coaching is recognised as a complex and dynamic task (Bowes & Jones, 2006), largely centred on knowledge constructed through the lived experiences of coaches interacting with those around them. It is through these experiences that practitioners create a sense of meaning and context, and despite noted attempts to capture this through formal and informal means of professional development, critiques remain as to the effectiveness of the support provided (i.e., mentoring programmes, communities of practice) (Stoszkowski and Collins, 2014; Leeder and Sawiuk, 2020). As such, learning designers are challenges as to how they might support and guide such interactions in a generative manner.

These interactions between coaches, athletes and key stakeholders can be thought of as taking place amid the interrelated socio-cultural arrangements of any given context, referred by some practice theorists as a 'practice architecture' (Kemmis, 2012), a set of conditions which shape the activity possible in any space and time. (Practice in this sense refers to any human behaviour, such as the development of institutional/organisational knowledge.) Proponents of

DOI: 10.4324/9781003253990-10

this theoretical lens would thus argue that to support learning and knowledge development, we must understand the interplay of situated actions, dialogues, structures and relationships in any coaching context. Indeed, each interaction thus plays a part in the construction of knowledge within a sporting programme.

Within this chapter, we suggest that the concept of practice architectures offers a unique perspective for exploring how professional sports coaches can improve their practice and cultivate training programmes that prioritise the construction of tacit knowledge in athletes to enhance performance. Using a contemporary case study from the England Men's U21 Futsal Performance Programme, this chapter seeks to identify lessons learnt from applying an intentional philosophical and pedagogical approach, designed to support athlete autonomy and accountability. It explores the broader ecology of the coaching workplace through a sociological lens, examining the use of language, actions and relationships when constructing a collaborative and effective coaching programme that consciously operates within a wider framework of time and space. In doing so, this chapter highlights the importance of retaining and safeguarding professional knowledge within elite sport settings, whilst providing a language for learning designers to challenge the complexity of learning in this context and carefully craft foundations for long-term athletic development.

Theoretical Background: Practice Architectures

The theory of 'Practice Architectures' (PAs) is a 'politicised' practice theory (Mahon et al., 2017), reflective of the work of Bourdieu, Giddens and Foucault, in that it pays attention to the 'everyday' 'lifeworld' (Reckwitz, 2002, p. 244), framing practices as situated, social and relational. The theory suggests that any human behaviour, or practice, is shaped by the historical and cultural conditions of a locality at any given moment. Specifically, practice (i.e., learning) is deemed to be conditioned by the result of three interdependent arrangements: cultural–discursive, material–economic and social–political.

The identification of these three intersubjective dimensions acts to highlight the complexity of practice sites, with particular attention paid to the complexity of relationships between distinct practices and sites (Schatzki, 2002). The cultural–discursive arrangements are those that represent the language of any practice, capturing the 'sayings' used to describe, interpret and justify behaviour. For example, a discourse predicated on winning and competition might foster a culture of 'performance over all else'. The material–economic arrangements are those that condition the 'doings' of practice, as they define 'what can be done amid the physical set-ups' of practice locations (Kemmis et al., 2014, p. 32). For example, this might encompass access to specialised equipment, performance support or simply the setup of a coach's workplace. The social–political arrangements are those that shape power and solidarity,

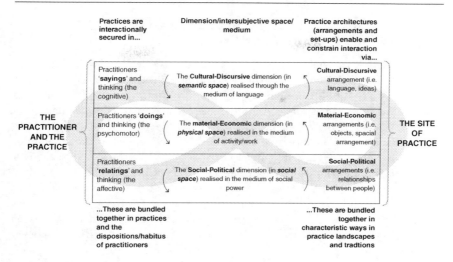

Figure 7.1 Illustration of the PA framework.
Source: Adapted from Hemmings et al. (2013).

conditions which relate to the understanding of roles, rules and organisational norms. For example, this could capture inherent hierarchies within a training centre or routines over who does what, when and where. Across these three dimensions, the roles of language, work and power are inextricably interconnected in the mediation of which practices are possible or not, whilst importantly considering the materiality and historied dimensions of practice (Marx, 1845; Shove et al., 2012).

A key implication of PA for coaching practitioners is that the interplay of the three interdependent arrangements (cultural–discursive, material–economic and social–political) enables and constrains practice through an individual's participation, where that participation is itself mediated by personal dispositions (Mahon et al., 2017) or habitus (Bourdieu, 1990). In doing so, acts of participation shape and reshape the particular 'site of practice', creating practice traditions through legacies of intersubjective interaction (Kemmis et al., 2014). Within any site of practice therefore, there exists a collective memory of practice that prefigures and pre-defines behaviour as the 'residue' of what has gone before and remains. Figure 7.1 clarifies the nature of this interdependence, demonstrating how the dispositions of 'individuals' (left) interact with the arrangements of the 'sites' (right) to create the various dimensions of intersubjective space (middle).

The value that PA offers is a unique perspective that emphasises knowledge creation and involves orchestration, of and between people and objects, within settings that are conditioned by time and space. Therefore, in order to think differently about the creation of professional sports coaches, PAs demand that we consider the broader ecology of the coaching workplace, namely, the space, time and language within which it operates.

Context: Developing a Performance Culture – England Futsal U21's Case Study

The following case study provides an account of the first and second authors' attempt to foster the construction of tacit knowledge within athletes on the England Men's U21 Futsal Performance Programme. In order to support the development of emerging talent between the ages of 16 and 21, it was deemed important to have a clear philosophy and pedagogical approach (see Table 7.1). This chapter frames some of the key coaching concepts that were applied to the programme over a period of three years and unpicks these in respect to the sociological tenets of PA. To this end, discussions are framed around the pragmatic details of interventions adopted and challenges faced in looking to support positive behaviour change in elite athletes.

Futsal is a fast-paced, dynamic invasion game with enormous demands placed on the physical, technical and mental capacities of an athlete. The key characteristics that define the sport are speed of movement and the ability to create space – both essential qualities of an elite Futsal player (Moore et al., 2014). The context of self, peers and sport-specific knowledge is invaluable – factors that coaching in a performance environment can significantly influence. The England Futsal Performance Programme has embraced an environment centred on the individual person, placing the athlete at the heart of development, driven by their specific needs. Over time, a clear coaching pedagogy emerged, in which coaches and athletes co-created the environment and co-produced learning (see Figure 7.1). A central thread to this pedagogy was to encourage performers to acquire critical thinking and reflection skills. The primary goal within the performance pathway was to develop the 'futsal literacy' of the players, which centres on the belief that, in order to master futsal, it is imperative to cultivate the tacit knowledge within athletes to perform on the international stage. In this instance, tacit knowledge is understood as information gained 'primarily from experience performing practical, everyday problems… often not openly expressed or stated', which must be acquired through individual experience (Nash & Collins, 2006, p. 469).

Developing international athletes with a tacit knowledge to perform on the world stage requires a considered pedagogy. Previously, the learning journey of U21 Futsal athletes was in its infancy, with little attention given to understanding self and others or critically analysing the habits of more advanced nations and questioning the purpose behind their actions. The process of developing the pedagogy of the England Futsal development pathway occurred over a three-year period as a result of multiple conversations with staff and athletes, trialling different coaching behaviours and implementing a variety of practice interventions. At its core was a clear understanding of the desired environment to establish and the culture surrounding it, which fostered a shift in the thinking and behaviours of the athletes towards considering why and how things happen on court, as much as what is happening. This lends itself to the pedagogical lens of PA, which enables a heightened sensitivity on 'what' is said and done, 'where' and 'how' they

Professional Knowledge Development   97

Table 7.1 Pedagogical Approach to England U21's Futsal Programme

Purpose:
The ability of an individual to constantly make effective decisions under
pressure in a changing environment through adopting performance
behaviours, knowledge and skills.

Pedagogical Approach	*Guiding Principles*
Co-create the environment and co-produce the learning.	To create an environment that athletes thrive, in which learning is determined by individual need.
Application of reflective practice to deepen perceptual understanding.	To support athletes to adopt an immersive perspective of self, peers, the environment and the specifics of the game in and on practice.

are said and 'who' says and does them. Within our practice environment, the importance of designing and implementing intentional and purposeful practices to consolidate key learning aligned to our pedological approach, which was driven by the recognition of limited contact time as a result of the amateur domestic game, coupled with a varying degree of athlete exposure to professional training environments.

The following sections present the authors' reflections on working within the U21 Futsal performance pathway as a form of narrative data, situating discussions within the theoretical framework of PA. Within this, themes that characterise behaviour amid the different arrangements of practice (cultural–discursive, material–economic, and social–political) are identified.

The Cultural–Discursive Space: Using Language to Promote Meaningful Learning

Schatzki (2005) argued that practices are always positioned in time and space, progressing through 'site ontologies' – an idea that was later expanded by Kemmis and Heikkinen (2011) to acknowledge that practices are not just embedded in, but shaped by, pre-existing cultures and conditions of specific locations at precise time periods. Traditionally, elite football programmes are dominated by a performance culture that places winning above all else. As a consequence, athletes can often be observed displaying behaviours that are not congruent to a high-performance environment. In contrast to this, we set out to establish a unique semantic space that prioritised a culture of behavioural excellence and collaborative learning, thus challenging the existing conditions prevalent in the football ecosystem during this time. To achieve this, deliberate effort was taken around the language used when communicating with athletes and staff, with the direct aim of inviting players to take a greater role in both their learning and the shaping of

98 Siôn Kitson et al.

that learning. In particular, the aim was to discuss, capture and consolidate their perspectives on what a high-performance environment should look and feel like and what behaviours should underpin that environment. By transforming the characteristic arrangements of typical football practices, we thus arrived at 'a new specialist discourse' (Kemmis & Heikkinen, 2011, p. 3) to form a less hierarchical social set-up.

Specifically, the intentions of each session were framed on a spectrum from 'explore' to 'execute'. For example, an explorative session would be characterised by flexibility, uncertainty and multiple opportunities for discussion, with an emphasis on language such as 'try', 'discover' and 'notice' as behavioural cues when learning about a new skill, tactical action or wider strategic objective. In contrast, during an execute session, the language shifted to refining, clarifying and honing technical actions as individuals, and tactical outcomes in pairs and small groups, with emphasis placed on attending to the information that matters most, magnifying cues and reducing distractions to maximise practice. In cultural–discursive terms, we sought to position the learning in multiple domains, placing equal weight on the importance of the 'physical, cognitive, social, and affective' (Goodyear et al., 2016, p. 6) in order to achieve a sustainable pedagogical approach.

Purposeful Conversations

Conversations were an important part of the U21's performance environment to ensure that meaningful learning emerged through facilitated interactions before, during and after practice. This offered opportunities to help athletes clarify intentions, collaboratively explore and exploit practice, and continually check and review agreed actions. These carefully crafted interactions within the session design offered flexibility to transfer focus from the individual to the whole group as required, which better supported the needs of each athlete (Bennett, 2019). To create the space for purposeful conversations, a variety of interventions were used:

- Carousal practice designed to enable a unit or team to review and reflect in and on practice.
- Empowering athletes to call 'live' time-outs within practice in order to address any behavioural, decision-making or technical/tactical actions in relation to the identified performance measures.
- Facilitated time-outs where teams were asked to review performance and agree action under a time constraint.
- Coach-initiated conversations relating to individual performance.

These interventions and subsequent conversations offered rich insights into the learning of our athletes and served to support their critical thinking, both in the moment and in future practices, in addition to improving the way in which these interactions take place. However, it is important to remain aware of individual

Professional Knowledge Development 99

perceptions, which alter the way each person approaches their understanding according to previous experiences (Kemmis & Heikkinen, 2011). Accordingly, there is a risk of individual bias when learning is filtered through each athlete's personal 'role frame' (consisting of personal attitudes towards practice), which could affect the amount of time they invest in engaging with conversations (Gilbert & Trudel, 2001). Over time, it became apparent that a small amount of facilitated learning was necessary in order to enable more deliberate conversations amongst players, identify problems more efficiently and devise solutions collaboratively so that we could build the group knowledge and understanding necessary to perform on the international stage. As a result, we introduced three questions to provide purpose to conversations, which helped athletes return to the task with greater clarity and understanding in their role and actions:

1   What is the task? What are our measures of success as a group?
2   What have we noticed as individuals in our behaviours, decisions and actions? What challenges/opportunities have emerged as a result?
3   What actions do we collectively agree on? (To explore the challenges and exploit the opportunities.)

This approach proved extremely valuable as a means for evaluating understanding in relation to actions, thus demonstrating that athlete-led and athlete-only interactions are valuable for learning but that some facilitation is beneficial to support performance. In essence, conversations do not automatically lead to improved performance but undoubtedly help athletes to align their thinking and accelerate their ability to perceive the game.

Coach Interventions

When there is a need for coaches to intervene, it is vital to stress the importance of deploying a range of coaching interventions to impact the individual. This could include some verbal cues during practice, individual conversations off court or even brief 'in-action' discussions when the task is explorative in nature. A coach might also pause practice and apply perception-based questioning to understand what information athletes are currently attending to as part of developing their critical thinking skills. The role of the coach is therefore to listen and guide athletes towards greater clarity in their thinking and equip them to interact with similar contexts in the future. In our work with the U21 Futsal performance athletes, we used the following questions to support conversations:

Perception

- Remind me of the task? What did you agree individual success looked like?
- What did you notice in this situation? How did it make you feel?
- What other information is available to you?
- If revisiting, what do you now notice?

Understanding

- What information matters the most right now?
- Why is this important?
- How will it influence your decision-making?

Interaction

- How will it impact your decision-making as an individual, a pair or a small group?
- What have you agreed? Has this been communicated effectively?
- What might you still have to consider?

The contextual example above illustrates a thirty-second conversation with two athletes who were able to return to practice with a shared knowledge of this particular situation. The perception-based approach gave the players a platform

---

Contextual Example of the Use of Perception-Based Questioning

Context: A coach intervening to question two players about their defensive strategy during a task on preventing forward play when pressing up court.

COACH: *Paul / Carlos, what is the problem?*
PAUL: *Our defensive line is getting broken too easily.*
COACH: *Ok, tell me what you have noticed?*
PAUL: *When the ball is played wide, we are closing down the line pass, but because we are defending with two on the front line, it's leaving the middle open.*
COACH: *Remind me of your goal as the first line of the defence?*
CARLOS: *Press the ball as a pair and where possible prevent the ball being played forward.*
COACH: *Ok great. So, the attackers are finding opportunities to break through the middle?*
PAUL: *Yeah.*
COACH: *And what else is happening?*
CARLOS: *It's bringing our second line defender up the court who is being played round too easily.*
COACH: *Ok. So, what do you want from the second line and where might the first line show the ball instead?*
PAUL: *They need to provide cover and not get drawn too close to our defensive line. We need to close the middle off, but that might open up the line pass.*

> COACH: *Fair point, but if you do show wide what might that allow you to do?*
>
> PAUL: *Well, our second defensive line can read the game a little earlier as he can use the touch line to defend.*
>
> COACH: *Right, so if we can't stop forward play, we can still prevent our first defensive line being broken by allowing them to play around, but not through or between us, and work with our second defensive line to protect the middle of the court still. Why do you think this important?*
>
> CARLOS: *Because if the ball is wide on the opposite side then our first line of defence has a better chance of offering cover. If the ball stays central, both of us are out of the game.*
>
> COACH: *Great, shall we give it a go? Just confirm what you've agreed first?*
>
> PAUL: *We will try to prevent forward play as a pair covering the middle more, but if the ball is switched quickly and we cannot prevent forward play then we'll encourage the line pass and defend with cover and balance, and try to force back so we can press again rather than leaving the middle open.*

to repeatedly review each other's progress and ask more purposeful questions of the coach if required. These questions sometimes required the coaches to step aside and observe the situation with a fresh lens before entering into immediate dialogue, thus relegating the coach to the role of an observant learner. At such times, it can be suggested that the coach and the athlete are equal co-constructors of knowledge, aligning with the goal of a non-hierarchical learning space (Heikkinen et al., 2012). In terms of the practice architecture, these findings suggest that athletes and coaches hold different parts of the knowledge, 'sayings' and language that together form the practice as a whole, thus holding it together collectively through 'discursive, material and social interactions' (Kemmis & Heikkinen, 2011, p. 4). Practice through this lens might therefore be understood as the outcome of socially established and cooperative human activity captured by forms of 'saying' (understanding). We would therefore argue that any pedagogical change initiative must be constructed, enacted and reconstructed through consistent engagement with all actors in a given context – in this space, coaching and athletes alike – in order to develop collective/shared meaning.

The Material–Economic Space: Contextualised Actions and the Constraints-Led Approach

The material–economic arrangements establish what can physically be done in a practice and how that can be used to predetermine the learning. As Simonton (1999) argues, environmental factors have a greater impact on variance in performance than innate capacity in every sphere of talent identification. The elite level facilities at St. George's Park, combined with the expertise of support staff, enabled a wide scope for varied futsal practices and fostered a culture of high expectations in regards to behavioural excellence (reinforced by our sayings). It also enabled us to control the direction of practices by manipulating or 'constraining' what could be done within the physical set-ups (Kemmis et al., 2014, p. 32). The aim was to design practices that replicated the most physically and mentally demanding moments of a game and incorporated elements of transition, in other words, to expose athletes to the physical, psychological, technical and tactical demands of the game on a frequent basis in order to impact the cognitive development of the players. Renshaw et al. (2019) term this the constraints-led approach, which strives to ensure that the 'cues' players receive in practice reflect game-related conditions. This method tests the decision-making skills and game intelligence of individual players, who must gather information from their surroundings in order to make an appropriate response under pressurised 'action constraints', such as time restrictions imposed by opponents (Williams, 2000). This secondary level of information is of particular value, as combining technical skills with decision-making creates an authentic environment, thus supporting Christensen's (2009, p. 375) notion that a reliable criterion for talent identification must be 'closely related to contextualized practice and…recognized in movement patterns related to real play'. The material space thus provided the opportunity to constrain activities in such a way as to afford players opportunities to learn in action, but the location of the practice brought mediating factors, such as access and prestige amid the practice traditions of the given space.

We delivered the content on court as much as possible in order to reduce the traditional classroom-based influence on learning. Additional constraints were introduced on court to better facilitate individual and group development. For example, when focusing on high defensive pressure, we constrained practice by changing the shape of the playing area, placing rewards on particular outcomes and limiting access to specific areas of the court in order to create relevant game context. In constraining practices, we aimed to reduce the spectrum for athlete interference, thus enabling them to hone their perceptual awareness on the elements that matter the most. Constraints should inspire learners to explore opportunities (or invitations) for action and always be linked to the session goals (Renshaw et al., 2019). Therefore, providing clarity in our intentions gave athletes the confidence to commit to agreed performance measures. Furthermore, having an increased understanding of how practice supports performance helped the players to apply relevant behaviours to accelerate their learning. The construction of knowledge and understanding that players were able to apply in partnership with teammates, through perceiving opportunities and sensing danger, enabled them to better recognise and select appropriate technical and tactical actions. In particular, understanding the 'why' behind what they do, and equally what their opponents intend to do, was the basis from which we aimed to invoke learning in our athletes. To achieve this, great emphasis was placed on three steps:

Professional Knowledge Development 103

1 Laying the foundation for each session with clear intentions and measures of success.
2 Ensuring practice is representative of the game and affords relevant development opportunities.
3 Building opportunities that allow for athlete, peer and coach-owned interventions.

Ecologies of Practice

The changeable nature of the U21's practice environment lent itself to learning in action and enabled 'live' conversations within games that further promoted the construct of knowledge. As studies have shown, practices are far from static but instead operate in 'constant motion', changing and developing over time, thus transcending the physical space of the practice (Kemmis & Heikennen, 2011, p. 12). We sought, therefore, to connect one principle, practice and training camp to another. An unintended constraint of the England Futsal practices was the limited contact time with players, restricted to several training camps a year. We therefore had to maximise our time with the athletes before, during and after every training camp in order to construct connected blocks of learning, building on what had gone before and what we were looking towards. In PA terms, this can be understood as 'nesting' the different learning platforms and external networks within one another (Kemmis & Heikkenen, 2011, p. 14). This idea is rooted in the theory of 'ecologies of practice', which highlights the influence and interdependence of related practices (Kemmis et al., 2017). In our context, this worked on both the level of interrelated practices at the site, such as athlete learning, coach learning, 'professional learning' and reflective practice (Kemmis et al., 2014), and practices that occurred externally at the athlete's individual clubs and training programmes. Under the lens of practice architectures, then, collaboration is key to gaining a clearer understanding of how these practices can inform and inspire progression by collectively agreeing 'intentions' and 'ends' for a project (Mahon et al., 2017). In this context, employers gave the coaching staff autonomy to experiment and implement a pedagogical approach within a physical environment which fostered a shared motivation between staff and players to collectively build a performance pathway conducive to the needs of their athletes.

The Social–Political Space: Co-created Learning and Critical Thinking

The social space of a practice environment is largely composed of relationships between individuals. These impact learning at both a formal level (recognised coaching measured by performance outcomes) and an informal level (unintentional learning within social conversations) (Kemmis & Heikennen, 2011). The social–political conditions act as 'the medium of power and solidarity' between those who are particularly invested in a specific practice and can be seen in the shared agreements between practitioners (Goodyear et al., 2016, p. 4). This aspect formed the umbrella of our coaching programme, within which the other two conditions of a practice architecture (the cultural–discursive and material–economic arrangements) were enveloped. Our role as coaching leads for the U21's Futsal squads was to facilitate athlete development and to reinforce in every practice, interaction and conversation that the 'influence' sits with the athlete and is something we nurture, through our sayings and doings, identifying the moments that matter the most to an individual's development. This was achieved through the demonstration of a clear set of behaviours and the creation of practices (as part of a wider ecology of practices) that understood the athletes we were supporting. Furthermore, we attempted to (co)design practice in a way that homed in on the things that, as a programme, stakeholders (athletes and staff) collectively felt mattered the most to support athlete progression.

The coach/athlete relationship is of paramount importance to the success of a training programme, which relies on a reciprocal process based on influential systems of interpersonal knowledge (Côté & Gilbert, 2009). Coaches need to understand the context in which they are working and select the best methodology depending on the needs of the players in front of them, supporting the argument that effective coaches adapt their behaviour in order to meet the demands of their environment (Nash & Sproule, 2009). However, as Kemmis and Heikennen (2011, p. 11) assert, social space is formed of not only the 'person-to-person' relations but also the system relationships that operate at a wider/higher level, and these 'metapractices' shape the ways in which 'conditions for learning' are created. For example, when an England Futsal player takes to the international arena, the question we are seeking to answer is 'can the individual problem-solve in the moment, whilst under pressure, rather than constantly seeking guidance from the coach?'

The unique demands of Futsal mean that games are often filled with instability and require high levels of independent analysis and tactical intelligence. This means that the traditional methods of the coach as teacher and athlete as learner are a false representation of the game and therefore not suitable to address athlete needs. Consequently, we committed to building a programme of learning through co-creation, whereby the role of the coach is a facilitator, guiding athletes towards meaningful knowledge and constantly transferring ownership and accountability within both the training and match environment. Every athlete had the opportunity to contribute to the expectations of the programme through a series of mini activities that empowered both the individual and the whole group to establish the social norms for our environment. The ultimate goal of this approach was to make athletes feel part of the collective whole of the project, in essence to 'stir' them into the overarching aims and goals, so that they can reach an understanding of how they are 'oriented in the practice as a whole' (Kemmis et al., 2011).

Professional Knowledge Development 105

In addition to establishing clear intentions, confirming the performance measures was also important to help both athletes and coaches understand what the goals are for a session. Accordingly, athletes were asked the question: What do you believe success looks like for this task? For example, the focus of the practice might be on 'Playing out of high defensive pressure'. In a national team, this may conjure up multiple meanings for athletes given a mix of experiences amongst the group. Therefore, it is imperative that clear performance measures are established at a group level so that everyone is held accountable. Below is an example of performance goals developed to align athlete learning with high performance demands of a particular situation in the game.

1   To increase space between the opposition when restarting play by adopting height and width in a 3-1 formation.
2   To perceive opportunities for numerical advantages to break first line defensive pressure with choreographed individual, paired and group movements.
3   To act with increased speed and commitment in our attacking intentions with quick thinking to exploit space created from breaking a defensive line.

As the session progresses, we would then begin to layer additional detail for individuals, units or the whole group underneath each performance measure. This offers the team a basis of knowledge in which they can spend deliberate time discussing 'what matters' in each aspect.

Critical Thinking (Tacit Knowledge)

An important goal of the England Futsal U21 programme was to help our athletes think for themselves, whilst developing self-awareness and understanding the environment in which they were performing. It was based on the belief that learning needs to be a meaningful process that stretches the cognitive capability of the athlete, whilst retaining at every step what success is. Whether we were in a training camp or an international environment, we would first review performance by focusing on our behaviours: the aspects of performance we can instantly control. A major aspect for this change in behaviour was to encourage critical thinking, which can be understood as 'the intellectually disciplined process of actively and skilfully conceptualising, applying, analysing, synthesising and/or evaluating information' (Scriven & Paul, 1987). Consequently, we strove to develop athletes who were hypersensitive to the multifaceted nature of the game, able to make sense of complexity, distil numerous cues and adapt decision-making in split seconds, applying technical actions for effective tactical outcomes. We witnessed enhanced athlete relationships through critical reflections and shared discussions on court, which was supported by a community made to feel comfortable and vulnerable to express their perceptions of learning and development. The relationship between peers was a critical marker to establish and evidence greater coherency and clarity of message within the training practices.

Conclusion

In consideration of the discussions above, the practice environment created within the England U21 Futsal Performance Programme afforded multiple opportunities for learning, both athlete-led and coach-led. By exploring the lens of PAs, the conditions of PA within this context have been examined with respect to the development of professional knowledge to support athlete learning via considered dialogue, situated actions and relationships. By recognising knowledge and language that coaches and athletes bring to an environment (Kemmis & Heikkinen, 2011), coaching practitioners are able to have a greater appreciation of the key components of embedding an effective pedagogical approach and in doing so leaving a residue for long-term programme sustainability. Coach interactions with athletes played a key role in positively or negatively impacting athlete development, which illustrates the level of influence attached to the role and highlights the responsibility of coaches to continuously reflect on the sayings, doings and relatings within the environments they inhabit. Furthermore, PA promotes the idea that innovations are influenced by a practitioner's pre-existing knowledge (Coburn, 2005) and their 'principles of vision and division' (Bourdieu, 1998, p. 25). Therefore, athletes, coaches and, importantly, those responsible for performance pathways have a responsibility to safeguard knowledge gathered through lived experiences in order to inform and improve athletic performance in the future. Yet, the critical challenge moving forward is how to ensure that learning designers can support, guide and, most importantly, reproduce such interactions. In essence, by acknowledging PA within the development of co-created and reflective environments, we can challenge coaching programmes and practices to support the growth of deep tacit knowledge connecting athletes across a programme that allows people to thrive in the most demanding moments of high-performance sport.

References

Bennett, M. (2019, October 04). Doing the best you can with what you have: A conversation with Mark Bennett MBE. [Audio podcast episode]. In *The talent equation podcast*. Stuart Armstrong. https://www.spreaker.com/user/thetalentequation/2017-09-26-t04-25-04pm-final-mix

Bourdieu, P. (1990). *The logic of practice*. Stanford, CA: Stanford University Press.

Bourdieu, P. (1998). *Practical reason. On the theory of action*. Cambridge: Polity.

Bowes, I., & Jones, R. (2006). Working at the edge of chaos: Understanding coaching as a complex, interpersonal system. *Sport Psychologist*, 20, 235–245.

Christensen, M.K. (2009). "An Eye for Talent": Talent identification and the "practical sense" of top-level soccer coaches. *Sociology of Sport Journal*, 26, 365–382.

Coburn, C.E. (2005). Shaping teacher sensemaking: School leaders and the enactment of reading policy. *Educational Policy*, 19, 476–509.

Côté, J., & Gilbert, W. (2009). An integrative definition of coaching effectiveness and expertise. *International Journal of Sports Science and Coaching*, 4(3), 310–311.

Gilbert, W., & Trudel, P. (2001). Learning to coach through experience: Reflection in model youth sport coaches. *Journal of Teaching in Physical Education*, 21, 16–34.

Goodyear, V.A., Casey, A., & Kirk, D. (2016). Practice architectures and sustainable curriculum renewal. *Journal of Curriculum Studies*, 49(2), 235–254.

Heikkinen, H.L.T., Jokinen, H. & Tynjälä, P. (Eds.). (2012). *Peer-group mentoring for teacher development*. Oxford: Routledge.

Hemmings, B., Kemmis, S., & Reupert, A. (2013). Practice architectures of university inclusive education teaching in Australia. *Professional Development in Education*, 39, 470–487.

Kemmis, S. (2012). Researching educational praxis: Spectator and participant perspectives. *British Educational Research Journal*, 38, 885–905.

Kemmis, S., Edwards-Groves, C., Lloyd, A., Grootenboer, P., Hardy, I.J., & Wilkinson, J. (2017). Learning as being "stirred in" to practices. In P. Grootenboer, C. Edwards-Groves, & S. Choy (Eds.), *Practice theory perspectives on pedagogy and education: Praxis, diversity and contestation* (1 ed., pp. 45–65). Dordrecht: Springer.

Kemmis S., & Heikkinen, H.L.T. (2011). Understanding professional development of teachers within the theory of practice architectures [Paper presentation]. European Conference of Educational Research, Berlin, Germany.

Kemmis, S., McTaggart, R., & Nixon, R. (2014). *The action research planner: Doing critical participatory action research*. Dordrecht: Springer.

Kemmis, S., Wilkinson, J., Edwards-Groves, C., Hardy, I., Grootenboer, P., and Bristol, L. (2014). *Changing practices, changing education*. London: Springer.

Leeder, T., & Sawiuk, R. (2021). Reviewing the sports coach mentoring literature: A look back to take a step forward. *Sports Coaching Review*, 10(2), 129–152.

Mahon, K., Kemmis, S., Francisco, S., & Lloyd, A. (2017). Introduction: Practice theory and the theory of practice architectures. In *Exploring education and professional practice* (pp. 1–30). Singapore: Springer.

Marx, K. (1845). Theses on Feuerbach. Retrieved from https://www.marxists.org/archive/marx/works/1845/theses/theses.htm

Moore, R., Bullough, S., Goldsmith, S., & Edmondson, L. (2014). A systematic review of Futsal literature. *American Journal of Sports Science and Medicine*, 2(3), 108–116.

Nash, C., & Collins, D. (2006). Tacit knowledge in expert coaching: Science or art? *Quest*, 58, 465–477.

Nash, C.S., & Sproule, J. (2009). Career development of expert coaches. *International Journal of Sports Science and Coaching*, 4, 121–138.

Reckwitz, A. (2002). Toward a theory of social practices: A development in culturalist theorizing. *European Journal of Social Theory*, 5(2), 243–263.

Renshaw, I., Davids, K., Newcombe, D., & Roberts, W. (2019). *The constraints-led approach: Principles for sports coaching and practice design*. Oxford: Routledge.

Schatzki, T.R. (2002). *The site of the social: A philosophical account of the constitution of social life and change*. University Park: Pennsylvania State University Press.

Schatzki, T.R. (2005). Peripheral vision: The sites of organizations. *Organization Studies*, 26, 465–484.

Scriven, M., & Paul, R. (1987). 8th annual international conference on critical thinking and education reform. Retrieved from https://www.criticalthinking.org/pages/defining-critical-thinking/766

Shove, E., Pantzar, M., & Watson, M. (2012). *The dynamics of social practices: Everyday life and how it changes*. Thousand Oaks, CA: Sage.

Simonton, D.K. (1999). Talent and its development: An emergenic and epigenetic model. *Psychological Review*, 106(3), 435–457.

Stoszkowski, J., & Collins, D. (2014). Communities of practice, social learning and networks: Exploiting the social side of coach development. *Sport, Education and Society*, 19(6), 773–788.

Vaeyens, R., Lenoir, M., Williams, M., & Philippaerts, R.M. (2008). Talent identification and development programmes in sport: Current models and future directions. *Sports Medicine*, 38(9), 703–714.

Werthner, P., & Trudel, P. (2006). A new theoretical perspective for understanding how coaches learn to coach. *The Sport Psychologist*, 20, 198–212.

Williams, A.M. (2000). Perceptual skill in soccer: Implications for talent identification and development. *Journal of Sport Sciences*, 18, 737–750.

Part III

Social Theories of Gender and Sexuality in Football

Chapter 8

Experiences of Female Football Referees

Using the Lack of Fit Model to Explore Gender Stereotypes in Football in England

Laura Grubb, Tom Webb and Mike Rayner

Introduction

A gender imbalance has existed in association football (hereafter football) in the United Kingdom (UK) since codification in 1863, with female involvement controlled by middle class men (Dunn & Welford, 2015), and entrenched beliefs leading to the perpetuation of stereotypes concerning the roles and positions of women as players, fans, administrators, board members and referees (Cleland et al., 2020). Some women defied the gender stereotypes and started to play organised football in the 1880s (Pfister & Gems, 2016). The first recorded women's match was played in Inverness, Scotland, in 1881 in a match where married women played single women, and in 1895, the Midland Challenge Cup was played between the North and the South and attracted 7,000 paying spectators (Williams, 2003). However, women's football increased its presence during World War I (Williams, 2007). Women's football was temporarily endorsed, and many workplaces created a women's football team to keep the workers healthy, promote local factories, boost morale and raise money for wounded soldiers (Pfister et al., 2002). Women's football maintained interest after the war and in 1920 saw a record crowd of 53,000 spectators at a match between Dick, Kerr Ladies and St Helen's (Williams, 2003). However, the success and growth of women's football were also a concern for the FA, who saw it as a threat to the men's game (Giulianotti, 1999). The FA declared that the game was 'unsuitable for women' after medical practitioners expressed concern for women's ability to have children if they participated in football, so women's football matches were banned on FA-affiliated pitches on 5 December 1921 (Williams, 2007). The ban lasted for 50 years, leading to a rapid decline in participation whilst marginalising women's football politically, socially and economically, which continues to exist and affect women in football (Pfister & Gems, 2016).

In recent years, there has been signs of a shift towards greater gender equality in football, in terms of participation and spectatorship (Cleland et al., 2020), growing a female fanbase (Toffoletti et al., 2019), more women working within

DOI: 10.4324/9781003253990-12

the sport (Clarkson et al., 2019) and the professionalisation of female footballers (Culvin, 2021). In the FA's latest strategy released in 2020, 'Inspiring Positive Change', they identified that there are 10.6 million male players, compared to 3.4 million female players; 234,551 male coaches, compared to 18,302 female coaches; and 27,451 male referees compared to 1,718 female referees (The FA, 2021). This increase in female involvement in football is considered by some to challenge the gender constraints that have historically restricted women's sport participation (Jeanes, 2011).

Issues related to sexism and gender discrimination are still present for women within football. Research conducted by Women in Football (WiF) found that more than 70% of women had witnessed sexist 'banter' or 'jokes' in the workplace, with 61.88% of women experiencing it themselves, 15% had been sexually harassed and 70% of participants agreed or strongly agreed that women have to be better at their jobs than their male colleagues to succeed in the football industry (WiF, 2016). Meanwhile, Women in Sport (WIS) explored women's experiences and identified that 38% of women encountered gender discrimination and 30% of women had experienced inappropriate behaviour from the opposite sex in the workplace (WIS, 2020). Whilst there is an emerging and evolving area of research around female football fandom (Gemar & Pope, 2021), female football participation, (Jeanes, 2011) female coach education (Lewis et al., 2018; Sisjord et al., 2020) and professionalisation of women's football (Culvin, 2021), minimal research has explored the experiences of female football referees (Webb, 2020). Extant literature that does exist has considered the mental health of female football referees (Webb et al., 2021) and experiences of females refereeing within the UK (Forbes et al., 2015). Therefore, to further extend the literature, this chapter explores the experience of female football referees and discusses the support they have (or have not) received throughout their career and also their personal professional development.

Female Referees in England

Football referees play an integral role in organised sport, ensuring that the laws of the games are understood by players, coaches and spectators and are executed fairly (Cleland et al., 2018). Historically, refereeing has been male-dominated and still is today (Webb, 2014), with few female referees at any level, although particularly working at the elite level in professional football. In the UK, the first female referee to officiate an English Football League's (EFL) men's match was in 2010, where Amy Fearn replaced the on-field referee due to injury (BBC, 2021). However, the first officially appointed female referee to an EFL game occurred in April 2021, when Rebecca Welch refereed the match between Harrogate Town and Port Vale (BBC, 2021), although other female officials have been involved in football in different capacities. For example, Sian Massey-Ellis has been an assistant referee in the Premier League since 2010 (Mason, 2021). Over recent years, the FA have sought ways to increase the number of female referees, with the 'Gameplan

Experiences of Female Football Referees   113

for Growth' strategy focused on the recruitment of more women into football, including refereeing (The FA, 2017). Joanna Stimpson was employed as the Women's Refereeing Manager responsible for recruiting, training and mentoring female referees in England to improve the number of female referees and to facilitate ongoing support to retain them. Between 2016 and 2020, there was a 72% increase in female referees, leading to 2,146 qualified female referees in England, a result of aiming to change perceptions so that women could see refereeing as a viable career option (The FA, 2020a). In the recent women's football FA strategy, *'Inspiring Positive Change'*, the FA state that they aim to support referees to officiate elite and international matches, whilst ensuring that 50% of female trainee referees transition into an active referee at the grassroots level (The FA, 2021). However, work is still required to ensure that women feel safe and supported to referee at all levels of the game and to change the historic, male-orientated perceptions around refereeing (Webb et al., 2021).

Lack of Fit Model

Given the gender imbalances and discrimination towards female players, coaches and particularly referees outlined above, it is imperative that there is a concerted focus on the factors that drive gender discrimination to ensure that it can be tackled effectively. For this chapter, the lack of fit model (Heilman, 1983, 2001, 2012) provides a framework for identifying strategies to minimise the effects of gender stereotyping in the workplace (for referees, the workplace is a football pitch and a football match), an issue that is prominent for female referees. Central to this model is the consideration of gender stereotypes and the preconceptions of men and women. Stereotypical beliefs are widely and consistently held, which have proven difficult to change despite decades of social change. Predominately, men are perceived to be agentic, assertive, bold and aggressive (Haines et al., 2016), whereas women are portrayed as more communal, helpful, understanding and friendly (Bosak et al., 2008). These stereotypes create challenges for women pursuing traditionally male work and past times. Female stereotypes do not match the attitude and skills which are perceived to be required within the workplace, and when someone does not match the stereotypical perception, they are viewed negatively or with suspicion (Eagly et al., 2000; Heilman, 2001; Johnson et al., 2008).

Stereotype-based expectations about women's competence can create bias regarding the way in which individuals perceive women. This biased perception can influence decision making, lead to people having negative performance expectations (Hollingshead & Fraiden, 2003) and also influence how information is interpreted (Madera et al., 2009). This misinterpretation can affect information processing and can make the evaluation process ambiguous, leading to cognitive distortion, which may reduce opportunities for women (Heilman & Haynes, 2008). As information processing is an important component of decision making in human resource departments (Murphy & Cleveland, 1995), the negative performance expectations that arise from the perception of the lack of fit between what women are like and what is required of them when working in a male-dominated environment can lead to gender bias in evaluative processes (Gaucher et al., 2011). Gender bias can affect selection (Biernat & Fuegen, 2001), performance appraisal (Bauer & Baltes, 2002), promotion (Lyness & Heilman, 2006) and salary (Castilla, 2008). As the FA are aiming to recruit more females into refereeing, these matters all need to be considered when encouraging females to get involved and when supporting their professional development, as women and girls have consistently struggled against sexism and gender stereotypes in order to be accepted into the football community (Caudwell, 2011).

Heilman's (2012) lack of fit model has two intervention strategies, firstly decreasing the lack of fit perceptions and secondly breaking the link between the expectations of incompetence that arise from lack of fit perceptions and the gender bias in evaluating performance it creates (Heilman & Caleo, 2018). To do this, gender stereotypes need to change, education and training should be delivered and changing the perceptions of what people believe to be a man's job needs to evolve. For example, football is perceived to be a man's game with careers being male-dominated. Therefore, for women to pursue opportunities within the game, the lack of fit model can support organisations to change perceptions and provide education regarding gender bias. The lack of fit model suggests that minimising either component of the model will lessen perceptions of unsuitability and therefore prevent negative performance expectations or biased decision making (Heilman, 1983, 2001, 2012). The model has been used as part of gendered research including gender bias and combatting gender discrimination (Heilman & Caleo, 2018); therefore, it has been used for this chapter to aid discussions around gendered experiences of female referees.

As part of a wider study, 12 female referees, who officiate matches in England, were interviewed to explore their experiences of mental health as a female referee (Webb et al., 2021). Within the data, it was identified that gender stereotyping exists for female referees; therefore, this chapter discusses those experiences. The referees ranged from level 3 to level 7 on the referee progression pathway and had a range of experiences refereeing fixtures from grassroots to elite level football. It is important to note that female referees are not professional in England and continue to work on a part time basis, sometimes whilst managing a full-time career in another industry. Semi-structured interviews were conducted over the telephone, and the data were analysed through deductive thematic analysis. To ensure confidentiality, each participant was allocated a pseudonym.

Discussion

Education and Training

To train as a referee in England, participants need to be at least 14 years of age and complete the Basic Referee Qualification, completing five online modules, attending 11 hours of face-to-face training and refereeing five matches (The FA, n.d). Research has identified that female-only training courses can encourage more women to attend as some women have reported being made to feel uncomfortable by men when participating in football qualification courses (Lewis et al., 2018), although there is an acknowledgement that this could be seen as positive discrimination. In Norway, a study exploring coaching pathways suggested that national governing bodies should create female-specific initiatives to encourage more women into football (Sisjord et al., 2020) and also lead to a fairer recruitment process by formalising the decision-making process and providing transparency in the decision-making structures (Schlesinger & Weigelet-Schlesinger, 2013). In England, initial referee courses are delivered by County FA's, with some opting to deliver female-only referee courses at a discounted rate to encourage more women to attend (The FA, 2019). Sian discussed the feedback to a female-only course by men in the county, 'My county introduced a female only referee course to try and get more females involved in the game and it went absolutely crazy, you had men complaining that they were doing a female only course'. The negative reaction by men could portray a concern that women are encroaching on a masculine sport and challenging the established hierarchies of football (Webb et al., 2021). Historically, women have been rejected within perceived 'male spaces', with women's sport being regarded as shameful; however, the position for women's sport has developed and is more accepted within today's society (Liston, 2021). The lack of fit model (Heilman, 2012) discusses the importance of changing perceptions of gender in the workplace, so it could be beneficial for County FA's to educate both their paid and voluntary workforce around the reasons for providing female-only courses. The lack of fit framework also raises the importance of breaking the link between perceived incompetence and performance expectations. Therefore, the provision of training courses will ensure that female referees are trained and therefore access the same opportunities as male referees. County FA's are also evaluated on their ability to help the FA reach their aims and objectives. This puts pressure on the County FA's to increase female engagement in participation, playing and refereeing as discussed in the FA's 'Inspire Positive Change' strategy (The FA, 2020).

Ongoing support is required for female referees to ensure that they have someone to talk to after a match and to support their professional development (Webb et al., 2021). The FA facilitates support for female referees by providing mentoring and educational workshops to enhance their development and aims to retain them within their role, in order to continue to reverse the gender imbalance within football. Each county has a Referee Development Officer (RDO), referee tutors deliver training and education and appropriately experienced mentors offer support and guidance to referees at different stages in their development (Webb, 2017). To establish these support networks, the FA has created a Female Development Group, which aims to provide a committed workforce, with knowledge skills, and expertise to continue to develop female referees (The FA, 2021). These female-only events have proved invaluable, providing a safe space for referees to discuss their experiences, as Stacey outlines:

> When I'm with the female development group I am so much more relaxed because I know we're all female, we can say things and everybody gets each other, it's a much nicer environment, but when I go to my Referee Association meetings, because I am the only girl I'm scared, I'm anxious that people are going to judge.

Some referees have found it difficult if they have been unable to access support in an all-female environment due to the perception that male referees do not fully understand the experiences of female referees. For example, Holly discussed the issues that exist with male coaches and colleagues and how a female instructor or colleague might be able to help:

> I have found working with male coaches and referees has been fine but then there are some sexist comments...I can't really speak to a male colleague about that you know, they don't really get it so it'd be nice to have a female that I could speak to.

It is important that female referees who experience sexist comments can discuss it with someone who has a similar lived experience to ensure that they feel listened to, can share their emotions and discuss ways to deal with those negative experiences (Webb et al., 2021). Some referees have also reported a lack of support from their County FA and RDO, and Rachel outlined how some female referees are unable to discuss their experiences with their RDO:

> I was speaking to a couple of female referees and they said they find it really hard to speak to their Referee Development Officer because they are male and they don't understand...he is a male referee but he doesn't see the impact abuse has on female referees.

The Referee Association (RA) is a membership organisation referees can join, providing a source of support as they aim to train, develop, support and mentor referees through regular meetings (The RA, n.d). However, not all female referees find these meetings welcoming. Poppy discussed how she is the only female at her RA and they address her incorrectly in emails. 'I'm the only [female] that goes to my Referee Association so that can be a struggle...I was getting a bit offended because the secretary would send out the monthly email and titled it with gents'. This experience links to the lack of fit model (Heilman, 2012) as the RA has neglected the female associates in this communication process, which may deter female referees from attending future meetings as it is unwelcoming and creates a barrier due to the perception that the group is male-orientated.

Male and female referees regularly face an abusive environment which is enshrined in a masculine ideology of football, with male dominance and a male-orientated outlook which was not designed or organised for female participation (Webb et al., 2021). As such, it is vitally important that female referees are supported if they encounter abuse during a game. Jane argues that she and her colleagues have all had issues around being a female official in a male-dominated environment, 'we've all received some sort of comment for being female on the football pitch'. This could show that some people have a negative preconception of female referees and believe that their fixture will be affected by having a female rather than male referee. When considering the lack of fit model (Heilman, 2012), these negative preconceptions could affect the professional development of female referees, so it is crucial that the FA raise awareness or create a diversity policy to publicly support female referees within football. Female referees follow the same pathway as their male counterparts, so both sexes receive the same education and training content. If we are to create a more welcoming and supportive environment for female referees, there needs to be a societal change where negative behaviour towards female referees is challenged in order for perceptions to change and women become 'normalised' within football, in all aspects of the game (e.g., refereeing, playing and coaching). This could be through coach qualification courses, educational workshops or disciplinary processes if discriminatory language or behaviour is reported.

Changing Gender Stereotypes

Research has identified that female referees face more barriers than their male counterparts, particularly regarding career progression, sexist comments and the environment in which they operate (Webb et al., 2021). Indeed, the presence of female referees can create a significant site of gender conflict (Mean, 2001). Serena exemplifies this notion of gender conflict through the description of a match she attended, although she was unable to access a changing room:

> I went to a match and as I walked around, I said who I was, the referee was male and the assistant referee was male, it was raining and the changing room only had one dressing room, I had to stand outside in the rain waiting for the men to get changed…it was a game I had to be smartly dressed for, I had nowhere to get changed, I need to get changed and we ask the club have you got somewhere for a female referee to get changed in private. They replied, 'the only place we can offer is a store cupboard'.

Serena's experience provides an example of the ingrained nature of gender stereotypes within football as the home team was not expecting a female referee and therefore had not organised a safe place for her to get changed. This aligns with the lack of fit model as it demonstrates the need to change perceptions within a traditionally male-dominated workplace (Heilman, 2012). Therefore, clubs need to take responsibility and identify who their referees are to ensure that they offer equitable areas for both male and female referees to provide appropriate working conditions. The FA also has the opportunity to change perceptions by developing a policy providing guidance and education to clubs, so they understand the needs of both female and male referees. Hannah also discussed her experience of refereeing and how she believes that she needs to work harder than her male counterparts:

> I'd have to work 10 times harder than any of the male referees and that's just me turning up to the game and because I'm a female and I have to prove a point 10 times more than any of the referees purely because of my gender so for us we have to deal with a lot in terms of before the game, during the game and after the game compared to a male referee.

Alice had experienced similar issues and commented on the perception of a female referee's ability before they had even started the match, 'I feel like some people have this thing where they see a female referee and immediately think of a much lower standard, I think it's a more traditional view but I feel like you've definitely got to overcome that initial assumption'. This perception of female referees provides a further example of the belief that a female referee will not perform at the same standard as a male referee [similar to historic preconceptions of female players; for example, some men felt women should not play football as it is a masculine sport and therefore they would not be able to perform as well (Jeanes & Kay, 2007)], and these negative, stereotype-based perceptions can have a detrimental effect when people evaluate the referee's performance, including the risk of gender bias informing selection or promotion (Biernat & Fuegen 2001; Gaucher et al., 2011; Lyness & Heilman 2006). This could lead to a lack of opportunity for female referees when they target promotion, selection and access to professional development opportunities and thus not being able to progress their career and links to Heilman's (2012) lack of fit model. Heilman raises concerns that the negative preconceptions of women working within a 'masculine domain' lead to gender bias when evaluating performance and could result in a lack of professional development and opportunities, something which female referees are evidently experiencing. Rachel has also heard other negative comments about her as a female referee during matches, 'I've given a couple of decisions that have not gone their way and they've made comments like, 'this is why females shouldn't ref'. Research has found that female football referees are questioned before they have even stepped on to the pitch which puts more pressure on the referee to get decisions correct in order to challenge and refute the gender stereotype (Forbes et al., 2015). The archetypal view that female referees are incompetent because of assumed biological differences is unjustified and sexist, and these perceptions need to change (Jones & Edwards, 2013) to support the professional development of female referees in football, as well as increase recruitment and retention numbers. To do this, the FA should involve female referees in developing a diversity

Experiences of Female Football Referees 119

policy to provide an uplift in knowledge for football clubs and coaches based on their experiences of being a female referee.

Changing social perceptions of females involved in football are discussed in the FA's 'Gameplan for Growth' (2017). The central concept is that by creating an engaging product and working with commercial partners, the number of women in coaching roles and refereeing will increase (The FA, 2017). To change social perceptions, people need to see females working within football; this will raise awareness of the career opportunities within football for females to pursue. At the professional end of the game, the FA have recently signed a multi-million-pound television agreement with Sky Sports and the BBC which will broadcast up to 44 matches live (The FA, 2021a). Barclays have also signed a three-year sponsorship deal worth £30 million, with that money being utilised to invest and continue the development of women's and girls' football (Barclays, 2021). With improved visibility of women's football, the traditional hegemonic stereotypes that women are not good enough to be involved in football as referees, players or coaches can potentially be challenged (Petty & Pope, 2019). Visibility has also raised the profile of women referees within the FA WSL, with these referees now working with the PGMOL to access support and training facilities which will help to professionalise the environment these referees have access to (The FA, 2021b). However, this visibility has also led to criticisms about the standards of the officials and the historic lack of professionalism of referees in the FA WSL. In order to change social perceptions, research has found that female sporting role models, if deployed carefully, can promote gender equity and empowerment (Meier, 2015). As more matches are broadcast live on television, female referees are seen by a wider audience and could be seen as female role models to those watching, potentially inspiring females to become referees.

Conclusion

This chapter has explored the experiences of female football referees in England. The lack of fit model was used to identify gender discrimination and recommend strategies to change behaviours and perceptions. Female referees have had negative experiences officiating football matches based on their gender and the historical practices and assumptions that football is a male domain. While the FA are working to overcome these social beliefs by encouraging more women to become referees and while this will continue to challenge the sexual division of labour, there are clearly still significant challenges that require attention. Changing perceptions is a key component of the lack of fit model, and the findings within this research allow for recommendations to be made. More support needs to be provided to female referees by expanding the female development network and providing more localised groups for regular meetings. Female-only referee courses should continue to be offered with ongoing opportunities to be mentored throughout their career. Educating their male counterparts on the appropriate support required when female referees face challenging situations such as abuse

120 Laura Grubb et al.

would be of benefit. The RA's should be modernised and provide a safe and welcoming environment for female referees to attend. Finally, the use of female referees as role models can encourage more females to become qualified, so raising awareness of their experiences should be used to recruit and retain female referees. Whilst progress has been made with more females officiating matches and with more females at the elite level, there is still work to do to ensure that gender stereotypes are removed from football.

References

Barclays, (2021). Barclays doubles investment in women's and girls' football. Retrieved from: https://home.barclays/news/press-releases/2021/12/barclays-doubles-investment-in-women-s-and-girls--football-acros/

Bauer, C. C., & Baltes, B. B. (2002). Reducing the effects of gender stereotypes on performance evaluations. *Sex Roles, 47*(9), 465–476. https://doi.org/10.1023/A:1021652527696

BBC, (2021). *English Football League Appoints Its First Female Referee*. Retrieved from: https://www.bbc.co.uk/newsround/56578525

Biernat, M., & Fuegen, K. (2001). Shifting standards and the evaluation of competence. Complexity in gender-based judgement and decision making. *Journal of Social Issues, 57,* 707–724. https://doi.org/10.1111/00224537.00237

Bosak, J. Sczesny, S., & Eagly, A. H. (2008). Communion and agency judgments of women and men as a function of role information and response format. *European Journal of Social Psychology, 38*(7), 1148–1155. https://doi.org/10/1002/ejsp.538

Castilla, E. J. (2008) Gender, race and meritocracy in organizational careers. *American Journal of Sociology, 113,* 1479–1526. https://doi.org/10.1086/588738

Caudwell, J. (2011). Gender, feminism and football studies. *Soccer & Society, 12*(3), 330–344.

Clarkson, B., Cox. E., & Thelwell, R. (2019). Negotiating gender in the English football workplace: composite vignettes of women head coaches' experiences. *Women in Sport and Physical Activity Journal, 27,* 73–84. https://doi.org/10.1123/wspaj.2018–0052

Cleland, J., O'Gorman, J., & Webb, T. (2018). Respect? An investigation into the experience of referees in association football. *The International Review for the Sociology of Sport, 53*(8), 960–974. https://doi.org/10.1177/1012690216687979

Cleland, J., Pope, S., & Williams, H. (2020). "I do worry that football will become over-feminized": ambiguities in fan reflections on the gender order in men's professional football in the United Kingdom. *Sociology of Sport Journal, 37,* 366–375. https://doi.org/10.1123/ssj.2019–0060

Culvin, A. (2021). Football as work: the lived realities of professional women footballers in England. *Managing Sport and Leisure,* 1–14. https://doi.org/10.1080/23750472.2021.1959384

Dunn, C., & Welford, J. (2015). *Football and the FA Women's Super League*. Basingstoke, UK: Palgrave Macmillan.

Eagly, A. H., Wood, W., & Diekman, A. B. (2000). Social role theory or sex differences and similarities: a current appraisal. In T. Eckes & H. M. Trautner (Eds.), *The Developmental Social Psychology of Gender,* (pp. 123–174). Mahwah, NJ: Erlbaum.

Forbes, A., Edwards, L., & Fleming, S. (2015). 'Women can't referee': exploring the experiences of female football officials within UK football culture. *Soccer & Society, 16*(4), 521–539. https://doi.org/10.1080/14660970.2014.882829

Gaucher, D., Friesen, J, & Kay, A. C. (2011). Evidence that gendered wording in job advertisements exists and sustains gender inequality. *Journal of Personality and Social Psychology, 101*, 109–128. https://doi.org/10.1037/a0022530

Gemar, A., & Pope, S. (2021). Women's consumption of men's professional sport in Canada: evidence of the 'feminization' of sports fandom and women as omnivorous sports consumers? *International Review of Sociology of Sport*, 1–23. https://doi.org/10.1177/10126902211026472

Giulianotti, R. (1999). *Football: A Sociology of the Global Game*. Oxford: Polity Press.

Haines, E. L., Deaux, K., & Lofaro, N. (2016). The times they are a-changing...or are they not? A comparison of components of gender stereotypes, 1983–2014. *Sex Roles, 40*, 353–363. https://doi.org/10.1177/0361684316634081

Heilman, M. E. (1983). Sex bias in work settings: the lack of fit model. *Research in Organizational Behavior, 5*, 269–298.

Heilman, M. E. (2001). Description and prescription: how gender stereotypes prevent women's ascent up the organizational ladder. *Journal of Social Issues, 57*, 657–674. https://doi.org/10.1111/0022–4537.00234

Heilman, M. E. (2012). Gender stereotypes and work-place bias. *Research in Organizational Behavior, 32*, 113–135. https://doi.org/10.1016/j.riob.2012.11.003.

Heilman, M. E. & Caleo, S. (2018). Combatting gender discrimination: a lack of fit framework. *Group Processes & Intergroup Relations, 21*(5), 725–744. https://doi.org/10.1177/1368430218761587

Heilman, M. E., & Haynes, M. C. (2008). Subjectivity in the appraisal process: a facilitator of gender bias in work settings. In E. Borgida & S. T. Fiske (Eds.), *Beyond Common Knowledge: Psychological Science in Court* (pp. 127–155). Mahwah, NJ: Lawrence Erlbaum Associates.

Hollingshead, A. B., & Fraiden, S. N. (2003). Gender stereotypes and assumptions about expertise in transactive memory. *Journal of Experimental Social Psychology, 39*, 355–363. https://doi.org/10.1016/S00221031(02)00549-8

Jeanes, R. (2011). "I'm into high heels and make up but I still love football': exploring gender identity and football participation with preadolescent girls. *Soccer & Society, 12*(3), 202–216.

Jeanes, R., & Kay, T. (2007). Can football be a female game? An examination of girls' perceptions of football and gender identity. In. J. Magee, J. Caudwell, K. Liston, & S. Scraton (Eds.), *Women, Football and Europe: Histories, Equity and Experiences* (pp. 105–129). Oxford: Meyer & Meyer Sport.

Johnson, S. K., Murphy, S. E., Zewdie, S., & Reichard, R. J. (2008). The strong, sensitive type: effects of gender sterotypes and leadership prototypes on the evaluation of male and female leaders. *Organizational Behavior and Human Decision Making Processes, 106*, 39–60. https://doi.org/10.1016/j.obhdp.2007.12.002

Jones, C., & Edwards, L. (2013). The woman in black: exposing sexist beliefs about female officials in elite men's football. *Sport, Ethics and Philosophy, 7*(2), 202–216.

Lewis, C. J., Roberts, S. J., & Andrews, H. (2018). "Why am I putting myself through this?" Women football coaches' experiences of the football association's coach education process. *Sport, Education and Society, 23*(1), 28–39. https://doi.org/10.1080/13573322.2015.1118030

Liston, K. (2021). Honour and Shame in Women's Sports. *Studies in Arts and Humanities, 7*(1), 1.

Lyness, K. S., & Heilman, M. E. (2006). When fit is fundamental: performance evaluations and promotions of upper-level female and male managers. *Journal of Applied Psychology, 91*, 777–785. https://doi.org/10.1037/0021–9010.91.4.777

122 Laura Grubb et al.

Madera, J. M., Hebl, M. R., & Martin, R. C. (2009). Gender and letters of recommendation for academics: agentic and communal differences. *Journal of Applied Psychology, 94*, 1591–1599. https://doi.org/10.1037/a0016539

Mason (2021). *Sian Massey-Ellis: Premier League Assistant Referee Discusses VAR, Online Hate and Inspiring Next Generation*. Retrieved from: https://www.skysports.com/football/news/11095/12257899/sian-massey-ellis-premier-league-assistant-referee-discusses-var-online-hate-and-inspiring-next-generation

Mean, L. (2001). Identity and discursive practice: doing gender on the football pitch. *Discourse Society, 12*(6), 789–815.

Meier, M. (2015). The value of female sporting role models. *Sport in Society, 18*(8), 968–982. https://doi.org/10.1080/17430437.2014.997581

Murphy, K. R., & Cleveland, J. (1995). *Understanding Performance Appraisal: Social, Organizational, and Goal-Based Perspectives*. Thousand Oaks, CA: SAGE.

Petty, K., & Pope, S. (2019). A new age for media coverage of women's sport? An analysis of english media coverage of the 2015 FIFA women's world cup. *Sociology, 53*(3), 486–502. https://doi.org/10.1177/0038038518797505

Pfister, G., Fasting, K., Scraton, S., & Benilde, V. (2002). Women and football – a contradiction? The beginnings of women's football in four European countries. In S. Scraton & A. Flintoff (Eds.), *Gender and Sport: A Reader* (pp. 66–77). Oxford: Routledge.

Pfister, G., & Gems, G. (2016). Gender. In E. Cashmore, & K. Dixon (Eds.), *Studying Football* (pp. 81–96). London: Routledge.

Schlesinger, T., & Weigelt-Schlesinger, Y. (2013). "Coaching soccer is a man's job!" - the influence of gender stereotypes or structures for recruiting female coaches to soccer clubs. *European Journal for Sport and Society, 10*(3), 241–265.

Sisjord, M. K., Fasting, K., & Sand, T. S. (2020). Gendered pathways to elite coaching reflecting the accumulation of capitals. *Sport, Education and Society, 26*(5), 554–566. https://doi.org/10.1080/13573322.2020.1732904

The FA. (n.d.) *FA Referee Course*. Retrieved from: https://www.thefa.com/get-involved/referee/general-information/the-fa-referee-training-course

The FA. (2017). *Gameplan for Growth*. Retrieved: http://www.thefa.com/news/2017/mar/13/fa-womens-football-strategy-gameplan-for- growth-double-participation-130317

The FA. (2019). *Female Only Referee Courses Available at Discounted Rate*. Retrieved from: https://www.northridingfa.com/news/2019/jul/23/female-only-referee-course-available-at-discounted-price

The FA. (2020a). *Find Out How We Helped Increase Number of Female Refs by 72 Percent Since 2016*. Retrieved from: https://www.thefa.com/news/2020/jun/03/gameplan-for-growth-refereeing-030620

The FA. (2020b). *Inspiring Positive Change*. Retrieved from: https://www.thefa.com/news/2020/oct/19/new-fa-womens-strategy-launched-191020

The FA. (2021a). *Barclays FA WSL on BBC & Sky*. Retrieved from: https://womenscompetitions.thefa.com/Article/Broadcast-announcement-20210322

The FA. (2021b). *Refs Ready for Step Up*. Retrieved from: https://womenscompetitions.thefa.com/en/Article/PGMOL-to-manage-FA-WSL-referees-20210420

The FA. (2021c). *Time for Change: The FA Strategy 2020–2024*. Retrieved from: https://www.thefa.com/about-football-association/what-we-do/strategy

The RA. (n.d.) *The Referee's Association*. Retrieved from: https://www.the-ra.org/about

Toffoletti, K., Pegoraro, A., & Comeau, G. S. (2019). Self-representations of women's sport fandom on instagram at the 2015 FIFA women's world cup. *Communication & Sport*, *9*(5), 695–717. https://doi.org/10.1177/2167479519893332

Webb, T. (2014). The emergence of training and assessment for referees in association football: moving from the side-lines. *The International Journal of the History of Sport*, *31*(9), 1081–1097. https://doi.org/10.1080/09523367.2014.905545

Webb, T. (2017). *Elite Soccer Referees: Officiating in the Premier League, La Liga and Serie A.* London; New York: Routledge.

Webb, T. (2020). Sports match official research: an evolving narrative, positioning future research. *Managing Sport and Leisure*, 1–8. https://doi.org/10.1080/23750472.2020.1762304

Webb, T., Gorcynski, P., Oftadeh-Moghadam, S., & Grubb, L. (2021). Experience and construction of mental health among English female football match officials. *The Sport Psychologist*, *35*(1). 1–10. https://doi.org/10.1123/tsp.2020–0086

Williams, J. (2003). *A Game for Rough Girls?: A History of Women's Football in Britain.* Oxford: Routledge.

Williams, J. (2007). *A Beautiful Game: International Perspectives on Women's Football.* Oxford: Berg.

Women in Football (2016). *Women in Football 2016 Survey Analysis.* Retrieved from: https://www.womeninfootball.co.uk/resources/women-in-football-2016-survey-analysis.html

Women in Sport (2020). *Empowering Women and Girls through Sport.* Retrieved from: https://www.womeninsport.org/wp-content/uploads/2020/03/Impact-report-18-and-19.pdf

Chapter 9

Critical Feminism and Football Pundits

Calm Down... It's Just a Woman Talking Football

Ali Bowes, Molly Matthews and Jess Long

Introduction

It has long been documented by feminist scholars investigating women in football that their involvement has been fragmented and rooted in discrimination. That being said, in the England the sport is increasingly significant for women. The formation of a formal semi-professional league in 2011 in the Football Association (FA) Women's Super League (WSL), which later fully professionalised in 2018, has contributed to growing numbers of girls participating, and women working in the sport (Culvin and Bowes, 2022). However, although there is increasing involvement of women within football in multiple ways, arguably the sport remains a bastion of male dominance. Often, disparities in media coverage between men's and women's football are a stark reminder of the gendered hierarchies that exist in the sport (Black and Fielding-Lloyd, 2019). However, much like participation rates and professional opportunities, there has been talk of a 'new age' of media coverage of women's football (Petty and Pope, 2019), which has included the emergence of women working in the sport media as pundits and commentators.

The increasing visibility of women involved in football within the sport media has occurred, yet it remains to be seen whether women *working* in the sport media are part of this change. While still vastly underrepresented in the sports media generally (Franks and O'Neil, 2016), women have been commentating on football since 2007, with trailblazer Jacqui Oatley featuring on Match of the Day, the first female commentator since the programmes launch in 1964. It has also taken time for women to feature more regularly as pundits during television coverage of matches, with former England international Eniola Aluko the first to feature in 2014. When both Aluko and her ex-England teammate Alex Scott featured on England's World Cup 2018 coverage, they were thrust into the media spotlight. They have since become prominent figures in the media, working on both men's and women's football while simultaneously paving the way for other women to do the same. However, their inclusion as pundits has provoked debates about the legitimacy of their involvement, discussions rooted in sexist discourse.

DOI: 10.4324/9781003253990-13

It is well known that there are increasing numbers of women who are taking part in, engaging with and consuming sport (Parry et al., 2021), yet the media coverage of women in sport continues to be problematic. Bruce's (2013; 2015) work draws together key findings on feminist sport media analyses, highlighting the subordinate and highly gendered nature of women's inclusion. More recent research on media representations of sportswomen has paid attention to technological changes in the media, incorporating online and new media analyses alongside traditional television and print media research. This body of work continues to highlight that sport is often presented as a male domain in both traditional and new, online spaces (LaVoi and Calhoun, 2014).

There is an emerging body of work that critically analyses the media coverage of women in football, centring primarily on analyses of women playing the sport. For example, Woodward (2019) explains that the women's game is much less visible than the men's game, given the historical and sociocultural roots of both the sport, and the sport media, as male-dominated spaces. The relatively limited research on the media coverage of women's football centres on the international scene. This research evidences that the initial boom in media interest around women's football was seen at the 1999 FIFA WWC, after it was hosted in and won by the USA (Ravel and Gareau, 2016). In the specific context of the England, research has shown that there has generally been a lack of media coverage of women's football (Pope, 2018). However, research on media coverage of the England national team at the 2015 FIFA Women's World Cup concluded an improved media representation of women's football (Petty and Pope, 2019). Attributing this beneficial change to a number of recent developments in women's sport, Petty and Pope (2019) put forward that we had entered a 'new age' of media coverage for women in football.

As the biggest sport in the UK, football pundits often are easy targets for ridicule (Hurrey, 2014), and for women intruding into this male domain, their involvement most definitely comes with difficulties. Birrell (2000: 61) highlights that critical feminist analyses have focused on the reproduction of gender relations, valorisation of male characteristics and evidence of male privilege through sport and sports media. From this perspective, it has been said that women breaking into the sport media are exposing themselves to unsavoury treatment (Etling and Young, 2007; Schultz and Sheffer, 2007), and are often considered less credible and less competent than men (Grubb and Billiot, 2010).

Using discourses on female pundits from both print and social media, this chapter will first outline a critical feminist approach to research women in football. To then consider the narratives around the increasing visibility of women as football pundits, and their continuing presence in a male-dominated profession, two case studies will be presented. These case studies present: (a) discussions about women's involvement as football pundits on social media, and (b) the media representations of women football pundits, before concluding on how critical feminist theory can be useful in research of this type.

Critical Feminism

Critical feminism as a theoretical approach exists within a myriad of different feminisms. Feminist research has long indicated that football has been, and remains, a male-dominated institution in most contexts. Most of this research takes a feminist standpoint, which exposes patriarchal notions that set up the male as the norm, and the female as 'the other', as we see in football (Bachman et al., 2018). In football, this privileging of men and men's activities can result in the reproduction of institutionalised practices and gendered roles, where women are marginalised and/or excluded. Considering this broad socio-historical and political context of a patriarchal society, a feminist perspective is adopted in this chapter. As Bachman et al. (2018: 3) note, there is no amalgamated perspective labelled 'feminist theory', feminist approaches have some common elements: 'attention to the status of women in society, the nature of gender and the interpretation of the condition of being a woman as a basic differentiating label organising different individual's lives'.

One such feminist approach has been termed critical feminism, an enmeshing of feminism with critical perspectives. Critical theories aim to identify the prevailing structures, practices and institutions that perpetuate and maintain disadvantage, inequality and/or oppression (Wood, 2015). When critical theories and feminist theories intersect, the focus is then to 'identify, critique and seek to change inequities and discrimination, particularly those that are based on sex and gender' (Wood, 2015: 206). Critical feminist perspectives thus begin with the assumption that society is organised in a patriarchal way, where gender is socially constructed and culturally defined to serve the needs and interests of powerful groups of society (in this way, men, and specifically white, middle-class men).

In relation to sport, Birrell (2000: 61) highlights that critical feminist analyses have focused on the reproduction of gender relations, valorisation of male characteristics and evidence of male privilege through sport and sports media. In practice, feminists have drawn attention to the ways in which sport was made by men for men, with women's history in sport fractured and fragmented. Indeed, Scraton and Flintoff (2013: 106) comment that 'questions of inequality remain on the agenda for gender and sport'. Equality of opportunity between the genders has been a central argument by feminists in their quest to gain resources for girls and women in sport, a perspective which has been accused of oversimplifying women's multiple and diversified identities.

Bachman et al. (2018: 1) highlight that 'media and their messages—including access to the production of these messages—have long been a key concern of feminist scholars', where the 'struggle over meanings and values of what it means to be a woman and what the category of gender entails' is as relevant today as it ever has been. Recent work on feminism and sports media has drawn attention to the multiple, complex and fragmented nature of feminisms (e.g. Bruce, 2015; Thorpe et al., 2017). As Wood (2015) explains, critical feminists are specifically interested in how power is deployed and resisted, including informal kinds of power such

Critical Feminism and Football Pundits 127

as media portrayals, and everyday practices that reproduce and sustain inequity. Sport is one such avenue when gender inequality persists (Bowes et al., 2021), and the sport media is an example of where critical feminism can be used to pay attention to the marginalisation and exclusion of women.

Twitter Responses to Women Football Pundits

Our first case study focused on the discussion of women football pundits on social media networking site Twitter during the 2019 Women's World Cup. Talia, Trunfio and Marozzo (2015) state that analysis of social media data can be used to understand the behaviour of people and the dynamics of public opinions. Relevant tweets were compiled using the Twitter search tool, using the following search criteria: 'football pundits', 'female football pundits', 'Alex Scott pundit', 'pundit women football world cup', totalling 53 different tweets and associated replies. This occurred during the time frame of the 2019 Women's World Cup: Friday 7 June to Sunday 7 July. As per the Twitter terms of service, by posting content on public profiles users grant access to use, copy and reproduce that content. However, as users have not provided informed consent, all Twitter user handles have been replaced with numbers, except for verified users, and minor changes made, to protect anonymity (Williams et al., 2017). The tweets about women football pundits collected were thematically analysed using a critical feminist perspective into three dominant themes: overt sexism, challenging equality and support for women pundits.

Overt Sexism

One of the dominant themes in the discussions of women football pundits was that of overt sexism and/or sexist abuse, which often positions women in a subordinate position. The inclusion of women as football pundits prompted scrutiny and disapproval. Some users disagreed with their involvement, and others likened women pundits as a tokenistic move by media companies:

> Female football pundits. No. Just no. #gohome (User 17)
> TV companies indulging in 'tokenism' by using female football pundits (User 29)

One example of overt sexism came in the obvious discussion of stereotypical gendered roles of women, problematising women's involvement in the male sphere of football (and punditry, specifically) and highlighting how gender is socially constructed and reinforced:

> When you watch the Women's World Cup, the female pundit gives her opinion... I am still waiting for her to finish off with... 'And then just pop it in the oven for 30 minutes' (User 52)

128 Ali Bowes et al.

Alongside this obvious gendering of women working as football pundits, there were examples of the sexualisation of women. For one user, this was due to women's (unexpected) knowledge of the sport, and for another, it was in marked contrast to women's involvement in football:

> I find female football pundits who know the offside rule to be strangely alluring #isthatsexist (User 19)
> Female football pundits are a disgrace. Take your clothes off or get off my screen #furious (User 18)

For one pundit, Alex Scott, online sexist abuse occurred 'every single day', and it is a clear issue for women involved in the profession. Given the increasing significance of social media usage, it appears women are exposed in new ways to sexist and/or sexualised views (Kavanagh et al., 2019).

Challenging Equality?

During the 2019 Women's World Cup, the selection of an all-women panel on the 9th June for England's game against Scotland sparked a 'reverse sexism' equality debate on social media. The initial tweet that sparked a magnitude of responses came from public figure Rebekah Vardy, the wife of former England men's footballer Jamie Vardy, who asked: 'Umm what happened to equality?'

Twitter user's responses centred on towards the BBC for broadcasting such 'inequality', as critics argued that an all-women panel of pundits was sexist towards men:

> Tell me why for men's football we have at least one female pundit however today, for the women's world cup game, all pundits were female and not one male in sight #imnotsexist (User 39)
> First game of the women's world cup and not one male pundit, yet with the men's game there are both male and female pundits? Equality my arse. (User 49)
> It is OK to have female pundits on the world cup; then male pundits do not get a look in when it is the women's world cup. I am not being sexist to anyone, but it is wrong when we are in the society of equality (User 46)

Alongside this debate was the notion of 'tokenism', when women are included on panels for the male game:

> 4 women pundits on the women's world cup coverage, 2 more on Sky Sports. Where is the token man pundit?? Like we must watch the female token pundit when we watch the premier league (User 48)

This incident highlighted some of the challenge's women face working in the sport media, and how difficult it can be to shift perceptions. However, as one user noted

Critical Feminism and Football Pundits 129

> A panel full of female football pundits is not discrimination, it is a breakthrough #WomensWorldCup2019 (User 15)

Clearly, this kind of narrative downplays the institutionalised sexism that women working in football have had to overcome. The 'reverse sexism' narrative is rooted in post-feminist sensibilities, and challenges to feminist thinking that frames feminism as 'out to get men' (García-Favaro and Gill, 2016). However, a critical feminist approach contests these ideas as ignorant to the institutionally gendered challenges women have faced in society, especially in the sport media landscape, with García-Favaro and Gill (2016) referring to narrative such as this as 'post-feminist sexism'.

Support for Women Pundits

While there were clear issues with sexist abuse towards women as pundits, and challenges to women's increased presence as pundits, this also prompted significant levels of support by twitter users:

> Just because we have vaginas does not mean we know fuck all about football (User 9)
> I am sorry lads, but football is our national sport and women are entitled to enjoy it too #WorldCup (User 7)

Opinions such as this complement the clear increase in coverage of female sports, and the increasing presence of women working in sport, such as pundits. This is often perceived as a positive movement for women and women's football:

> My daughter is a bit too young for football but how is it that as she grows up she will be in the generation where having female commentators and pundits is the norm #WorldCup (User 10)

This idea of advocates for equality in football is also supported by Premier League Tonight presenter, Jake Humphrey, who took to social media when voicing his opinions on female football pundits and the sexist abuse they receive online, stating: 'any form of discrimination is wrong. Football is for everyone; it should be empowering our daughters as well as our sons'. This overt support for women as pundits, and the challenges to obvious power inequalities within football and the mediatisation of football, demonstrate the importance of critical feminist thought in highlighting gendered issues.

In summary, our first case study utilised a critical feminist lens in analysing social media communication about women football pundits. This has revealed some of the challenge's women football pundits face, demonstrating a double-edged sword where sexism was rife, but also challenged. What was evident is the initial responses to women as football pundits highlighted the gendered hierarchy of football. There was clear abuse directed at women based on their gender, and expected gendered stereotypes, and the implication that football remains a male-dominated culture. When that idea was challenged – with the all-female panel – the outrage was tangible. The discussion of 'reverse sexism' highlights a lack of awareness of institutionalised sexism in the sport, and the challenges that women have had to overcome. However, there was clearly a wealth of support for women as football pundits, seemingly rooted in an awareness of the marginalisation of women in football, and as football pundits.

Print Media Representations of Women Football Pundits

Despite a shift in audiences interacting with online media platforms, print media are still a prominent media source (Velija and Silvani, 2020). In our second case study, print media data on women as football pundits were collected using Nexis database, using UK print media sources. The time frame of the search was between the year 2018 and 2021, using the keywords: 'women football pundits', 'female football pundits', as well as focusing on leading women football pundits during this period: 'Jacqui Oatley', 'Karen Carney' and 'Alex Scott'. In total, 47 newspaper articles within the set timeframe were identified. As with case study 1, the dataset was thematically analysed using a critical feminist lens. Dominant themes identified were positive descriptors, narratives of change and challenging sexism.

Positive Descriptors

Using a critical feminist lens and drawing on a wealth of work regarding women in the sport media (e.g. Bruce, 2013; 2015), it was expected that the media representation of women football pundits would be problematic. However, the print media coverage was distinctly positive about the emerging involvement of women working as football pundits within football media, with the following headline proclaiming:

> Female pundits set for star roles as BBC and ITV battle for World Cup ratings.
> (The Observer, 10 June 2018)

Writing about the all-woman pundit team for the England versus Scotland Women's World Cup game, the positive narrative manifested into a call for equality via levelling the playing field:

> It's high time we had level playing field; Talented all-female World Cup presenting team even the score for football fan Jean.
> (Sunday Mail, 16 June 2019)

For some of the leading women, such as Alex Scott, the media were conscious to highlight how much she deserved, or has earnt her place in football media:

Alex Scott deserves her place alongside football's male pundits.

(The Times, 12 August 2018)

THE WORLD AT HER FEET; In her early years at Arsenal Alex Scott did the laundry for the men's team to make ends meet. Now she's one of the football's star pundits.

(Sunday Times, 18 October 2020)

The women were framed as capable, with the following descriptors used to describe women working as football pundits: 'exceptionally informed'

(The Independent, 16 January 2020)

'Scott's commenting success has soared'

(The Mail, 20 December 2018)

'well-informed'

(Daily Mail, 30 December 2020)

and 'respected'

(The Guardian, 30 December 2020)

This is a notable shift in the ways in which women in sport have typically been written about by the print media, moving away from the previous research studies suggesting that women in the sport media are often feminised and sexualised (Bruce, 2013; 2015).

Breaking the Glass Ceiling

In light of the first theme, which highlighted the positive discussions in the print media of women football pundits, women's involvement in football in this way was described as a significant moment for women in sport. It was evident throughout the dataset that women in punditry, like Jacqui Oatley, were trailblazers. This supports Schmidt's (2018) recent research that the media are giving significant coverage to advocators of social issues:

'Jacqui took a bullet for us': the women with key World Cup reporting roles; There will be more women than ever before broadcasting to British homes from Russia

(The Guardian, 14 June 2018)

However, this 'breaking' of the glass ceiling was not something that was reported lightly, with stories of women pundits challenging the sexist cultures of sport and navigating sexist abuse in a variety of forms:

> No, the world isn't ending, it's just a women hosting Sunday Supplement; The hugely experienced and pedigreed Jacqui Oatley is the new host of Sunday Supplement and the sexist reaction to the announcement from Sky Sports was as pathetic as it was expected
>
> (The Independent, 15 January 2020)

> 'Breaking glass ceiling wasn't without pitfalls'; Women now play a prominent role on the front line of TV coverage, but as Sally Jones, the first female sports reporter on BBC Breakfast News, recalls it was a tough battle to break down the gates to male-dominated world.
>
> (The Daily Telegraph. 16 May 2019)

At this stage, while we can acknowledge the significance of the print media's positive reporting of women football pundits, it is also important to see how the media adopt a critical feminist stance in highlighting the gendered inequalities women face, and the gendered hierarchy that has persisted in the sport media.

Challenging Sexism

Leading on from the following theme, in which breaking the glass ceiling for women football pundits often meant confronting sexism, the print media were open to presenting issues related to sexism and sexist abuse of women football pundits.

> From breast-grabbing to 'hottest fan' galleries, is this World Cup the most sexist?; Female presenters, pundits and fans are on our screens in unprecedented numbers. It looks as if the sport has progressed – but the rate of sexual harassment and assault tells a disturbing story
>
> (The Guardian, 2 July 2018)

For one notable sports media figure, Clare Balding, the abuse received on social media when reporting on football was enough to prevent her continued employment in this space:

> 'VILE ABUSE' BBC star Claire Balding refuses to cover men's football over 'vile abuse' on 'toxic' social media
>
> (The Sun, 29 November 2020)

A specific feature of the print media dataset was the focus on Karen Carney, who received a barrage of abuse for her comments about Leeds United in 2020. The newspapers were quick to condemn the sexist abuse she received on social media, as well as the reaction of the club itself:

> Club's irresponsible action opened the door to sexist trolls:? Leeds should have known better than to single out a female pundit who would be attacked for her gender
>
> (The Daily Telegraph, 31 December 2020)

> The abuse received by Carney was undeniable. In public messages seen by the Guardian, Carney was called a "silly bitch", a "stupid slag" and "twat of the week" and was told to "get back in the kitchen", or to "put your mic down and get yourself home there's dishes to wash and clothes to iron". Other users wrote they were "sick of this shit women pundits", while another quipped "women's lives matter but come on, women and football? Get kettle on love!"
>
> (The Irish Times, 21 January 2020)

The media reports also suggested that Leeds United should be:

> bringing in representatives from Women in Football and educating their staff, coaches, owner and seemingly alien world of sexist abuse.
>
> (The Guardian, 2020)

In this way, the media are advocating for women, challenging dominant belief systems about women's role as football pundits, and reprimanding sexist 'trolls' on social media, like the users seen in our first case study.

In sum, our second case study provides a critical feminist analysis of the representation of women in sport media, in particular women football pundits. Unlike Fink's (2015) findings that women in the sport media are rarely noted by their success, the women football pundits in this study are praised for their skillset and supported by the media in this way. It is reported that more women are breaking through the glass-ceiling into traditionally male held roles within football, such as punditry. The majority of the findings within the study reflected the positive representation of female football pundit by the media, against a backdrop of sexist problems.

Conclusion: Researching Football Pundits Using Critical Feminist Theory

As we enter 'the new age of media coverage' of women's football, there is an increasing visibility of women working in the football media. This chapter highlights how critical feminist approaches can be used to help understand the presentations of women football pundits in traditional media and online media spaces. Drawing on both case studies here, the focus is very much on the double-edged sword of media involvement for women football pundits, in which there is an increasing acceptance of, and support for them working in a culture that is inherently and institutionally sexist, gendered and hierarchical.

Our first case study highlights how the gendered hierarchy of football plays out in online spaces in discussions of women working in the game. It is evident from the data collected that the perceptions of female football pundits are both problematic, but also supportive. The support is seemingly cognisant of the perpetual subordination of women within football, and of the power imbalances between women and men in sport hierarchies. However, there are concerns at the accessibility of women pundits on social media, as they navigate through targeted sexism and sexist abuse from football fans. Our second case study evidences the significance of the print media in challenging the inherently sexist sport media institution. In this chapter, we have seen a snapshot of how journalists can frame women pundits as worthwhile of their place in the gendered cultures of football. Again, while it is apparent that the power in football rests in men's hands, the push back from print media journalists is encouraging.

Currently, we are still at the stage where gender seems a significant aspect of a football pundits' identity, in the sense of how they experience the sport media workplace. It could be suggested that the discussions of women pundits – both in print and online – is out of the *uniqueness* of women in the role of pundit, emphasising the gendered nature of the profession. Alex Scott, an ex-England footballer-turned football pundit, suggests that:

> It's going to get to the stage where I am not regarded as a female pundit. I don't want to be regarded as a female pundit, I'm a pundit.
>
> (Wrack, 2019)

Until that is the case, critical feminist approaches, alongside other feminist theories, will continue to be a useful lens to understand women's experience in football. As Bachman et al. (2018: 18) state, 'feminist theory is a broad theoretical perspective, one that serves as connective tissue binding raw data and observation with critical thought about gender and identities'. However, feminism has at times been called out for its narrowness and white centrism, and contemporary, intersectional feminist theory can enable a more nuanced consideration of subordination and dominance that goes beyond gender. Future analyses of women in punditry would benefit from a diverse range of feminist perspectives (Thorpe et al., 2017).

References

Bachmann, I., Harp, D., & Loke, J. (2018). Through a feminist kaleidoscope: Critiquing media, power and gender inequalities. In D. Harp, J. Loke & I Bachmann (Eds.). *Feminist Approaches to Media Theory and Research*. Palgrave Macmillon. 1–15.

Birrell, S. (2000). Feminist theories for sport. In J. Coakley and E. Dunning (Eds.). *Handbook of Sports Studies*. Sage Publications, 61–76.

Black, J., & Fielding-Lloyd, B. (2019). Re-establishing the 'outsiders': English press coverage of the 2015 FIFA Women's World Cup. *International Review for the Sociology of Sport, 54*(3), 282–301.

Critical Feminism and Football Pundits   135

Bowes, A, Lomax, L., & Piasecki, J. (2021). A losing battle? Women's sport pre- and post-COVID-19. *European Sport Management Quarterly, 21*(3), 443–461.

Bruce, T. (2013). Reflections on Communication and Sport: On Women and Femininities. *Communication & Sport, 1*(1–2), 125–137.

Bruce, T. (2015). Assessing the sociology of sport: On media and representations of sportswomen. *International Review for the Sociology of Sport, 50*(4–5), 380–384.

Culvin, A., & Bowes, A. (2022). *Women's Football in a Global, Professional Era.* Emerald.

Etling, L., & Young, R. (2007). Sexism and the authoritativeness of female sportscasters. *Communication Research Reports, 24*(2), 121–130.

Fink, J. S. (2015). Female athletes, women's sport, and the sport media commercial complex: Have we really "come a long way, baby"?. *Sport Management Review, 18*(3), 331–342.

Franks, S., & O'Neill, D. (2016). Women reporting sport: Still a man's game?. *Journalism, 17*(4), 474–492.

García-Favaro, L., & Gill, R. (2016). "Emasculation nation has arrived": Sexism rearticulated in online responses to Lose the Lads' Mags campaign. *Feminist Media Studies, 16*(3), 379–397.

Grubb, M. V., & Billiot, T. (2010). Women sportscasters: Navigating a masculine domain. *Journal of Gender Studies, 19*(1), 87–93.

Hurrey, A. (2014). *Football Cliches.* Hachette UK.

Kavanagh, E., Litchfield, C., & Osborne, J. (2019). Sporting women and social media: Sexualization, misogyny, and gender-based violence in online spaces. *International Journal of Sport Communication, 12*(4), 552–572.

LaVoi, N. M., & Calhoun, A. S. (2014). Digital media and women's sport: An old view on 'new' media? In A. C. Billings & M. Hardin (Eds.). *Routledge Handbook of Sport and New Media.* Taylor and Francis, 320–330.

Parry, K. D., Clarkson, B. G., Bowes, A., Grubb, L., & Rowe, D. (2021). Media framing of women's football during the covid-19 pandemic. *Communication & Sport.* (Ahead of Print). https://doi.org/10.1177/21674795211041024.

Petty, K., & Pope, S. (2019). A new age for media coverage of women's sport? An analysis of English media coverage of the 2015 FIFA Women's World Cup. *Sociology, 53*(3), 486–502.

Pope, S. (2018). 'Who could name an England women's footballer?': Female fans of men's football and their views of women's football in England. In G. Pfister & S. Pope (Eds.). *Female Football Players and Fans: Intruding into a Man's World.* Palgrave Macmillan, 125–153.

Ravel, B., & Gareau, M. (2016). 'French football needs more women like Adriana'? Examining the media coverage of France's women's national football team for the 2011 World Cup and the 2012 Olympic Games. *International Review for the Sociology of Sport, 51*(7), 833–847.

Schmidt, H. (2018). Sport reporting in an era of activism: Examining the intersection of sport media and social activism. *International Journal of Sport Communication, 11*(1), 2–17.

Schultz, B., & Sheffer, M. L. (2007). Sports journalists who blog cling to traditional values. *Newspaper Research Journal, 28*(4), 62–76.

Scraton, S., & Flintoff, A. (2013). Gender, feminist theory and sport. In D. Andrews & B. Carrington (Eds.). *A Companion to Sport.* Malden, MA: Blackwell Publishing Ltd, 96–111.

Talia, D., Trunfio, P., & Marozzo, F. (2015). *Data Analysis in the Cloud: Models, Techniques and Applications.* Elsevier.

Thorpe, H., Toffoletti, K. & Bruce, T. (2017). Sportswomen and social media: Bringing third-wave feminism, postfeminism, and neoliberal feminism into conversation. *Journal of Sport and Social Issues, 41*(5): 359–383.

Velija, P., & Silvani, L. (2021). Print media narratives of bullying and harassment at the football association: a case study of Eniola Aluko. *Journal of Sport and Social Issues*, *45*(4), 358–373.

Williams, M. L., Burnap, P., & Sloan, L. (2017). Towards an ethical framework for publishing Twitter data in social research: Taking into account users' views, online context and algorithmic estimation. *Sociology, 51*(6), 1149–1168.

Wood, J, T. (2015). Critical feminist theories: Giving voice and visibility to women's experiences in interpersonal relations. In D. O. Braithwaite & P. Schrodt (Eds.). *Engaging Theories in Interpersonal Communication: Multiple Perspectives (2nd Edition)*. Sage Publications, 203–215.

Woodward, K. (2019). The gendering of defining moments: Heroic narratives and pivotal points in footballing memories. *Soccer & Society, 20*(7–8), 1108–1117.

Wrack, S. (2019, 9 May). *Alex Scott: 'I Wouldn't Want Graeme Souness to Change because I'm Female'*. The Guardian. https://www.theguardian.com/football/2019/may/09/alex-scott-what-keeps-me-going-is-helping-change

Chapter 10

Towards the Application of Feminist-Informed Pedagogical Principles into Coaching Practice

Personal Narratives and Implications for Football Coaches

Adi Adams, Alice Hunter and Ellie Gennings

Introduction

This chapter develops a feminist-informed pedagogy via three personal narratives (one from each author), to explore concerns arising at the intersection of gender and football coaching practice. First, we draw on our narratives to stimulate coaches' own reflections on their practice and bring feminist theory and masculinities theory to life through interpretations of our personal experiences. Next, we contextualise our stories by tracing hegemonic patterns of masculinity in football coaching and borrow from existing scholarship to outline a feminist-informed pedagogy. This framework departs from dominant masculine models of leadership and coaching and has value for coaches in a variety of ways: re-thinking power and authority in coaching; challenging competitive individualism; creating communal environments; respecting and increasing diversity; and providing life-changing learning through social action opportunities. We conclude with some thoughts around how such an approach may be taken-up by football coaches to meaningfully inform more ethical, inclusive and sustainable football coaching methodologies. Implications for coaching practice are threaded through the work, and relate to interpersonal coaching interactions, practice design and the organisational structure of football coaching settings. We begin with our three author narratives.

Co-author Personal Narratives

Alice: My coaching and playing experience span many different worlds within the sports multiverse, and the only common denominator is my sporting persona, though this has taken many forms. When I first started coaching, I was only 16 years old and immediately found myself in a male-dominated environment, and though at the time I didn't realise it, this shaped my coaching practice from day

DOI: 10.4324/9781003253990-14

138   Adi Adams et al.

one. Over a decade later, I've had experiences of coaching from grassroots to international level, and now predominantly find myself in co-ed sports (mixed gender) and I'm still learning to appreciate my own 'more-feminine' coaching voice.

Many of my initial experiences in coaching were within multi-sports camps (some more akin to babysitting than coaching), but these tended to be staffed by male, student coaches and were predominantly football focused. Normally, I'd be assigned the children who chose multi-sports rather than football and would coach skills-based sessions through a game-sense approach in a variety of game focuses such as net and wall games or invasion games. During the breaks in the day, coaches would normally discuss their sessions and any issues they faced, but rarely would my voice be called on unless I voluntarily interjected, and I was tentative as to the voice I used – would my opinion be seen as a 'coach's' or a 'female coach's'? I made my coaching persona crass and abrasive around others, I didn't want to seem 'soft' but then when I was naturally empathetic with children, I felt this was almost looked down upon by other coaches. I present these examples not to discourage female coaches or to generalise that all male coaches or male environments are similar, but instead to educate as to the environments that we create, as coaches: we focus on the learning environments of our players – this could be described as our main focus – but are we then neglecting the environment we create for coaches? As a young and inexperienced (female) coach, one might look for social inclusion to be accepted into an established coaching team – but we need to ensure that these environments are encouraging.

When coaching at a higher level, I've felt more accepted than at grass-roots level, mainly because I have developed a confidence in my coaching ability that pays no attention to my own gender or of others around me. However, I have relied heavily on engaging in reflection to have an awareness of my coaching practice that doesn't dismiss my feminine coaching voice – something I had consciously done to myself for so long.

Ellie: I remember walking into a football coaching workshop and receiving welcoming looks and smiles with a slight hint of judgement. They are surprised that a girl is on the coaching course. I immediately feel seen as a female first and then a coach. I am questioning: 'Do I belong here?'

On the board, there are different pictures of animals… Gorilla, shark, lion, snake. The course leader begins to talk about coaching styles. We had to pick which animal represents us as a coach. I am not loud, aggressive or have a dominant voice. Nor do I want to have that – does this mean I am not a 'good' coach? It's time to go round the room and state which animal relates to our coaching style and why. Everyone is choosing and I am thinking, 'I am none of these, but which one could I be'.

I do not have a traditional authoritative leadership style. I am a petite young female. I do not have a loud voice – something which I think we (other coaches, players, parents) expect coaches to have. These characteristics, along with masculinist social norms reinforced within football, mean that – in this moment – I do not think I am a good coach, and I don't feel like I belong here.

Personal Narratives and Implications for Football Coaches   139

Six years on, I am comfortable with my coaching style and if I was to undertake that same task of 'what animal best describes your coaching style?' I would describe myself as a deer; curious, gentle and warm. I became comfortable with this through the sharing of my learning and ideas with a mentor and other female coaches. I received support that my 'non-traditional' pedagogy was ok, and this generated a sense of belonging which I did not have before. Through talking and developing a communal environment for my coach development I was able to meet other like-minded female coaches. I then focused on developing my own coaching pedagogy and moved away from trying to fulfil others' expectations and incorporate elements of masculine pedagogies into my own.

Football is a powerful institution. It has the power to help reshape social norms which are representative of feminist pedagogies. If female coaches feel like they don't belong in the football coaching community they will not continue with their coach development. The reason I stayed in coaching is because I was able to connect with diverse communities. This gave me a sense of belonging and an understanding that I have a choice in how I proceed as a coach, and that a masculine/authoritarian coaching pedagogy is only one way of coaching.

Adi: As the first author on this chapter discussing feminist pedagogy, I was conscious of my own voice as a white, hetero, cis-gender, now-middle-class academic male to lead and dominate the starting point and subsequent direction of the chapter. The decision to lead the chapter with our personal narratives came from Alice and Ellie and, as it turned out, their completion of their narratives before mine meant that as first author for the chapter I subsequently had the privilege to read their narratives while re-ordering our initial first draft of the work and constructing my own narrative. I was stirred by the stories and experiences of Alice and Ellie above, and I am grateful to them since their commentaries provoked my own reflections and affected my contribution to this narrative opening to our chapter. Below, I offer two connected personal narratives: the first explores my own on-field football coaching pedagogy and the second reflects on a formative football experience.

Being an academic for the past decade and a football player and coach of 20 years – with 10 years coaching in English professional football club youth 'academies' – my practice is informed by an array of personal experience, and social and pedagogical knowledges. As well as being influenced in my professional practice by various coaching and teaching pedagogies (e.g. nonlinear/constructivist pedagogies such as ecological dynamics, constraints-led coaching and game-sense approaches), some of my academic work has also explored issues relevant to the sport←→masculinities and feminist pedagogy literature discussed later in this chapter: for example, a recent study problematising gendered humour among male coaches within a football academy (Adams, 2020). In short, my coaching pattern interweaves the personal, pedagogical and sociological, and has broadly resulted in a tendency towards 'game-relevant' or 'game-realistic' practices incorporating problem solving, discussion and respecting/considering the thoughts of others. My intention is to avoid over-controlling in my coaching as

140   Adi Adams et al.

part of a strategy to support performance/development and build positive relationships. As well as being in line with my constructivist/nonlinear coaching tendencies, this approach is also in line with feminist principles, in that strategies incorporating problem-solving, discussion and respecting the thoughts of others are also building blocks of a feminist football coaching pedagogy: they are strategies which problematise the traditional masculine tropes within coaching, and disrupt views of male coaching authoritarianism in the classroom by attempting to distribute power, influence and autonomy more widely among players and other coaches involved in the process alongside me. In other words, it may be that the constructivist/nonlinear approaches of many contemporary football coaches – in activities such as questioning to facilitate problem solving, promoting listening and collaboration, respecting the thoughts of other people and developing an understanding of their viewpoints – may also be generating more actively welcoming football spaces, as well as fostering the skills and qualities (that is, 'feminist building blocks') of young people which later set them up to listen and work with diverse groups of people within and beyond football spaces (e.g. girls, women, and LGBT+ colleagues, students and coaches). Indeed, in an attempt to connect these thoughts about my current coaching practice and its pedagogical/nonlinear and sociological/feminist components to my own formative football experiences, it is to this influence of coaches and diverse workspaces on young people's feminist sensibilities within football spaces that I turn to next.

Alice and Ellie's narratives above on being female coaches add an important dimension to this chapter, given the historical male dominance in football coaching practice and literature. Their stories affected me, as I hope they do other readers, and evoked one of my earliest memories of playing football and being coached within a formal team: at primary school, in the early-mid 1990s. This is probably the case for many boys (and, nowadays, girls – our primary school back then had no girls team). However, what makes this moment in my life stand out to me as an important formative football experience is that our coach – Ms Foulkes – was a woman. My lasting recollections of Ms Foulkes' are of an energetic, knowledgeable and skilful coach. At the time, when the boy's team were informed that 'Miss'[1] would be our new coach, I think we were all a bit surprised and unsure what girls/women knew about football that they could teach us – because deep down we thought about football as the terrain of boys, *ours*, something *we* had control of. None of the other school teams in the area were coached by women – there was some fear among us that we would be mocked by the boys from the other schools' teams and other pupils attending to watch the games. However, we grew to know Ms Foulkes – a warm person who loved football and wanted to help give us the chance to play organised football. Without realising this at the time, I can see now that Ms Foulkes – a female coach in a male dominated space (both within our school and across the district) – was engaged in what is conceptually discussed below as 'boundary crossing' and 'transformation' of this particular sport context from the inside. The positively 'disturbing' impact that this Ms Foulkes' presence within our school football world had on me as a young boy and the fact that this

Personal Narratives and Implications for Football Coaches   141

experience lives long in my current memory as an adult – now a football coach myself – demonstrates the potential importance of feminist principles of raising up the voices and influence of female coaches, valuing their knowledge and experience, and in particular where men (male-allies) can help to achieve this gender diversity within football. Whether or not Ms Foulkes understood this, her presence problematised our boys-only football space; it confronted me with the prejudices of other boys both within my school and in other schools, and it provoked me at the time to reckon with and reflect on my own emerging beliefs about 'what a coach looks like' and the place of women and girls in 'our' (male) football world.

Of course, it is easy to over-romanticise this moment – boys with a female coach – as being a panacea for challenging dominant enactments of masculinities in football and challenging boys to re-think 'who' has/can have power and authority in football. However, it is also important not to entirely dismiss such formative personal moments. As feminist theory highlights, the personal can be political, and therefore, such moments can be instructive in guiding future coaching practice: indeed, the feminist principles of communality, collegiality, diversity, inclusion and respect that arise in the story above also underpin further personal interactions and working relationships I have experienced with female and LGBT+ players, coaches, referees, academic colleagues, guest speakers and students – all cumulatively transformative in terms of allowing me opportunities to listen to and work with people from a diverse spectrum of gender and sexuality.

Contextualising Our Stories: Masculinities and Football Coaching Pedagogies

In this section, we seek to contextualise our personal stories by exploring and unpacking some of the existing academic research in relation to some of the experiences raised in our own narratives. Drawing on the work of Acker (1990) and Connell (1995, 2002, 2005, 2008), gender relations are conceptualised here as relations *between* and *within* female/male gender categories: what Connell (1995) describes as inter-gender and intra-gender relations. Gender is understood as socially (re)constructed and embedded in organisational and educational contexts through divisions of labour, power relations, emotional relationships and organisational cultures (Acker, 1990; Connell, 2002, 2008). Central to Connell's theorising on contemporary masculinities is gender as a relational concept.

'Gender' is interpreted not as a fixed or static 'property' that individuals bring with them into 'neutral' contexts, but something relational and malleable which is reconstructed within what Acker (1990) calls 'gendered organisations'; that is, organisations which may already have established sets of gender practices and ideologies, for example, around 'masculinities' (i.e. the gender practices defining 'manhood'). According to Connell (1995, 2005), when men can approximate socially esteemed and dominant patterns of gender practice within a society they are dominant or *hegemonic*. In reality, few men actually achieve and maintain this socially idealised status, but many men – whom either aspire to or support the hegemonic form and/or do not challenge the hegemonic, patriarchal (male-dominated) status quo – can retain alliance with and benefit from it. In Connell's parlance, *complicit* men reap the reward of a system which privileges some men more than other men (intra-gender relations), but *all* men over women (inter-gender relations) – this is what Connell calls the *patriarchal dividend*. Other forms of masculinity in this structure of masculini*ties* (pluralised by Connell, due to multiple formations of masculinities rather than one masculinity) are described as *subordinated* and *marginalised* (Connell, 1995, 2005).[2]

Messner's (1992) work on hegemonic masculinities in the context of sport helps us further understand how this system functions in athletic worlds, and how an *athletic center (sic)* is maintained in relation to (inter- and intra-) gender relations: typically through mechanisms such as physical violence on and off the field (using the body as a weapon against other men and women), homophobia (intra-gender violence against gay men but also straight men), sexism and misogyny (inter-gender violence against women) and sexual violence (rape). Men who want to retain the benefits of being 'real men' (i.e. approximating the socially constructed hegemonic form) use these mechanisms, actively encourage other men to use them and/or remain complicit; that is, they remain silent and do not contest others who use them. In these ways, particular patterns of (violent and dominating) masculinities remain hegemonic within a society or sub-culture of society.

More specifically, professional football has been shown to be a powerful institution: one in which individual identities are subject to re-shaping in line with deeply embedded knowledges, norms and values (Kinkema & Harris, 1998; Meân, 2001; Parker, 2006). Competitive professional football, youth academy settings and football coach education have been shown to work along such lines with deeply gendered structures and norms (e.g. Adams, Anderson, & McCormack, 2010; Cushion & Jones, 2006, 2014; Kelly & Waddington, 2006; Norman, 2012, 2013; Parker, 1996, 2001, 2006; Roderick, 2006; Sawiuk, Lewis & Taylor, 2021). We can see some of this playing out in Alice and Ellie's narratives above, with formative coaching experiences of 'not fitting in' to male-dominated spaces or feeling the need to 'put on' a more abrasive or authoritarian tone to be respected as coaches. Furthermore, recent research in these masculinity-saturated spaces demonstrate that football coaches influence, and are influenced by, complexities of practice imbued with dominant masculine values and common beliefs, transmitting both explicit and 'hidden' ideas about 'acceptable masculine practice' (see Cushion & Jones, 2006, 2014; Potrac & Jones, 2009; Thompson, Potrac, & Jones, 2015). In this context, what might more aptly be described as belligerent (masculinist) coaching behaviour is viewed as 'necessary' by male coaches, and players themselves, in preparing boys and men for life in professional/competitive football (Cushion & Jones, 2006, p. 148). Compliance, fear of exclusion and an obligation to be silent and not challenge, resist or question coaches' practices are all known parts of this process in men's football settings and men's coaching practice – accepted by players in order to maintain their own position and participation in the setting (Cushion & Jones, 2006; Parker & Manley, 2017). Within football coach education settings more specifically, Sawiuk et al. (2021) recently found that women experience toxic masculinity, sexualised language, dismissive practices and ignorance of women's football, in addition to the men's game dominating examples within the learning content and curriculum. In summary of current research exploring masculinities in the context of men's football, it is evident that the day-to-day pedagogical activities of male coaches, players and coach educators are problematic, with highly gendered, masculine, intimidatory and sometimes violent and abusive norms and practices enacted and communicated by coaches.

Towards a Feminist-Informed Coaching Pedagogy

While the research on masculinities within football is critical of coaching practice, it is important to reiterate (as discussed above, and in our narratives) that gender discourses and patterns of masculinities are not static or fixed, and that they *can* and *have been* negotiated, transgressed and transformed (see also Gill, 2007; McGuffey & Rich, 1999; Theberge, 2003). This is also true in the context of contemporary sport and physical cultures (see Barker-Ruchti, Grahn, & Lindgren, 2016). As Barker-Ruchti et al (ibid) outline, the literature on this topic provides multiple and various contemporary moments of, for example, men/boys participating in 'non-traditional' male sport and physical activities (Chimot & Louveau, 2010), the co-training of boys and girls, men and women (Wachs, 2005), and the creation of alternative corporeal (and) gender ideals (Anderson, 2012; Azzarito, 2010; Kelly, Pomerantz, & Currie 2006; Ross & Shinew, 2008; Thorpe, 2009) and sexuality (Ravel & Rail 2006; Travers & Deri 2010).

Like Barker-Ruchti et al. (2016), this chapter attempts to avoid a 'deficit approach' of solely examining and identifying gender 'inequalities', 'barriers' and 'disadvantages': instead, taking opportunities to turn this approach on its head, *studying up* power structures rather than down, and actively and consciously focusing on how patterns of gender (hegemonic masculinity and men's coaching practice) are and (importantly for the future) *could* be re-imagined, challenged and transformed at the micro-level of coaching practice. Indeed, going further than the micro-level thoughts and actions of coaching interaction, to challenge patterns of masculinity embedded in meso-level spaces, and macro-level power structures. Echoing and responding to Barker-Ruchti et al (ibid), the argument and personal author narratives set out in this chapter are a contribution to a vision for change, a vision of transformation, and a vision of 'alternative ways of being and doing' in sport coaching. In this way, this chapter contributes further to the literature on the 'unsettling' patterns of deeply embedded gender behaviour and thinking in high-performance sport organisations. We are keen to stimulate thought on how football coaches could 'be' and 'do' coaching to challenge and transform the settings in which they work, to help 'unsettle' patterns of masculinity which reinforce discourses of 'fixed' gender patterns to the detriment and exclusion of more dynamic, gender-inclusive and– to put it bluntly –more sensible, realistic and real-to-life conceptions of gender which have been established in existing gender and masculinities literature.

To enable this, we now move on to attempt to outline in more clarity a feminist-informed pedagogy for sport coaches. We draw on existing feminist theory and teaching principles in an attempt to show how feminism can be integrated with other pedagogical ideas perceived as contributing to 'effective' coaching. Inter-woven into our narratives and this subsequent contextualisation, theoretical discussion and analysis is an attempt to re-imagine the future of football coaching practice, along with a sensibility to the gender and masculinities literature discussed above; an understanding of how gender boundaries are socially con-structed, and how they can be negotiated, shifted, crossed and transformed from within. Perhaps more specifically, this chapter speaks to the idea of coaches' roles in shifting, crossing and transforming boundaries (Barker-Ruchti et al., 2016). In particular *transforming boundaries*, in which coaches pro-actively alter and trans-form (or facilitate others to transform) the 'membrane' previously defining that which is on the 'inside' and on the 'outside' of their particular sporting context.

Defining Feminist Coaching Principles

Chawansky (2005) utilises the work of Forrest and Rosenberg (1997) to outline some principles of feminist pedagogy. Here, briefly, we undertake a similar task while also directing readers to engage with Chawansky's (2005) work, within the context of US college basketball, which influences this current chapter in its attempt to interpret football coaching practice with feminist pedagogy litera-ture. According to Forrest and Rosenberg (1997, p. 179) pedagogy, 'In its simplest form…is focused on the process and methods of teaching', while feminist peda-gogy 'is the infusion of feminist values into the process and methods of teaching'. In reviewing feminist pedagogy literature, Forrest and Rosenberg (ibid) usefully distinguish between writing on feminist pedagogy (focused on process and meth-ods of teaching) and feminist curricula development (focused on content), while also highlighting the interplay (perhaps, inseparability) between content and process.

Feminist pedagogy focuses on women's lives. However, importantly, Forrest and Rosenberg (ibid, p.180) also summarise feminist pedagogy as attending to women's oppressions and 'gender analyses of historical and sociocultural influences'. This is important because feminist pedagogies[3], while focused on women's lives, *also re-quire attentiveness to men's lives*: the ways that men oppress women and other men and contribute to the maintenance of oppressive structures. As Connell (1995) describes, and something which comes through in our own gendered narratives at the top of this chapter, it is important to examine both 'intra-gender' and 'inter-gender' relationships; that is, relationships among men and between men and women. In short, feminism and feminist pedagogy are not simply to be reduced to examining women's lives or 'women's issues'. Feminism is not simply a 'women's problem', and not to be dismissed as irrelevant to or for men's (coaching) lives

Personal Narratives and Implications for Football Coaches   145

and their gender relations with other men and women (within football spaces). To reaffirm the importance of this point and focus, re-read our narratives and note that each involves descriptions of intra-gender relations (between women *and* men) within coaching spaces (e.g. Alice describes changing her 'coaching persona' to be included in a male-dominated coaching team; Ellie's initial feelings of 'being judged' and feeling like she is 'too quiet' to be within a coach education space where only male constructions of coaching styles are offered; and Adi's tale of being affected and challenged in his formative years through having a female coach).

To this end, we are also influenced by and highlight the work of Light and Kentel (2010) on 'soft' pedagogies for 'hard' sports, and the possibilities of what they call 'non-genderist' pedagogy informed by feminist theory, in their efforts to transform the coaching of young men within rugby. Light and Kentel's (ibid) work is a valuable resource for our own, in examining the possibilities for disrupting the influence of hegemonic masculinity in sport/coaching.

Returning to Forrest and Rosenberg (1997), we note they outline various guiding principles for feminist educators. For football coaches searching for practical meaning and workable strategies within the theoretical preamble above, we have borrowed and re-presented these principles below, with some reworking and additions based on our reading of Light and Kentel (2010). These form a set of feminist-informed coaching principles:

- Rethinking power and authority in coaching spaces;
- Collaboratively solving problems through talking, discussion and negotiation;
- Challenging (hyper) competitive individualism;
- Problematising dominant enactments of masculinity;
- Creating communal, collegial and reciprocal coaching/learning environments;
- Respecting, making visible and increasing diversity in coaching spaces;
- Integrating and valuing the knowledge of personal (player/coach) experience, and;
- Incorporating (player/coach) learning through social and political action opportunities.

Forrest and Rosenberg (1997) provide a full discussion of many of these principles, and Chawansky (2005) provides insightful interpretation and examples of how these were put to work in her own coaching practice (in a US college basketball context).

Some Conclusions and Final Thoughts

We invite readers to (re)evaluate, (re)interpret and reflect on our personal author narratives – and their own and others' coaching practice – using the conceptual framework and principles outlined above. Our narratives aim to stimulate reflection by football coaches on their own experiences. We do this by asking coaches to

146 Adi Adams et al.

'think with' the feminist principles outlined above to develop personal interpretations of our stories, towards incorporating these principles and developing more specific context-relevant strategies and actions to be implemented into their coaching practices. We ask: What do these principles mean for coaches in their own contexts? How can they be enacted in meaningful concrete terms, and what strategies and practices can follow on from these guiding principles? In short, following Chawansky's (2005) lead, we have attempted to sketch out some of the edges of what 'feminist coaching' might take into consideration and what it might look like. More specifically (diverging from Chawansky's female-coach/female-sport context), we are interested in what feminist coaching does and could look like within cross-gender coaching and coach development contexts, and male-dominated high-performance (youth) sporting institutions which have been traditionally (either consciously or unconsciously) determined to keep authoritarian conceptions of masculinity on the inside, and women (vis-à-vis feminism) on the outside.

In concluding, we have some final thoughts for (1) coaching academics and (2) coaches and coach developers. First (1), we highlight feminist-informed coaching principles as a guiding framework for future academic research. Exploration of coaching and masculinities remains relatively limited. The principles outlined offer important foci for future research: Concepts such as *intra-gender, inter-gender* and *boundary shifting/crossing/transforming* can all help to focus attention on particular coaching relationships, in terms of who, what and how we study a variety of perspectives. Second (2), we (t)ask coaches and coach developers to reflect on their own playing and coaching experiences, their intra- and inter-gender relations, with other men/boys in their playing and coaching contexts, with women/girls and female coaches, how they support women and girls in their clubs and beyond, and how they could 'think forward' with these feminist-informed principles to generate positive and inclusive change in their everyday coaching practices and wider spheres of influence.

Notes

1 'Miss' was a term used in our school to address our female teachers.
2 While there has been some critique of Connell's work in recent years, this has primarily been framed around the contemporary 'inclusive masculinities' of young people in society and sport and has not explicitly examined sport coaches or coaching, which is the focus of this chapter. Indeed, where coaches and coaching have been mentioned in the masculinities literature, they have tended to uphold Connell's theorising (e.g. Adams, Anderson, & McCormack, 2010; Anderson & McGuire, 2010; Adams, 2020).
3 There are multiple feminist pedagogies, rather than a unitary pedagogy – see Forrest and Rosenberg (1997) for more on this.

References

Acker, J., 1990. Hierarchies, jobs, bodies: A theory of gendered organizations. *Gender & Society,* 4(2), pp.139–158.

Personal Narratives and Implications for Football Coaches 147

Adams, A., Anderson, E. and McCormack, M., 2010. Establishing and challenging masculinity: The influence of gendered discourses in organized sport. *Journal of Language and Social Psychology*, 29(3), pp.278–300.

Adams, A., 2020. Humour, masculinities and youth sport coaching: 'Good morning, ladies!'. *Sport, Education and Society*, 25(4), pp.463–474.

Anderson, E., 2012. *Inclusive Masculinity: The Changing Nature of Masculinities*. New York: Routledge.

Anderson, E. and McGuire, R., 2010. Inclusive masculinity theory and the gendered politics of men's rugby. *Journal of Gender Studies*, 19(3), pp.249–261.

Azzarito, L., 2010. Future girls, transcendent femininities and new pedagogies: Toward girls' hybrid bodies? *Sport, Education and Society*, 15(3), pp.261–275.

Barker-Ruchti, N., Grahn, K. and Lindgren, E.C., 2016. Shifting, crossing and transforming gender boundaries in physical cultures. *Sport in Society*, 19(5), pp.615–625.

Chawansky, M., 2005. That takes balls: Toward a feminist coaching methodology. *Women's Studies Quarterly*, 33(1/2), pp.105–119.

Chimot, C. and Louveau, C., 2010. Becoming a man while playing a female sport: The construction of masculine identity in boys doing rhythmic gymnastics. *International Review for the Sociology of Sport*, 45(4), pp.436–456.

Connell, R., 1995. *Masculinities*. Berkeley: University of California Press.

Connell, R., 2002. *Gender*. Cambridge: Polity Press.

Connell, R., 2005. *Masculinities (2nd edition)*. Cambridge: Polity Press.

Connell, R., 2008. Masculinity construction and sports in boys' education: A framework for thinking about the issue. *Sport, Education and Society*, 13(2), pp.131–145.

Cushion, C. and Jones, R., 2006. Power, discourse, and symbolic violence in professional youth soccer: The case of Albion Football Club. *Sociology of Sport Journal*, 23(2), pp.142–161.

Cushion, C. and Jones, R., 2014. A Bourdieusian analysis of cultural reproduction: Socialisation and the 'hidden curriculum' in professional football. *Sport, Education and Society*, 19(3), pp.276–298.

Forrest, L. and Rosenberg, F., 1997. A review of the feminist pedagogy literature: The neglected child of feminist psychology. *Applied and Preventive Psychology*, 6(4), pp.179–192.

Gill, F., 2007. 'Violent' femininity: Women rugby players and gender negotiation. *Women's Studies International Forum*, 30(5), pp.416–426.

Kelly, D.M., Pomerantz, S. and Currie, D.H., 2006. "No boundaries"? Girls' interactive, online learning about femininities. *Youth & Society*, 38(1), pp.3–28.

Kelly, S. and Waddington, I., 2006. Abuse, intimidation and violence as aspects of managerial control in professional soccer in Britain and Ireland. *International Review for the Sociology of Sport*, 41(2), pp.147–164.

Kinkema, K. and Harris, J., 1998. 'MediaSport studies: Key research and emerging issues', in L. Wenner (ed.) *MediaSport*, pp.27–54. London: Routledge.

Light, R., Kentel, J.A., Kehler, M. and Atkinson, M., 2010. Soft pedagogy for a hard sport: Disrupting hegemonic masculinity in high school rugby through feminist-informed pedagogy. *Boys' Bodies: Speaking the Unspoken*, 5(3), pp.323–338.

McGuffey, C. and Rich, B., 1999. Playing in the gender transgression zone: Race, class, and hegemonic masculinity in middle childhood. *Gender & Society*, 13(5), pp.608–627.

Meân, L., 2001. Identity and discursive practice: Doing gender on the football pitch. *Discourse & Society*, 12(6), pp.789–815.

Messner, M., 1992. *Power at Play*. Boston: Beacon Press.

Norman, L., 2012. Gendered homophobia in sport and coaching: Understanding the everyday experiences of lesbian coaches. *International Review for the Sociology of Sport*, 47(6), pp.705–723.

Norman, L., 2013. The concepts underpinning everyday gendered homophobia based upon the experiences of lesbian coaches. *Sport in Society*, 16(10), pp.1326–1345.

Parker, A., 1996. Chasing the "Big-Time. *Football Apprenticeship in the 1990s', unpublished PhD thesis, University of Warwick*, pp.72–4.

Parker, A., 2001. Soccer, servitude and sub-cultural identity: Football traineeship and masculine construction. *Soccer & Society*, 2(1), pp.59–80.

Parker, A., 2006. Lifelong learning to labour: Apprenticeship, masculinity and communities of practice. *British Educational Research Journal*, 32(5), pp.687–701.

Parker, A. and Manley, A., 2017. Goffman, identity and organizational control: Elite sports academies and social theory. *Sociology of Sport Journal*, 34(3), pp.211–222.

Potrac, P. and Jones, R., 2009. Micropolitical workings in semi-professional football. *Sociology of Sport Journal*, 26(4), pp.557–577.

Ravel, B. and Rail, G., 2006. The lightness of BeingGaie' discursive constructions of gender and sexuality in Quebec women's sport. *International Review for the Sociology of Sport*, 41(3–4), pp.395–412.

Roderick, M., 2006. *The Work of Professional Football*. Abingdon: Routledge.

Ross, S. and Shinew, K., 2008. Perspectives of women college athletes on sport and gender. *Sex Roles*, 58(1), pp.40–57.

Sawiuk, R., Lewis, C.J. and Taylor, W.G., 2021. "Long ball" and "balls deep": A critical reading of female coach-learners' experiences of the UEFA A licence. *Sports Coaching Review*, 10(1), pp.110–127.

Theberge, N., 2003. "No fear comes" adolescent girls, ice hockey, and the embodiment of gender. *Youth & Society*, 34(4), pp.497–516.

Thompson, A., Potrac, P. and Jones, R., 2015. 'I found out the hard way': Micro-political workings in professional football. *Sport, Education and Society*, 20(8), pp.976–994.

Thorpe, H., 2009. Bourdieu, feminism and female physical culture: Gender reflexivity and the habitus-field complex. *Sociology of Sport Journal*, 26, pp.491–516.

Travers, A., and J. Deri., 2010. Transgender inclusion and the changing face of lesbian softball leagues. *International Review for the Sociology of Sport*, 46(4), pp.488–507.

Wachs, F., 2005. The boundaries of difference: Negotiating gender in recreational sport. *Sociological Inquiry*, 75(4), pp.527–547.

Chapter 11

English (Men's) Football, Masculinity and Homophobia
From Hegemonic to Inclusive Masculinity

Jay Willson and Rory Magrath

Introduction

English (men's) football has traditionally been a hostile environment for sexual minorities (e.g. Clayton & Humberstone, 2006). Gay male athletes – or even those suspected of being gay – have, historically, been shunned, excluded and marginalised by the 'toxic jock' (Miller, 2009, p. 72); that is, ostensibly heterosexual men attempting to (re)prove, (re)establish and consolidate their own heteromasculine identities – thus distancing themselves from homosexuality (Connell, 1987). Rich (1980), therefore, argues that, in sport, particularly combative team sports like football, any form of non-heterosexuality is perceived on 'a scale ranging from deviant to abhorrent'.

Since the turn of the millennium, however, attitudes towards sexual minorities in the Western world have improved considerably (Kranjac & Wagmiller, 2021; Watt & Elliot, 2019). Moreover, lesbian, gay and bisexual (LGB) people now enjoy greater social and legal freedoms than ever before. Football has also undergone a significant transformation with respect to equity, diversity and inclusion. As we outline in greater detail throughout this chapter, a plethora of scholarly research – in both the United Kingdom (UK) and United States (US) – has countered outdated assumptions about sport's (lack of) acceptance of sexual minority athletes (Anderson, Magrath & Bullingham, 2016).

In this chapter, we provide an outline of English football's evolution from hostility to inclusivity, with a specific focus on the theoretical implications. We do so by first providing the historical context of the game's masculine foundations, which were largely established against the backdrop of a fast-changing society. Next, we outline how attitudes towards sexual minorities have improved, and how – as above – research investigating sporting terrain has also acknowledged these improvements. Finally, we outline how the dominant theoretical apparatus underpinning these findings has evolved over the past decade, away from Connell's (1995) Hegemonic Masculinity Theory (HMT) and towards Anderson's (2009) Inclusive Masculinity Theory.

DOI: 10.4324/9781003253990-15

The Foundations of Football, Masculinity and Homophobia

While the invention of machinery and transportation necessary for industrialisation began in the early-1700s, the antecedents of today's sporting culture can largely be traced to the second Industrial Revolution – the mid-1800s through to the early 1900s. It was around this time that farmers exchanged their time-honoured professions for salaried work, and families replaced their farm's rent for life in the city. The allure of industry, and the better life it promised, influenced a significant wave of migration. Cancian (1987), for example, shows that the percentage of people living in cities increased 50% – from 25% to 75% – in around a century. It was also around this time that the organisation, regulation and codification of most dominant sports – including football – occurred. Men's team sports, in particular, were considered to replicate qualities that were valuable to factory employers. Indeed, factory workers were expected and required to show sacrifice and dedication which, in turn, was also taught to boys (Anderson, 2009).

As men became sole 'breadwinners', working long hours, many of them spent little time raising their children, which became the role of their mother. During this time, gender-segregated sport played a vital role, instilling masculinity in a way that a mother supposedly could not (Anderson, 2015). Indeed, by participating in sport in the company of a dominant male figure – the coach – boys were able to 'align their gendered behaviors with idealized and narrow definitions of masculinity' (McCormack & Anderson, 2014, p. 114). Thus, by suppressing pain, concealing same-sex desire and behaviours, and committing acts of violence against oneself and others, boys were able to avoid the supposed 'risk' of homosexuality – while also simultaneously preparing them for labour-intensive work and participation in the military (Raphael, 1988). The male sporting body, then, is appropriately described by Polley (1998, p. 109) as an 'idealised, orthodox, heterosexual sign'. Moreover, by making women unwelcome in the sporting arena, men's sporting prowess was uncontested proof of their superiority in masculine domains.

Football, among other contact team sports, gained mass popularity throughout this period, providing a medium through which an orthodox form of masculinity could be embodied and embraced (Dunning, 1999). While this was primarily among boys and men, the women's game also began to gain a significant amount of traction in the early part of the twentieth century. However, deemed both a threat to the men's game, and as an 'unsuitable' game for women (Williams, 2021), the women's game was banned (from FA-affiliated facilities) in 1921, for a period of 50 years. The banning of women's football during this time further ensured that it was framed as a sport only for men – a 'male preserve' (Dunning, 1986, p. 86).

In *The Rites of Men*, Varda Burstyn (1999) argues that it was mostly through sport that boys and men could exhibit 'hypermasculinity' – so much so that masculinity essentially became synonymous with homophobia (Kimmel, 1994). Men who played sport were, therefore, not thought likely, or even possible, to be gay.

English (Men's) Football, Masculinity and Homophobia 151

Thus, sport has served to privilege not all men, but specifically heterosexual men (Anderson & McCormack, 2010). Given the hypermasculine environment evident throughout English football's history, any alternative sexuality has been emphatically and explicitly rejected.

A (further) Shift Towards Hostility

Almost a century after the antecedents of industrialisation in the West, sport once again took on renewed cultural significance for boys and men; another opportunity to emphasise orthodox notions of masculinity in what Anderson (2009) describes as a culture of homohysteria (a concept which refers to the fear of being homosexualised). Indeed, the increased visibility of (male) homosexuality in the 1980s had significant consequences for the gay community. The conservative sociopolitical response to the HIV/AIDS crisis – which became intimately associated with the gay community – increased cultural stigma (Goh, 2008). This was also influenced by the then UK prime minister Margaret Thatcher's views that homosexuality was a threat to traditional family values. This was perhaps best evidenced by the introduction of Section 28; legislation introduced by Thatcher's government in the UK which effectively banned the promotion of homosexuality in British schools – making teachers fearful of combating homophobia (Nixon & Givens, 2007). In the US, while comparable legislation did not exist, similar homophobic perspectives were also evident with Ronald Reagan's Republican administration.

These deleterious attitudes are best evidenced by the British Social Attitudes Survey (BSA). At the start of the decade, 62% of the UK population believed that same-sex sex between consenting adults was 'always wrong' or 'mostly wrong'; by 1987, this figure had increased to 75% (Clements & Field, 2014). Similar trends were also evident in the US (e.g. Loftus, 2001) and across Western Europe (e.g. Gerhards, 2010). This led Anderson (2009, p. 89) to conclude that '1987 or 1988 seems to be the apex of homophobia in both countries [the UK and the US]'. Desperate to avoid homosexual stigma, men went to extraordinary lengths, including excessive steroid use (Halkitis, Green & Wilson, 2004), to align their image with dominant notions of masculinity. Kellner (1991) refers to this as the 'Rocky-Rambo Syndrome' of the Reagan era.

Sports research at this time, and bleeding into the following decade, reflects the broader societal hostility. In the US, Messner (1992, p. 34) describes the levels of homophobia in men's sport at this time as 'staggering' and argued that 'to be gay, to be suspected of being gay, or even to be unable to prove one's heterosexual status is not acceptable'. Similarly, Curry (1991, p. 130) found that, 'Not only is being homosexual forbidden, but tolerance of homosexuality is theoretically off limits as well'. In Canada, Pronger (1990, p. 26) wrote that the gay men he interviewed were 'uncomfortable with team sports'. In Europe and the UK, comparable research is lacking – although, in the Netherlands, Hekma (1998, p. 2) wrote that,

'Gay men are seen as queer and effeminate are granted no space whatsoever in what is generally considered to be a masculine preserve and a macho enterprise'. However, research on men's football at this time is lacking entirely.

The toxic environment of the game, however – notably at the elite level – was evident when Justin Fashanu came out in 1990. Having learned that details of his private life were about to be revealed in a national newspaper, Fashanu agreed to an exclusive with British tabloid newspaper, *The Sun*. Under the now-infamous headline, '£1m Football Star: I AM GAY', the wheels were set in motion for an explicit wave of homophobia (Gaston, Magrath & Anderson, 2018). Indeed, while he initially claimed that he had been accepted by his teammates, Fashanu suffered severe backlash from the football community, and although the admission of his sexuality did not end his career outright, he never signed a professional contract again (Mitchell, 2012) – and eventually retired from the game in 1997. The following year, after being accused of assaulting a 17-year-old boy in the US, Fashanu took his own life. He has since become what Magrath (2017a) has previously described as a 'trendsetter' for football's fractious relationship with homosexuality – breathing life into football's homophobic (and racist) subculture.

A Shift towards Inclusivity

Since 2000, cultural attitudes towards homosexuality in Western cultures have improved significantly. Evidencing this, Watt and Elliot's (2019) analysis of the BSA found that only 16% of those sampled believed in same-sex sex to be 'always wrong' or 'mostly wrong' (down almost two-thirds from three decades earlier). Again, similar trends have also been apparent elsewhere, with two-thirds of American adults who now believe that homosexuality should be accepted by society (Twenge, Sherman & Wells, 2016). In addition to general attitudes, the legalisation of same-sex marriage in multiple nations is also testament to the changing social and legal rights of LGB people. Indeed, since the Netherlands became the first country in the world to introduce same-sex marriage, in 2001, it is now legal in over 30 countries. While these are mostly in the West – many countries outside of the West continue to hold more conservative attitudes towards homosexuality (e.g. Masci & Desilver, 2019) – these continue to grow at a rate of knots.

While sport – and football, in particular – is frequently criticised for being slower to accommodate social change than broader society, a plethora of academic evidence now shows that this is not the case (Anderson, Magrath & Bullingham, 2016). This has been identified not only among players, but also fans and the media, too. Magrath (2017a) carried out semi-structured interviews with 60 academy-level English footballers, investigated the construction of male friendships, coming out, team relationships and gay-friendliness. Excluding a small number of individuals who were influenced by religion (see Magrath, 2017b), Magrath's findings identified overwhelming support of homosexuality, same-sex marriage and (hypothetically) 'out' gay teammates. One participant, for example, stated that, 'I'm very open about what I believe, and I've got no issues at all. It's just basic human rights' (Magrath, 2017a, p. 15). Other recent research with footballers has found similarly positive attitudes (Cleland & Magrath, 2020; Magrath, Anderson & Roberts, 2015; Magrath, 2021a). These positive attitudes have also been mostly evident upon the coming out of gay male footballers across differing levels across the world, including Anton Hysén (Cleland, 2014), Thomas Hitzlsperger (Cleland, Magrath & Kian, 2018) and, most recently, Josh Cavallo (Zeigler, 2021).

This shift in attitudes has also been documented among football fans. Perhaps most notably, Cashmore and Cleland's (2012, p. 377–378) research documented a 'new and surprising image' regarding football's growing acceptance of homosexuality. Specifically, their research showed that 93% of 3,500 fans in their sample had no objection to an 'out' gay player being contracted to the team they support. These fans resented being held accountable for the lack of gay male footballers, and almost half believed that clubs, agents and governing bodies were truly responsibly for this trend. When this research was replicated almost a decade later, Cleland, Cashmore, Dixon and MacDonald (2021) found that the overall figure of acceptance had increased to 95% (among 2,663 survey respondents). Despite these inclusive findings, however, Pearson's (2012) ethnography of English football fans identified the prevalence of terms such as 'gay' and 'queer', with such language likely to have 'made it very uncomfortable for an openly gay fan to join a trip with the carnival fans' (p. 168).

While some organisations, such as Stonewall – the UK's most influential LGBT+ advocacy charity – suggest that sexual minority fans' experiences are overwhelmingly negative (see Stonewall, 2016), the academic research has increasingly shown that the opposite is true. Indeed, Magrath's (2021b) research, one of the first scholarly projects examining the experiences of LGBT fans, confirms the positive shift in attitudes towards homosexuality. In his analysis of gay male football fans, for example, 26 of the 35 participants said they felt 'safe' attending matches, as opposed to previous feelings of anxiety and intimidation. Recent research on the experiences of bisexual football fans found similar levels of safety and inclusion, despite social media remaining a prominent issue (Magrath, 2022). Letts and Magrath (2022) also show that despite these changes, gay male football fans felt that the Rainbow Laces campaign was largely tokenistic, and they would like to see more proactive work from the game's governing body to ensure that English football was an increasingly inclusive space for sexual minorities.

Theorising Football, Masculinities and Sexualities

Hegemonic Masculinity Theory

The most dominant theoretical paradigm for understanding men and masculinity has been (Raewyn) Connell's (1995) Hegemonic Masculinity Theory (HMT). It has become the most influential theory for understanding the unequal distribution of male privilege and articulates two social processes: (1) how all men benefit from the existence of patriarchy – the 'patriarchal dividend' (Connell, 1995,

p. 26); and (2) that multiple masculinities exist in an intra-masculine hierarchy, with one archetype of masculinity 'culturally exalted above all others' (Connell, 1995, p. 77). Based on a lack of empirical evidence on the first of these contentions (e.g. Anderson & McCormack, 2018), we focus here only on the second; that of an intra-masculine hierarchy.

Hegemony refers to the maintenance of power in social groups, in which any challenge to these hierarchies can be viewed as 'weak, soft, unathletic and feminine' (Lucyk, 2011, p. 67). Patterns of masculinity hold the dominant position, usually associated with strong, successful, capable and reliable men (Kimmel, 1994). Such a multitude of attributes can be earned (displaying homophobia or competitiveness) while others are permanent (heterosexuality or Whiteness) (Howson, 2006). However, possessing and maintaining hegemony requires the reproduction of regulatory behaviours, such as sexism, misogyny, homophobia and violence. Connell (1995) argued that material domination and discursive marginalisation are key processes to the maintenance of hegemonic masculinity; so much so that inferior men deem those who hold power to be deserving of rule without challenge from oneself. Furthermore, Connell (1995) refers to three forms of masculinity that derive from the process of hegemony: complicit, marginalised and subordinate.

Complicit masculinities make up the majority of men; those with little association to hegemonic masculinity, but who still benefit from male privilege. While there may be behaviours and attributes that meet the definition of hegemony, the difference lies in, as Connell (2005, p. 79) states, they 'respect their wives and mother, are never violent toward women, do their accustomed share of the housework, [and] bring home the family wage'. Marginalised masculinity describes men who are marginalised by their class or race, while subordinate masculinity, whom Connell (1995, p. 79) describes 'the most conspicuous', refers to gay and/or effeminate men.

Although the intra-masculine hierarchy has been a model of great value, it has received significant critique in recent years. Moller (2007), for example, argues that the wide endorsement of HMT has led to scholars interpreting patterns of hegemonic masculinity too easily, overlooking potentially more complex patterns of masculinity. Indeed, Moller (2007) writes:

> The concepts of hegemonic and hierarchical masculinities do little to help researchers understand diversity and complexity...they *reduce* our capacity to understand the ways in which the performance of masculinity may be productive of new socio-cultural practices, meanings, alliances and feelings.
> (p. 275)

Alongside this, Howson (2006) has critiqued the central components of the intra-masculine hierarchy, which have been only loosely explained in Connell's work. Anecdotally, this definitional uncertainty is evident each time the second author of this chapter asks his students to consider how we might conceptualise professional footballers according to Connell's hierarchy, especially given the complexity of athlete identities which are often impacted by class, race, sexuality and so on. In Magrath's (2017a) analysis of HMT, in the context of football, he writes:

> There is perhaps little argument that a footballer represents a hegemonic form of masculinity. But how might one theorize the position of a football hooligan? Both are dominant, albeit relatively separate, notions of masculinity in their own right. How might one also theorize the class elements affecting English professional footballers, most of whom hail from the working classes.

But perhaps the most significant critique relevant to this chapter has been that, while HMT made sense and was accurate at the time it was devised – in the 1980s – cultural homophobia has since declined, and sexual minorities no longer face extreme marginalisation in the West (Anderson & McCormack, 2018). Consequently, Connell's intra-masculine hierarchy fails to account for the varying masculinities that researchers have found flourishing without hierarchy or hegemonic in numerous contexts.

Inclusive Masculinity Theory

Anderson's (2009) theory of Inclusive Masculinity (IMT) has become a more accurate means of theorising contemporary masculinity. While Anderson drew on Connell's scholarship in his early work (e.g. Anderson, 2002), antecedents of IMT emerged in Anderson's (2005) men's cheerleading research in the US, in which he found 'two contrasting and competing forms of normative masculinity...orthodox [and] inclusive' (p. 337). However, as he found Connell's work to be increasingly incapable of explaining the reduction of homophobia, increased inclusivity of sexual minorities, and the reduction of homophobic discourse, IMT was formally published in his seminal text, *Inclusive Masculinity: The Changing Nature of Masculinities*.

Central to Anderson's theorising is the concept of *homohysteria*, which seeks to explain the power dynamics of heterosexual masculinities within a historical frame. It is best defined as a 'homosexually panicked culture in which suspicion [of homosexuality] permeates' (Anderson, 2011b, p. 83). Anderson further argues that, in order for a culture of homohysteria to exist, three social factors must coincide: (1) mass cultural awareness of homosexuality, (2) a cultural zeitgeist of disapproval towards homosexuality, (3) cultural disapproval of men's femininity, as displaying these behaviours becomes closely associated with homosexuality.

In a Feminist Forum debate in the *Sex Roles* journal, McCormack and Anderson (2014) discuss three conditions through which a culture historically moves: (1) *homoerasure* – describing a severely homophobic culture, but one which fails to recognise the existence of homosexuality as a static part of their population,

(2) *homohysteria* – a combination of the acceptance of, and antipathy toward, homosexuality, such as Western cultures in the 1980s (e.g. Watt & Elliot, 2019), and (3) *inclusivity* – a culture in which homosexual stigma is minimal, and men are not required to alter their expression of masculinity (Anderson & McCormack, 2015).

Evidencing these softer versions of masculinity, a considerable body of work has documented how heterosexual boys and men are no longer bound by the rigid practices of previous generations (e.g. Anderson, 2014; Anderson, Ripley & McCormack, 2019; Magrath & Scoats, 2019). Anderson and McCormack (2015, p. 223), for example, document how young men are able to engage in 'prolonged acts of homosocial tactility – namely cuddling and spooning' without the threat of homophobic policing. Aside from a show of celebration among sporting men, such displays were seen as simply demonstrations of love and affection for one's close friends. An extension of gendered male behaviours is also notable through the development of emotionally open and intimate friendships – labelled by Robinson and Anderson (2022) as the 'bromance'. Interestingly, men in this research even prioritised their bromantic relationships over their romantic ones. This was because these were deemed to have fewer boundaries and be more judgement free, thus allowing men to 'push the margins of traditional masculinity' (Robinson, & Anderson, 2022, p. 96). While most research on the bromance has been restricted to university friendships, Magrath and Scoats (2019) show that these friendship bonds frequently continue years after graduation.

Although IMT initially emerged in relatively restricted populations – such as middle-class, university-educated men – it has also increasingly incorporated the behaviours of working-class men, such as those involved in sport (e.g. Magrath, 2017a). Moreover, Roberts' (2013) research on young working-class men in the retail sector also documents the emergence of a softer version of masculinity. Interestingly, he also writes that 'positioning working-class masculinity in opposition to middle-class masculinity…is entirely problematic and a simplistic misrepresentation' (p. 683). Softer forms of masculinity have also been evident among young, working-class men in education; such as those in Blanchard, McCormack and Peterson's (2017) analysis of a sixth form in Northeast England.

Since its publication over a decade ago, IMT – and its associated concept, homohysteria – has been prolific in its theorising of contemporary masculinities. It has been used in hundreds of separate academic studies, some of which we outline earlier in this chapter. Although IMT has mostly been applied to sporting locales, it has also been applied to research in education (McCormack, 2012), the media (Kian, Anderson & Shipka, 2015) and the workplace (Magrath, 2020; Roberts, 2018). It has, therefore, emerged as a more adaptable heuristic tool in explaining the contemporary stratification of Western men. It has, therefore, emerged into a more adaptable heuristic tool in explaining the contemporary stratification of Western men. With this flexibility, it has helped to move standpoints from a vertical one (in Connell's model of masculinity) to a horizontal one (in Anderson's theory), as homophobia continues to decline.

English (Men's) Football, Masculinity and Homophobia   157

It has been so widely employed that Borkowska (2020) has argued that the most recent phase of masculinities research – the 'third phase' – should be described as 'Andersonian' because this work has 'moved away from the hierarchical order of social relations where men attempt to distance themselves from femininity or position themselves within the orthodox ideologies of manhood' (p. 411).

Interestingly, perhaps owing to the sport's popularity, and subsequent range of publications, it is, perhaps, in football, that IMT has been applied most. Indeed, as evidenced in the earlier sections of this chapter, declining homophobia in the game has been documented in research on fans (e.g. Cashmore & Cleland, 2012; Cleland, Magrath & Kian, 2018; Magrath, 2018, 2021b), players (Anderson, 2011a; Magrath, 2017a, 2017b, 2021a; Magrath, Anderson & Roberts, 2015) and the media (Cleland, 2014, 2018). Softer, more inclusive forms of masculinity have also been detected among young, elite footballers, too – such as the physical tactility and emotional intimacy discussed earlier in this section. Interestingly, though, this is less pronounced than in other research, something that Roberts, Anderson and Magrath (2017) attribute to the competitive environment of professional football. In other words, where young elite footballers effectively compete with one another to maintain their professional status, this restricts the closeness of their friendships with teammates.

While IMT has previously been critiqued for its failure to acknowledge the effect that changing masculinities has on women, this has, recently, been included in football-based research. Indeed, Pope, Williams and Cleland's (2022) analysis of nearly 2000 male football fans extended IMT by presenting a new model to incorporate attitudes towards women – and women's sport. This included what they referred to as 'progressive masculinities', 'overtly misogynistic masculinities' and 'covertly misogynistic masculinities'.

Other critiques of IMT have included De Boise's claims that 'a combination of underdeveloped theoretical arguments, inadequate consideration to research design and a selective use of examples means that a theory of inclusivity is difficult to accept' (p. 333). This included suggestions that homophobia has not shown decline, that continued presence of heterosexism is just as severe as homophobia, and attitudes are still as traditional in other parts of the world. However, Anderson and McCormack (2018) addressed these critiques in the *Journal of Gender Studies*, and drew on a range of international studies to show that declining homophobia is sustained and profound across most Western nations. There still remains some claims that declining homophobia in sport – and football in particular – has not followed these trends (e.g. Allison & Knoester, 2021); however, by drawing on a broad range of the scholarly research, such as that in previous sections of this chapter, there is no evidence that football is inherently more homophobic than broader society. Naturally, though, more research is still required.

Concluding Thoughts

This chapter has provided an outline of how English (men's) football has shifted from a culture of hostility, to one that is characterised by greater levels of inclusion than ever before. Where homophobia in the game was once endemic, as perhaps best evidenced by the experiences of Justin Fashanu after he came out, a plethora of scholarly literature has documented positive attitudes (e.g. Cashmore & Cleland, 2012), improved experiences (e.g. Magrath, 2021b) and a greater commitment to equality, diversity and inclusion than in previous generations (Letts & Magrath, 2022). While there do, of course, remain significant issues – the prevalence of homophobia on social media is likely the best example of this (Hansen et al., 2022) – Eric Anderson's (2009) Inclusive Masculinity Theory has become a more dominant theory to underpin the changing nature of the game. As homophobia remains low in Western society, and if research continues to document positive attitudes in English football, IMT's dominant position is likely to remain.

References

Allison, R. & Knoester, C. (2021, April 6). Sports remain hostile territory for LGBTQ Americans. *The Conversation.* https://theconversation.com

Anderson, E. & McCormack, M. (2010). 'It's just not acceptable anymore': The erosion of homophobia and the softening of masculinity at an English sixth form. *Sociology,* 44(5), 843–859.

Anderson, E. (2002). Openly gay athletes: Contesting hegemonic masculinity in a homophobic environment. *Gender and Society,* 16, 860–877.

Anderson, E. (2005). Orthodox and inclusive masculinity: Competing masculinities among heterosexual men in a feminized terrain. *Sociological Perspectives,* 48(3), 337–355.

Anderson, E. (2009). *Inclusive masculinity: The changing nature of masculinities.* Routledge.

Anderson, E. (2011a). Updating the outcome: Gay athletes, straight teams, and coming out in educationally based sport teams. *Gender & Society,* 25(2), 250–268.

Anderson, E. (2011b). Inclusive masculinities of university soccer players in the American Midwest. *Gender and Education,* 23(6), 729–744.

Anderson, E. (2014). *21st century jocks: Sporting men and contemporary heterosexuality.* Palgrave.

Anderson, E. (2015). Assessing the sociology of sport: On changing masculinities and homophobia. *International Review for the Sociology of Sport,* 50(4–5), 363–367.

Anderson, E. & McCormack, M. (2014). Theorizing masculinities in contemporary Britain. In: S. Roberts (Eds.). *Debating modern masculinities: Change, continuity and crisis?* (pp. 125–144). Palgrave Macmillan.

Anderson, E. & McCormack, M. (2015). Cuddling and spooning: Heteromasculinity and homosocial tactility among student-athletes. *Men and Masculinities,* 18(2), 214–230.

Anderson, E. & McCormack, M. (2018). Inclusive masculinity theory: Overview, reflection and refinement. *Journal of Gender Studies,* 27(5), 547–561.

Anderson, E., Magrath, R. & Bullingham, R. (2016). *Out in sport: The experiences of openly gay and lesbian athletes in competitive sport.* Routledge.

Anderson, E., Ripley, M. & McCormack, M. (2019). A mixed-method study of same-sex kissing among college-attending heterosexual men in the US. *Sexuality and Culture,* 23(1), 26–44.

Blanchard, C., McCormack, M. & Peterson, G. (2017). Inclusive masculinities in a working-class sixth form in northeast England. *Journal of Contemporary Ethnography,* 46(3), 310–333.

Borkowska, K. (2020). Approaches to studying masculinity: A nonlinear perspective of theoretical paradigms. *Men and Masculinities*, 23(3–4), 409–424.

Burstyn, V. (1999). *The rites of men: Manhood, politics, and the culture of sport*. University of Toronto Press.

Cancian, F.M. (1987). *Love in America: Gender and self-development*. University of Cambridge Press.

Cashmore, E. & Cleland, J. (2012). Fans, homophobia and masculinities in association football: Evidence of a more inclusive environment. *The British journal of Sociology*, 63(2), 370–387.

Clayton, B. & Humberstone, B. (2006). Men's talk: A (pro) feminist analysis of male university football players' discourse. *International Review for the Sociology of Sport*, 41(3–4), 295–316.

Cleland, J. (2014). Association football and the representation of homosexuality by the print media: A case study of Anton Hysén. *Journal of Homosexuality*, 61(9), 1269–1287.

Cleland, J. (2018). Sexuality, masculinity and homophobia in association football: An empirical overview of a changing cultural context. *International Review for the Sociology of Sport*, 53(4), 411–423.

Cleland, J., Cashmore, E., Dixon, K., & MacDonald, C. (2021). Analyzing the presence of homosexually-themed language among association football fans in the United Kingdom. *Communication and Sport* (Online First).

Cleland, J. & Magrath, R. (2020). Association football, masculinity, and sexuality: An evolving relationship. In: R. Magrath., J. Cleland & E. Anderson (Eds.). *The Palgrave handbook of masculinity and sport* (pp. 341–357). Palgrave.

Cleland, J., Magrath, R. & Kian, E., (2018). The internet as a site of decreasing cultural homophobia in association football: An online response by fans to the coming out of Thomas Hitzlsperger. *Men and Masculinities*, 21(1), 91–111.

Clements, B. & Field, C. (2014). Public opinion towards homosexuality and gay rights in Great Britain. *Public Opinion Quarterly*, 78(2), 523–547.

Connell, R. W. (1987). *Gender and power*. Wiley.

Connell, R. W. (1995). *Masculinities*. Polity Press.

Connell, R. W. (2005). Change among the gatekeepers: Men, masculinities, and gender equality in the global arena. *Journal of Women in Culture and Society*, 30(3), 1801–1825

Curry, T. J. (1991). Fraternal bonding in the locker room: A profeminist analysis of talk about competition and women. *Sociology of Sport Journal*, 8(2), 119–135.

De Boise, S. (2015). I'm not homophobic "I have gay friends" evaluating the validity of inclusive masculinity. *Men and Masculinities*, 18(3), 318–339.

Dunning, E. (1986). Sport as a male preserve: Notes on the social sources of masculine identity and its transformations. *Theory, Culture and Society*, 3(1), 79–90.

Dunning, E. (1999). *Sport matters: Sociological studies of sport, violence and civilization*. Routledge.

Gaston, L., Magrath, R. & Anderson, A. (2018). From hegemonic to inclusive masculinities in English professional football: Marking a cultural shift. *Journal of Gender Studies*, 27(3), 301–312.

Gerhards, J. (2010). Non-discrimination towards homosexuality: The European Union's policy and citizen's attitudes towards homosexuality in 27 European countries. *International Sociology*, 25(1), 5–28.

Goh, D. (2008). It's the gays' fault: News and HIV as weapons against homosexuality in Singapore. *Journal of Communication Enquiry*, 32(4), 383–399.

Halkitis, P, N., Green, K. A. & Wilson, L. (2004). Masculinity, body image, and sexual behavior in HIV-seropositive men: A two-phase behavioral investigation using the internet. *International Journal of Men's Health*, 3(1), 27–42.

Hansen, M., Kavanagh, E.J., Anderson, E., Parry, K.D., & Cleland, J. (2022). An analysis of responses on Twitter to the English Premier League's support for the anti-homophobia Rainbow Laces campaign. *Sport in Society* (Online First).

Hekma, G. (1998). "As long as they don't make an issue of it..." Gay men and lesbians in organized sports in the Netherlands. *Journal of Homosexuality*, 35(1), 1–23.

Howson, R. (2006). *Challenging hegemonic masculinity*. Routledge.

Kellner, D. (1991). Film, politics and ideology: Reflections on Hollywood film in the age of Reagan. *Velvet Light Trap*, 27(2), 9–24.

Kian, E. M., Anderson, E. & Shipka, D. (2015). 'I am happy to start the conversation': Examining sport media framing of Jason Collins' coming out and playing in the NBA. *Sexualities*, 18(5–6), 618–640.

Kimmel, M. S., (1994). Masculinity as homophobia: Fear, shame and silence in the construction of gender identity. In: H. Brod & M. Kaufman (Eds.). *Theorizing masculinities* (pp. 119–141). Sage.

Kranjac, A.W. & Wagmiller, R.L. (2021). Attitudinal change, cohort replacement, and the liberalization of attitudes about same-sex relationships, 1973–2018. *Sociological Perspectives* (Online First).

Letts, D. & Magrath, R. (2022). English football, sexuality, and homophobia: Gay fans' perspectives on governance and visibility. In: D. Coombs & A. Osborne (Eds.). *Routledge handbook of sport fans and fandom* (pp. 192–203). Routledge.

Loftus, J. (2001). America's liberalization in attitudes toward homosexuality, 1973 to 1998. *American Sociological Review*, 66(5), 762–782.

Lucyk, K. (2011). Don't be gay, dude! How the institution of sport reinforces homophobia. *Constellations*, 2(2), 66–80.

Magrath, R. (2017a). *Inclusive masculinities in contemporary football: Men in the beautiful game*. Routledge.

Magrath, R. (2017b). The intersection of race, religion and homophobia in British football. *International Review for the Sociology of Sport*, 52(4), 411–429.

Magrath, R. (2018). 'To try and gain an advantage for my team': Homophobic and homosexually themed chanting among English football fans. *Sociology*, 52(4), 709–726.

Magrath, R. (2020). "Progress... slowly but surely": The sports media workplace, gay sports journalists and LGBT media representation in sport. *Journalism Studies*, 21(2), 254–270.

Magrath, R. (2021a). Inclusive masculinities of working-class university footballers in the South of England. *Sport in Society*, 24(3), 412–429.

Magrath, R. (2021b). Gay males football fans' experiences: Authenticity, belonging and conditional acceptance. *Sociology*, 55(5), 978–994.

Magrath, R. (2022). The experiences of bisexual soccer fans in the UK: Inclusion, engagement, and digital lives. *Journal of Bisexuality* (Online First).

Magrath, R., Anderson, E. & Roberts, S. (2015). On the door-step of equality: Attitudes toward gay athletes among academy-level footballs. *International Review for the Sociology of Sport*, 50(7), 804–821.

Magrath, R. & Scoats, R. (2019). Young men's friendships: Inclusive masculinities in a post-university setting. *Journal of Gender Studies*, 28(1), 45–56.

English (Men's) Football, Masculinity and Homophobia 161

Masci, D. & Desilver, D. (2019, October 29). *A global snapshot of same-sex marriage*. Pew Research Center. https://www.pewresearch.org/fact-tank/2019/10/29/global-snapshot-same-sex-marriage/

McCormack, M. (2012). Queer masculinities, gender conformity, and the secondary school. In: J. Landreau & N. Rodriguez (Eds.). *Queer Masculinities: A critical reader in education* (pp. 35–46). Springer.

McCormack, M. & Anderson, E. (2014). Homohysteria: Definitions, context and intersectionality. *Sex Roles*, 71, 152–158.

Messner, M. A. (1992). *Power at play*. Beacon.

Miller, K. E. (2009). Sport-related identities and the "Toxic Jock". *Journal of Sport Behavior*, 32(1), 69–91.

Mitchell, J. (2012). *A culture of silence: Football's battle with homophobia*. JMitchell Media.

Moller, M. (2007). Exploiting patterns: A critique of hegemonic masculinities. *Journal of Gender Studies*, 16(3), 263–276.

Nixon, D., & Givens, D. (2007). An epitaph to Section 28? Telling tales out of school about changes and challenges to discourses of sexuality. *International Journal of Qualitative Studies in Education*, 20(4), 449–471.

Pearson, G. (2012). *An ethnography of English football fans: Cans, cops and carnivals*. Manchester University Press.

Polley, M. (1998). *Moving the goalposts: A history of sport and society since 1945*. Routledge.

Pope, S., Williams, J. & Cleland, J. (2022). Men's football fandom and the performance of progressive and misogynistic masculinities in a 'new age' of UK women's sport. *Sociology* (Online First).

Pronger, B. (1990). *The arena of masculinity: Sport, homosexuality, and the meaning of sex*. GMP.

Raphael, R. (1988). *The men from the boys*. University of Nebraska Press.

Rich, A. (1980). Compulsory heterosexuality and lesbian existence. *Women: Sex and Sexuality*, 5(4), 631–660.

Roberts, S. (2013). Boys will be boys... won't they? Change and continuities in contemporary young working-class masculinities. *Sociology*, 47(4), 671–686.

Roberts, S. (2018). *Young working-class men in transition*. Routledge.

Robinson, S. & Anderson, E. (2022). *Bromance: Male friendship, love and sport*. Palgrave.

Stonewall. (2016). Homophobic views still prevalent in sport. Available at: www.stonewall.co.uk

Twenge, J. M., Sherman, R. A. & Wells, B. E. (2016). Changes in America adults reported same-sex sexual experiences and attitudes. *Archives of Sexual Behaviour*, 45(7), 1713–1730.

Watt, L. & Elliot, M. (2019). Homonegativity in Britain: Changing attitudes towards same-sex relationships. *Journal of Sex Research*, 56(9), 1101–1114.

Williams, J. (2021). *The history of women's football*. Pen and Sword.

Zeigler, C. (2021, October 29). *Josh Cavallo received support from these 38 pro soccer players and clubs after coming out as gay*. https://outsports.com

Part IV

Social Theories of 'Race' and Ethnicity in Football

Chapter 12

The Racialised Construction of Black Professional Footballers in Engl(ish) Football

Love the Game, Hate the Player

Jason Arday

Introduction: Football's Coming Home

On July 7, 2021, for the first time in their footballing history, England reached the final of the UEFA European Championships. Morale had lifted and sporting nationalism was at the social and political centre, with the idea that 'our boys' might bring it home this year. When England players took the knee before the start of each game in protest against racism, what had started as booing from various sections of England supporters was slowly overtaken by applause. Gareth Southgate and his team came to represent England's 'progressive patriotism', challenging 'what it means to be English' (Clavane & Long, 2020). On the eve of the final, the Queen wrote to Southgate and spoke of the 'spirit, commitment and pride' of the team.

Four days later Italy won the Euros, following a tense penalty shootout in which two players scored and three players missed. In an instant these three players – Marcus Rashford, Jadon Sancho and teenager Bukayo Saka – went from English to Black ('they're colour blind when you're winning, but can only see colour when you lose', Grant, 2021). Twitter removed 1,000 posts sharing hateful content, and the UK's Football Policing Unit received 600 reports of racist comments sent via social media to England's Black players. Of these, 207 were judged to be criminal and 11 arrests were made (National Police Chief's Council, 2021).

The stark contrast before and after the final betrayed the truth of the matter. To the Black England players, it said: '*We decide if (and when) you are English. You are not one of us. We win, but you lose*'. The power to assign (and withdraw) the status of 'English' remains in possession of those who are White. It speaks to 'whiteness as property' (Harris, 1993), the value that whiteness holds in relation to other races (Mensah & Jackson, 2018). The limited access to Englishness for Black footballers illustrates 'the fundamental precept of whiteness – its exclusivity' (Harris, 1993, p. 1789). In the context of the Euros, this created a separation not just in the loss of the final (e.g. 'well it took three ethnic players to f*** it up'; Metro, 2021), but also in the aftermath. Instead of grieving together – perhaps a true mark of sporting nationalism – it became 'them' who lost 'us' the game. This itself speaks to an entitlement found football fans (Međedović & Kovačević,

DOI: 10.4324/9781003253990-17

166 Jason Arday

2021), creating a sense of persecution which was also reinforced by the media (e.g. 'English football fans have suffered enough', Daily Mail, 2021). It also speaks to the objectification and dehumanisation of footballers and other athletes (Dwyer et al., 2021; Slater, 2020), who are seen as vehicles of entertainment for their fans.

Dehumanisation and Objectification in Football

Dehumanisation in sport tends to take the mechanistic form; that is to say, the likening of humans to machines (Slater, 2020). This happens frequently in the media, such as in an article in the Daily Mail referring to Sebastian Haller as a '£35-million rated Ajax goal machine' (2022), or another referring to Italy's Euros' team as 'engines' (2021). In doing so, even in seemingly 'positive' terms, it denies players their humanness and those attributes which characterise what it means to be human (Haslam & Loughnan, 2014).

Related to mechanistic dehumanisation is objectification. This is the process of reducing a person to the ways in which they can facilitate personal gain (Slater, 2020), or seen as a means to one's ends (Nussbaum, 1999). When a target is objectified, their personal attributes become peripheral while their usefulness becomes the focus (Wang & Krumhuber, 2017). This is why it is possible for a teenage Bukayo Saka to shoot a high-stakes penalty in front of 328 million people worldwide, and the focus for some to be on his output, not his bravery.

Dehumanisation and Objectification of Black Footballers

The centrality of whiteness means that it is considered the 'norm or standard for human' (Menakem, 2017, p. xix). As Menakem says, this positions people of colour as a 'deviation' from that norm; an actress becomes a *Black* actress, a footballer becomes a *Black* footballer and so on. In the context of racism, it is often animalistic, not just mechanistic, dehumanisation that occurs. UEFA has conducted several investigations of monkey chants being directed at Black footballers during Euros games, and former Italy striker Mario Balotelli had a banana thrown at him during a Euros game in 2012. When Marcus Rashford, Jadon Sancho and Bukayo Saka missed their penalties, one social media user put an orangutan emoji underneath Marcus Rashford's Instagram post, while one of the Facebook responses of an English football fan was a call to 'sack the three monkeys' (Metro, 2021).

As well as racialised notions of sub-humanness, Black footballers are also subjected to impositions of super-humanness. Many exist both within and beyond the pitch; for example, research suggests that White people have associated Black people as 'possessing supernatural, extrasensory and magical qualities' (Waytz et al., 2015, p. 358). There are also studies into racial bias, indicating that Black people are perceived to have thicker skin and be more impervious to pain (e.g. Hoffman et al., 2016). Often present in these themes is the hyperfocus on the Black body (e.g. Mills, 1997); that is to say, reducing Black excellence to physical

The Racialised Construction of Black Professional Footballers 167

attributes in favour of other qualities. The media has been instrumental in constructing narratives concerning Black professional footballers in Britain.

Dehumanisation and Objectification of Black Footballers through the Media

Understanding the way the media is positioned through the lens of race is important when we consider how footballers from this diaspora have been portrayed and how these narratives endure. A principal way in which the media interact with consumers is through direct address. In the sporting context, any meanings that the consumer constructs thus become likely affected by the choice of descriptors, metaphors and analogies utilised by analysts 'which constantly reproduces particular inflections and ascriptions about Black people which are digested and maintained by stakeholders at every level of the game' (Whannel, 1992).

The media often associates Black male and female athletes with natural athleticism and physicality (Carrington, 2001; Hylton, 2015). Such dominant discourses have always provided the subtext to Black footballers and how they have been viewed under the racialised British gaze. This was found to be the case within football commentary in a seminal study by RunRepeat and the Professional Footballers' Association (2019). They analysed 2,073 statements from commentators in 80 football matches across the 2019/20 season, which discussed 643 players of various races and skin tones. They found bias from commentators who praised players with lighter skin tones as being more intelligent, as being of higher quality and working harder than players with darker skin tones. On the other hand, players with darker skin tones were significantly more likely to be reduced to their 'form' and physical characteristics or athletic abilities than their lighter-skinned counterparts. For example, when talking about *power,* commentators were 6.59 times more likely to be talking about a player with darker skin tone, and when talking about *pace/speed,* they were 3.38 times more likely to be talking about a player with darker skin tone. When talking about *intelligence,* two-thirds (62.6%) of the praise was aimed at players with lighter skin tones and two-thirds (63.33%) of criticism was aimed at players with darker skin tones – consistent with other research in sport (Frisby, 2015; Hoffman et al., 2016). Comments around leadership and cognitive ability were referenced more frequently when talking about lighter-skinned players. Again, this is reflected in earlier research finding that white athletes are more often associated with technical prowess, dedication and intelligence. This has been solidified as the 'invisible norm' against which Black athletes are constructed as extraordinary 'natural' athletes (Bradbury, 2010; Dwyer et al., 2022; Hylton, 2009). Highlighting problematic nature of these portrayals, Rada and Wulfemeyer (2005) state that:

> Portraying African Americans/[Black people] as naturally athletic or endowed with God-given athleticism exacerbates the stereotype by creating the impression of a lazy athlete, one who does not have to work at his craft.

The written and televised sporting message, in this context the representation of both Black and White athletes, embodies and rationalises a value-laden structure where we frame 'ability' according to dominant white supremacist thinking. This has implications for the cultivation of nationalism and ethnocentrism, in addition to solidifying negative enduring discourses which rely on binary thinking associated with other discriminatory intersections: xenophobia and racism (Rose & Friedman, 1997). At a deeper level, according to Maguire (1993), mediated sport discourses serve to uphold systems of domination such as white supremacist thinking, as they 'continually make implicit and explicit statements' which sustain cultures of oppression firmly embedded in the political and lived experience. Such contexts are considered by Sabo and Jansen (1994) to have the capacity to mould and create the 'pictures in our heads' – and with all the resultant implications.

Audience interpretation and engagement with Black footballers are thus shaped by our societal and political conceptualisations of race and racism. Media presentations co-opt thinking in a myriad of ways, and in some ways continue to be designed to position social actors towards 'preferred' while 'othering' (Hall, 1980). These interpretations invariably happen at the expense of others. Hence, through their language, commentators, journalists and spectators 'frame' individuals, which, in turn, profoundly affects the football consumer's construction of Black footballers against a current of racialised societal norms. Indeed, in providing knowledge and constructing narrative information, media accounts of Black footballers 'give the football enthusiast the tools they need to sustain exclusionary and discriminatory cultural norms' (Rose & Friedman, 1997). Unspoken narratives such as 'brawn over brains' reinforce the ongoing dehumanisation of Black people in sport as well as stereotypes of the Black athlete. By focusing on strength, power, pace and other physical attributes, it facilitates the objectification of Black bodies as superhuman, fetishised (for example, in 2017 Romelu Lukaku had to ask Manchester United supporters to stop chanting a song claiming he had an oversized penis) and as instruments for entertainment. As Billy Hawkins writes in *The New Plantation*, 'did it put them at ease and make them feel comfortable seeing Black males in a prescribed role of using our physicality to amuse a White audience?' (2010, p. 6).

Football as the New Plantation

There are many writers and scholars who have spoken to the concept of Black people fulfilling roles of entertainment (i.e. music and sport) and servitude (i.e. health and social care). Menakem (2017, p. 28) writes that

the Black body was forced to serve white bodies. It was seen as a tool, to be purchased from slave traders...made to plant, weed, and harvest crops; pressed into service in support of white families' comfort; and used to build economy.

The Racialised Construction of Black Professional Footballers   169

Hawkins (2010) goes on to say that 'the Black body has been a valued commodity in generating revenue and wealth for the White establishment' (2010, p. 1). He locates this pattern not just in history (i.e. slavery) but also in the modern-day plantations such as football pitches and basketball courts. He positions Black male athletes' experiences within the broader historical and social context of exploitation, and how:

> athletic departments, like colonisers, prey on the athletic prowess of young Black males, recruit them from predominantly Black communities, exploit their athletic talents, and discard them once they are injured or their eligibility is exhausted.

This 'plantation model' is characterised by White-dominated leadership (i.e. club owners, football managers), and Black-dominated playing teams. Though this model refers to American football and basketball leagues, the English context is not wholly distinct. A recent report (Szymanski, 2022) found that nearly half (43%) of English Premier League footballers are Black, compared to just 4% holding managerial positions and 1.6% in executive, leadership and ownership positions. It is certainly consistent with the findings from RunReport (2019), where leadership and cognitive abilities were undervalued in darker-skinned footballers and power and pace were overvalued. It is also consistent with the research around objectification, which instrumentalises footballers' physical abilities over other human attributes and qualities.

Almost certainly this impacts on fan–player discourse. The anger and aggression towards football players by their fans, which has been linked to entitlement (Međedović & Kovačević, 2021), manifests as racism and dehumanisation in the context of Black footballers. Perhaps if the Black body is seen as property, as has been the case throughout history, then a loss or poor performance attributed to (a) Black footballer(s) might even be experienced as a form of insubordination. The rage and racism that is directed at Black players during and after matchdays might also answer a different but related question: 'why are football crowds so white?' (The Athletic, 2020). The answer is probably also in statistics that show that of 2,663 fixtures in English football there was a hate crime incident recorded in 287 matches; this translates to there being a one in ten chance of encountering marginalisation during the match-going experience (Home Office, 2020). As a Black man who has been to games and been on the receiving end of racial abuse and violence, I know my answer. It feels safer to stay at home than be in pubs or football grounds – especially if 'we' lose.

Responding to Racism in Football

The influence of Black professional footballers on the English game is a well-documented story, which has often been in opposition to a sport that has extolled the virtues of anti-racist endeavour despite proclamations of being 'The People's

Game'. The contradiction to this mantra resides in the membership of the beautiful game and ultimately who has historically had access to this. While racism in football is far from stamped out, there are a number of initiatives that have attempted or are attempting to eliminate it.

'Kick It Out' has been the English game's answer to ensuring this membership is as inclusive as possible. However, the effectiveness of this intervention has been undermined by the lack of a sustained commitment by the FA to address this issue and invest in anti-racist education for all stakeholders in football as part of a wider suite of interventions. Despite this, the charity is maybe the most recognisable organisation committed to tackling racism in football in the world. Since its inception, Kick It Out has worked to promote awareness of the benefits of inclusion and diversity in football, as well as challenging all aspects of discrimination at all levels of the game. Other campaigns such as 'No Room for Racism' also aim to do so, through a range of interventions such as increasing research and statistics, providing easier and more accessible means to report hate crimes, diversifying and enhancing coaching and player pathways, supporting communities, and engaging in relevant training and education. The FA, the English Premier League, the English Football League, Premier League, UEFA and FIFA as organisational bodies all endorse race (and other) equity initiatives and campaigns. There have been a number of statements that have asserted their positions, such as those issued by the Football Association and UEFA after the Euro 2020 final:

> The FA strongly condemns all forms of discrimination and is appalled by the online racism that has been aimed at some of our England players on social media.
>
> – Football Association (2021)

> UEFA strongly condemns the disgusting racial abuse directed at several England players on social media after the EURO final, which has no place in football or society.
>
> – UEFA (2021)

While well meaning, statements that use language such as *'we will not accept'*, *'we will not tolerate'*, or *'we condemn'* are problematic when not accompanied by wider action. They can place distance between the institution and those people they are condemning, without recognising the power that it has to effect necessary change. A statement of unacceptance in many ways rejects the lived reality of Black footballers and Black football supporters whom, regardless of how unacceptable, intolerable or appalling it is, experience significant racism in the footballing sphere. This denial of the principle–implementation gap (Dixon et al., 2017), which refers to the gap between the principle and the implementation of racial equity, is often what can undermine meaningful action and change. The institutional power and privilege held within clubs, management and associations within football is not to be underestimated – or understated. As Rio Ferdinand stated, '...for too long now, European football authorities have not taken the problem of racism in the game seriously and refuse to acknowledge how widespread the problem is'.

Conclusion

There are many shades of racism in football, whether it be overt racism and dehumanisation, or more cover forms such as super-humanisation, fetishisation and objectification. The implications of both sub- and super-human biases are significant, across fans, football teams and franchises. Firstly, there is a reduction and/or removal of social protections for those who are targets of this bias, which increases the likelihood not only of mistreatment but also legitimisation of its continuation. Secondly, it maintains an already deeply unjust society by perpetuating disrespect and disregard for Black lives. The denial of subjectivity and identity through objectification of the Black body can be considered a reinforcement of white supremacy, and not wholly dissimilar to the plantation models described in American football (Hawkins, 2010). Added to this is the ongoing reinforcement of these biases in media and football commentary.

Football has always held a hallowed place within popular culture in regard to the British context in that it has provided one of the key vehicles for the ritual articulation of identity, intertwined within the politics of social stratification and class. This has historically also been categorised through regional and local pride, and national patriotism. Of course, the tribal nature of this participation facilitates an abandonment of behavioural standards that society requires for harmony and cohesion to flourish. Football in some way, shape or form has always been a means for expression particularly among enthusiasts of the beautiful game. This expression has simultaneously been inclusive, exclusive, xenophobic and racist; a rather accepted norm culturally within British football. Evidence of racism in football is hardly surprising given that football is a microcosm of society, as a subject of widespread concern it was the 1970s and 1980s that illuminated how deeply entrenched this became within the terraces. The increase in racist behaviour was in part due to increase in racist behaviour throughout society and attempts by extreme right-wing movements to use football as a basis for recruitment.

Though decades have passed, racism is still problematic in sport and in society. A radical acceptance of the state of racism in football provides an axis on which to pivot towards change. Only then can the chasm between ideology and reality meaningfully reduce, thus redefining how Black excellence, and especially Black athletes, are represented and treated within English football.

References

The Athletic (2020). Why are football crowds so white? Available at: https://theathletic.com/1876499/2020/06/28/football-crowds-supporters-diversity-fans-ethnicity/

Bradbury, S. (2010). From racial exclusion to new inclusions: Black and minority ethnic participation in football clubs in the East Midlands of England. *International Review for the Sociology of Sport*. https://journals.sagepub.com/doi/10.1177/1012690210371562

Carrington, B. (2001). Fear of a Black athlete: Masculinity, politics and the body. *New Formations*, (45), 25–29.

Clavane, A. & Long, J. (2020). Bigger than ourselves: The Southgate narrative and the search for a sense of common purpose. *Cultures, Commerce, Media, Politics*, 24(1), 56–73. https://doi.org/10.1080/17430437.2020.1810021

Dwyer, D. B., Di Domenico, I., & Young, C. M. (2022). Technical performance in elite women's Australian football–comparisons with men's football, identifying important performance characteristics and apparent trends. *International Journal of Performance Analysis in Sport*, 22(1), 29–37.

Daily Mail (2021). A look at both sides' tournament stats as they prepare for Sunday's final. Daily Mail Online. https://www.dailymail.co.uk/sport/football/article-9772079/Euro-2020-look-England-Italys-key-tournament-stats-ahead-Sundays-final-Wembley.html

Daily Mail (2022). Manchester United could target £35m-rated goal machine Sebastian Haller. Daily Mail Online. https://www.dailymail.co.uk/sport/football/article-10758257/Manchester-United-target-Ajaxs-35m-rated-goal-machine-Sebastian-Haller-summer.html

Dixon, J. Durrheim, K., & Thomae, M. (2017). The principle-implementation gap in attitudes towards racial equality (and how to close it). *Advances in Political Psychology*, 38(S1) 91–126.

Dwyer, B., Larkin, B., & Goebert, C. (2021). Fantasy sports participation and the (de)humanisation of professional athletes. *Sport in Society*. https://doi.org/10.1080/17430437.2021.1900827

Frisby, C. M. (2015). Race and gender representations in sports. In M. L. Rios & E. Perry (Eds.), *Cross Cultural Journalism: Communicating Strategically about Diversity* (pp. 297–319). Routledge.

Grant, D. (2021). [Twitter]. 12th July 2021. Available at: https://twitter.com/dionnegrant/status/1414357994041659400

Hall, S. (1980) Cultural studies: Two paradigms. *Media, Culture & Society*, 2(1), 57–72.

Harris, C. I. (1993) Whiteness as property. *Harvard Law Review*, 106(8), 1707–1791.

Haslam, N., & Loughnan, S. (2014). Dehumanization and infrahumanization. *Annual Review of Psychology*, 65, 399–423.

Hawkins, B. (2010). *The New Plantation: Black Athletes, College Sports, and Predominantly White NCAA Institutions*. Palgrave MacMillan, USA.

Hoffman, K. M., Trawalter, S., Axt, J. R., & Oliver, M. N. (2016). Racial bias in pain assessment and treatment recommendations, and false beliefs about the biological differences between blacks and whites. *PNAS*, 113(16), 4296–4301.

Home Office (2020). Football-related arrests and banning order statistics: England & Wales, 2019/20. https://assets.publishing.service.gov.uk/government/uploads/system/uploads/attachment_data/file/920624/football-related-arrests-banning-orders-1920-hosb2720.pdf

Hylton, K. (2009). *Race and Sport: Critical Race Theory*. London and New York: Routledge.

Hylton, K. (2015). 'Race' Talk! Tensions and contradictions in sport and PE. *Physical Education and Sport Pedagogy*, 20(5), 503–516.

Maguire, J. (1993). Bodies, sportscultures and societies: A critical review of some theories in the sociology of the body. *International Review for the Sociology of Sport*. https://journals.sagepub.com/doi/10.1177/101269029302800103

The Racialised Construction of Black Professional Footballers   173

Metro (2021). England fan who racially abused black players after Euro 2020 final spared jail. Metro. https://metro.co.uk/2021/09/08/euro-2020-england-fan-who-racially-abused-black-players-spared-jail-15228527/

Međedović, J., & Kovačević, U. (2021). Sadism as a key dark trait in the link between football fandom and criminal attitudes. *Journal of Individual Differences*, 42(1), 9–18.

Menakem, R. (2017). *My Grandmother's Hands*. Penguin, UK.

Mensah, F., & Jackson, I. (2018). Whiteness as property in science teacher education. *Teachers College Record*. https://journals.sagepub.com/doi/10.1177/016146811812000108

Mills, C. W. (1997). *The Racial Contract*. Cornell University Press, USA.

National Police Chief's Council (2021). *Hate crime investigation following Euro 2020 final leads to 11 arrests*. NPCC. Available at: https://news.npcc.police.uk/releases/hate-crime-investigation-following-euro-2020-final-leads-to-11-arrests

Nussbaum, M. (1999). *Sex and Social Justice*. Oxford University Press, Oxford.

Rada, J. A., & Wulfemeyer, T. (2005). Colour-coded: Racial descriptors in television coverage of intercollegiate sports. *Journal of Broadcasting & Electronic Media*, 49(1), 65–85.

Rose, A., & Friedman, J. (1997). Television sports as masculine cult of distraction, In Baker, A., Boyd, T. (Eds.), *Out of Bounds: Sports, Media, and the Politics of Identity* (pp. 1–15). Bloomington: Indiana University Press.

RunRepeat & The Professional Footballers' Association (2019). *Racial bias in football commentary (study): The pace and power effect*. RunRepeat. https://runrepeat.com/uk/racial-bias-study-soccer

Sabo, D., & Jansen, S. C. (1994). Seen but not heard: Black men in sports media, In M. Messner & D. Sabo (Eds.), *Sex, Violence, and Power in Sports: Rethinking Masculinity* (pp. 150–160). Freedom, CA: Crossing Press.

Slater, M. J. (2020). *Coaches' dehumanisation in sport: Exploring antecedents and relationships with wellbeing*. Durham theses, Durham University. Available at Durham E-Theses Online: http://etheses.dur.ac.uk/13501/

Szymanski, S. (2022). *Soccernomics*. Available at: https://www.espn.co.uk/football/english-premier-league/story/4593700/les-ferdinand-forms-diversity-campaign-groupsays-fa-only-interested-in-tokenism

Wang, X., & Krumhuber, E. G. (2017). The love of money results in objectification. *British Journal of Social Psychology*, 56, 354–372.

Waytz, A., Hoffman, K. M., & Trawalter, S. (2015). A superhumanisation bias in Whites' perceptions of Blacks. *Social Psychological and Personality Science*, 6(3), 352–359.

Whannel, G. (1992). *Fields in vision: Television Sport and Cultural Transformation*. Routledge, London.

Chapter 13

Black Professional Football Players, Social Capital and Social Change

A Case Study of Marcus Rashford's Child Poverty Campaign

Keon Richardson

Introduction

Young Black British men – of both African and Caribbean heritage – have faced structural racism within criminal justice, education, employment and many other systems, precluding their prospects of achieving upward social mobility. Black male unemployment has remained double that of the White male population over the past two decades, standing at 10.4% for the former and 4.8% for the latter (House of Commons Library, 2021). Similar disparities are apparent in education attainment: 42% of Black Caribbean male students in London achieved 5 GCSEs A*–C, compared to 65% of their White male student counterparts (Greater London Authority, 2017). The disparities within these multi-tiered systems have provided greater financial rewards for young White men more than young Black men, who have been excluded from numerous career sectors, restricting their opportunities and confining them to the least important areas of the labour market (Cashmore, 2000). Resultingly, young Black men have been allowed to, predisposed to and even encouraged by the Black community, family members and the media to circumvent their way out of difficult socio-economic conditions through pursuing careers as sport athletes, entertainers or music artists (Brooke, 2019; Chaplin, 2019). A professional football career in England has been traditionally viewed by many young Black males from low socio-economic backgrounds as a legitimate means to confer upward social mobility (Richardson and Fletcher, 2018). This imagination of upward social mobility is compounded by media rhetoric which is inundated with headline stories of Black male players in Europe with lucrative sponsorship deals, huge salaries, ostentatious lifestyles, expensive cars, palatial homes and model girlfriends, all earned through meritocracy (Ungruhe and Esson, 2017). Outside of football, they seemed to have little going for them, having experienced fragile childhoods typically in impoverished community settings, often infested with crime, unemployment and other indictors of deprivation (Spaaij, 2012).

However, this 'dream of social mobility' is considered problematic for young Black males because the over-represented high-profile cases portraying upward

DOI: 10.4324/9781003253990-18

career paths often conceal far more common occurrences of unfulfilled dreams and promises of a professional football career. According to Calvin (2017), only 180 of the 1.5 million boys who play organised youth football in England at any one time will become a Premier League player, leaving a tiny success rate of 0.012%. Young people from lower socio-economic backgrounds, as Collins (2010) argues, tend to possess insufficient social capital, or the skills to acquire it, to progress through and compete within the football 'system'. This is corroborated by Agergaard and Sørensen's (2009) study of young Black and ethnically diverse men from deprived areas in Denmark, which concluded that upward social mobility through a professional football career was unlikely due to difficulty developing peer relationships with White teammates, coaches and leaders; Black and ethnically diverse players feeling a sense of non-belonging – outsiders in their new environment and network, and outsiders in their original network – and limited economic capital, meaning getting to and from training and matches becomes difficult, if not impossible.

Even if they make it as professional footballers, fewer Black players transition into senior authoritative position such as first-team managers, directors of football, chief executive officers and club owners after retiring (Cashmore and Cleland, 2011). According to Szymanski (2022), out of 326 senior and lesser coaching roles[1] at Premier League and Championship clubs in England during 2021, occupied by former professional players between 2004 and 2020, only 30 (9%) were occupied by Black players.

Findings from Bradbury's (2016) study on the progression of Black and minority ethnic footballers into professional football coaching found these players were constrained by 'racially closed' methods of coach recruitment often favouring White coaches drawn from within dominant social and cultural 'insider' networks. This involved an over-reliance on networks-based (rather than qualifications-based) methods of coach recruitment at professional clubs, premised on processes of personal recommendation, patronage and sponsored mobility. Consequently, a Black player's upward social mobility might be transitory and only last while their physical capital is deemed useful to specific football clubs (Bandyopadhyay, 2013).

While there is ample research on Black male footballers acquiring social capital, along with other forms of capital, to attain professional football status and upward social mobility (Richardson and Fletcher, 2018; Ungruhe and Agergaard, 2020), research appears to be limited in examining how Black Premier League players generate and mobilise social capital as professional footballers to create social change. Numerous sport content editors have highlighted the work of Black Premier League footballers – emanating from low socio-economic backgrounds – using their wealth and professional football status to tackle social issues. Recent examples include Raheem Sterling, who latterly developed a charitable foundation to improve social mobility among young people from deprived backgrounds in England and Jamaica (Flood, 2020). However, there remains a limited sociological examination of how Black Premier League players exchange and leverage capital to campaign for pertinent social issues. Through adopting Putnam's notions of social capital, this chapter analyses the effectiveness of England and Manchester United striker Marcus Rashford in tackling Britain's child food poverty crisis through his child food poverty campaign.

Capital – From Bourdieu to Putnam

A number of sociological theorists have discussed and expanded the notion of capital. There are several forms of capital that Marcus Rashford appears to possess, embody and exchange throughout several social spaces for his child food poverty campaign. These include the following: human capital, economic capital, cultural capital, physical capital, social capital, symbolic capital and linking capital.

Human capital originated as an economic conceptualisation of the competencies, knowledge and personality attributes – embodied by and inseparable from the individual – which produce economic value (Becker, 1964). Economic capital can be viewed as material assets which can be immediately and directly convertible into money and can be institutionalised in the form of property rights. Marcus Rashford has a large volume of economic capital as a Premier League professional footballer. With a net worth of £65 million, Rashford earns approximately £10.4 million yearly playing for Manchester United and £2 million from his five-year Nike contract (Kelly, 2020; Miller, 2016). Furthermore, he purchased five properties in 2020 estimated to be worth £2 million (Buckwell and Aitchison, 2020). Cultural capital refers to cultural goods, knowledge, skills, education, experience, style of language and other cultural advantages an individual possess which can be converted into economic capital and thereby confirm a higher status in society. Physical capital is viewed by Bourdieu as a subdivision of cultural capital. However, Shilling (1991) contended that 'the physical' was important to be viewed merely as a component of cultural capital. Shilling (1991, p. 564) defined physical capital as 'the social formation of bodies by individuals through sporting, leisure and other activities in ways which express a class location and which are accorded symbolic value'. Rashford's muscular physique, speed, shot power, dribbling, agility and ball-carrying skills can be viewed as physical capital which holds significant value among fans, young aspirant footballers and professional football clubs. Social capital describes an individual's social connections, group memberships and interactions with others and the shared values derived from these networks (Baker, 2000). Unlike human capital, which is embodied within individuals, social capital is embodied within relationships and networks with people, institutions or events (Danes et al., 2009). This form of capital identifies that it takes more than simply money to produce desired social change. At the surface level, social capital is a relatively straightforward notion regarding the social connectedness of individuals within a wider community, and as Nicholson and Hoye (2008, p. 3) contend, 'there is an inherent logic in the idea that the more connections individuals make within their communities the better off they will be emotionally, socially, physically and economically'.

A Case Study of Marcus Rashford's Child Poverty Campaign   177

Symbolic capital is based on capital movements (cultural, economic, social and other capital forms) through social space, which once perceived and recognised as legitimate, can be capitalised upon (Skeggs, 1997). The forms of capital described above can function as, and feed into, the volume of symbolic capital an individual possesses. Social capital, for example, always functions as symbolic capital, since it is 'governed by the logic of knowledge and acknowledgement' (Bourdieu, 1986, p. 257). Symbolic capital is predicated upon that which it is valued by others in a specific social field (Siisiainen, 2000). Although capital is earned on an individual basis, it can also be bestowed upon by someone without a purposeful effort being made to acquire it. The transmission of a family name, and implicitly a transmission of social capital, is a basic element in hereditary symbolic capital supporting this process (Bourdieu, 1998). Symbolic capital is 'rational' in that it can be freely converted into leveraging advantage within social and political spheres. This is a common occurrence within professional football where former players use their playing renown and coveted list of honours and awards as a form of symbolic capital not only to springboard into management (Morrow and Howieson, 2018), but also to enter politics and tackle social issues. Liberian football legend George Weah, for example, was able to leverage his revered playing career with AC Milan, Chelsea and AS Monaco (cultural capital), achievement of being the only African player to win the Ballon d'Or and FIFA's world player of the year (cultural capital), business degree from DeVry University (cultural capital) and personal experience of living in a slum within the Liberian capital of Monrovia (human capital) as symbolic capital which poor and young voters recognised and valued, leading to him winning Liberia's presidential election in 2017 (BBC, 2019).

Bourdieu envisioned a process wherein one form of capital can be transformed or converted into another. For example, economic capital can be converted into cultural capital, while cultural capital can be readily translated into social capital. Shilling (1991) suggested that physical capital can be converted into economic capital (in the form of money from professional football contracts), cultural capital (in the form of enhanced education) and social capital (in the form of social networks and connections through charities and sports organisations). For this study in particular, it is worth stressing that capital is not easily transferred from one social space to another; meaning that capital acquired prior to and during Rashford's professional football career is not necessarily recognised or appreciated outside of it, or other forms capital may be more of recognised as more or less valuable than others.

Although Bourdieu identified social capital as a primary asset for privileged groups in society to maintain their superiority, a notable flaw in his conceptualisation is fully recognising the importance of social capital for individuals from low socio-economic backgrounds (Field, 2008). This chapter undertakes Putnam's (2009, p. 9) view of social capital, which focuses on the value of social networks both individually and collectively: 'social networks have value... [social capital refers to] connections among individuals – social networks and the norms of reciprocity and trustworthiness that arise from them'. Putnam's definition of social capital aptly fits into the framework of this chapter, given that it places an important emphasis on civic engagement, association and volunteering as they bolster the efficiency of communities and enable them to be more effective in the pursuit of collective interests.

Putnam distinguished two primary forms of social capital: bonding and bridging. Bonding capital refers to maintaining pre-established social ties with people sharing similar backgrounds, interests and values to oneself, which tend to corelate with horizontal relationships referred to above. Putnam (2000, p. 23) advocates for bonding capital as the 'sociological superglue' that holds communities together. This type of social capital is typically associated with positively perceived outcomes, such as educational attainment and reduced costs of job searches (Field, 2008). However, Putman issues a caveat of bonding capital possessing a 'dark side' which can lead to inward looking, reinforced exclusive identities and homogenous groups. This not only contributes to the exclusion of 'outsiders' but may also hinder the development of individuals within that group and stifle their own social mobility (Portes, 1998). Bridging capital, on the other hand, has the potential to create social change, as the process involves an individual connecting with different people that they have 'weak ties' with. This form of social capital is usually associated with resources that help individuals to acquire broader identities and reciprocity (Putnam, 2000). Putnam (2000) appears to place a higher value bridging capital than bonding capital; bonding capital is good for 'getting by', whereas bridging capital is essential for 'getting ahead'. As Putnam (2000, p. 22) posits, bridging networks with loose ties are 'better for linkage to external assets and for information diffusion', such as better jobs, career advancement and resources that are not generally available by the more exclusive and resource-poor networks of bonding social capital. Woolcock (2001) extends Putnam's work through the idea of linking capital, which involves individuals strengthening ties with representatives of institutionalised networks of power and authority to accumulate a greater range of resources than the ones available within their community. This form of capital is concerned with vertical connections between the various levels in the social stratification. Therefore, linking capital is important to negotiate social change as it can perform a profound role in the exchange of power, wealth and status between socioeconomic groups (Portes and Landolt, 2000). This is extrapolated in the analysis to follow.

Bonding Social Capital with FareShare

Perhaps cognisant that the physical capital which facilities entry and progression into professional football holds little to no relevance to institutional agents (e.g. charities and British government) within child poverty, Marcus Rashford generated other forms of capital to gain entry to this space – specifically bonding social capital. During the UK's first coronavirus lockdown in March 2020, and in response to imminent school closures, he partnered with food poverty charity FareShare (2020) as an ambassador to provide food security for vulnerable children, families and individuals at risk of hunger, with the safety net of free school meals and

A Case Study of Marcus Rashford's Child Poverty Campaign 179

breakfast clubs removed. Establishing strong bonding relationships with a charity aligned with his objective not only enabled Rashford to gain entry into child poverty, but to also leverage his pre-existing human capital to address child hunger:

> FareShare's work fighting hunger in the nation's most vulnerable communities, especially our ActiveAte campaign helping vulnerable children at risk of hunger over the summer holidays, is aligned to Marcus' personal mission. His own family relied on breakfast clubs, free school meals and at times, food banks. Raised by mum Melanie Maynard, who worked full time earning minimum wage, it was often not enough. As Marcus explains: "the system not built for families like mine to succeed, regardless of how hard my mum worked".
>
> (FareShare, 2020).

The statement above by FareShare is reflective of bonding social capital – that is, the formation of Rashford's strong social ties with charity employees and beneficiaries sharing very similar cultural and social backgrounds, in addition to personal experiences of and attitudes towards child poverty (Putnam, 2000). This is reinforced by the fact that Rashford himself received free school meals while growing up in a low-income household in Wythenshawe, Manchester. As a result, he was able to deploy his pre-existing human capital in the form of knowledge of the welfare system, alongside his trustworthiness, credibility and leadership skills to raise £20 million in economic capital for FareShare to distribute the food equivalent of 21 million meals for vulnerable children and families (Whitehead, 2021). Bonding capital is frequently criticised throughout literature for being inward facing and discouraging individuals from pursuing relationships with people from outside their immediate community. However, in Rashford's case, accumulating this form of capital was a valuable resource for introducing him to institutional agents working in child poverty, meeting families experiencing similar challenges he once faced and subsequently identifying a financial solution towards feeding these families throughout the school closure period.

Bridging Capital and Linking Capital through Social Media

According to Putnam (1995), bridging social capital refers to the process where an individual gets to know people who might be different to oneself (e.g. people belonging to another ethnic group or social class), with whom we share weak ties (e.g. an interest in football). Literature has highlighted young Black males' limited success in bridging social capital to achieve professional football status or social integration due to insufficient forms of capital and dependency on institutional agents (Agergaard and Sørensen, 2009; Richardson and Fletcher, 2018). However, Rashford's symbolic capital in terms of celebrity status and playing renown as a current Manchester United and England striker provided him with significant influence to independently bridge social capital between FareShare and his fans through social media. Rashford donated his own money (economic capital) to FareShare and also called out to his global social network of fans on Facebook (8.7 million followers), Twitter (5.3 million followers) and Instagram (12.4 million followers) to also donate, leading to the total £20 million raised. This reiterates Putnam's thesis of bridging capital being critical for 'getting ahead'.

While Rashford raised significant levels of economic capital through bonding and bridging social capital, he needed to build connections with the British government to influence their policies on reducing child poverty. This point brings us to the idea of linking social capital. The concept of linking capital is a process involving an individual building vertical connections with people in dissimilar social stratifications to accumulate a greater range of resources than those available within their immediate community (Woolcock, 2001). A key function of linking capital, therefore, is the ability to leverage resources, information and ideas from formal institutions' relations and structures, (e.g. government, political regime and judiciary system) and apply them to other contexts. On June 15, 2020, Rashford wrote an open letter to the British Members of Parliament (MPs), appealing they reconsider the government's decision to stop free school meal vouchers over the school holidays; an excellent example of linking capital, according to Woolcock. Following the government's refusal of the appeal, Rashford leveraged his power within the social space of the internet by creating the #MakeTheUTurn campaign and asking his fans online to repost his open letter across various social media platforms and tag their local MPs. With the mounting pressure of approximately 700,000 social media engagements from schools, celebrities, campaigners, unions and Rashford's fans, Boris Johnson performed the U-turn on and created a 'COVID summer food fund' of £120 million to extend free school meals over the summer for 1.3 million children (Syal et al., 2020).

Crucially, Rashford's eventual success in linking capital to influence policy change was made possible by connecting his large social network of fans on the internet with his appeal to the government, which is generally a form of social capital that charities and individuals addressing child poverty do not possess. It is apparent that an appropriate balance of all three forms of capital discussed – bonding, bridging and linking capital – were critical for Rashford to raise funds and influence policy change on extending free school vouchers. Bridging social capital and linking capital through the internet in particular were key in Rashford diffusing information to a wider network. However, it would be remiss to assume that these forms of capital solely lead to positive experiences or outcomes as Woolcock and Putnam hypothesise. This is discussed in the final section.

The 'dark side' of Bridging Capital and Linking Capital – UEFA Euro 2020 Final

Previous literature has highlighted the problematic nature of bonding capital, in that it is thought to promote inward looking and exclusive identities (Nicholson

A Case Study of Marcus Rashford's Child Poverty Campaign 181

and Hoye, 2008). Putnam himself describes this as the 'dark side' of bonding capital; in contrast, bridging capital is aligned with resources that help individuals acquire broader identities. While sport is praised as an arena to build bridging capital, numerous studies have highlighted negative encounters (e.g. discrimination and aggression) in bridging and linking capital between ethnically diverse groups and dominant social groups (Krouwel et al, 2006; Spaaij, 2011; Verhagen and Boonstra, 2014; Walseth, 2008). Within football, this is exemplified by black players being routinely subjected to racial abuse from spectators, overt and tacit discrimination based on racial stereotypes of abilities by white managers, and unfair and unequal recruitment practices in coaching and management (Maguire, 1988). Thus, bridging and linking capital within football can present a 'dark side', which exposes young Black players to racist abuse from individuals of different dominant social groups seeking to diminish their racial identity rather than broaden it.

For Rashford, bridging capital and linking capital both present a double-edged sword. While these forms of capital were effective in leveraging his social media platforms to build bridges and linkages between British MPs, football fans and vulnerable children, Rashford, alongside Jadon Sancho and Bukayo Sako, was racially abused online after missing penalties in England's defeat to Italy in the Euro 2020 final on July 11, 2021 (Morse, 2021). Additionally, Tory MP Natalie Elphicke mocked Rashford in a WhatsApp group chat with other MPs, claiming he was 'playing politics' instead of practising football after the penalty miss (Kaplan, 2021). Rashford's weak ties with fans who have supported his campaign seems to be a performative relationship dependent on the successful display of his physical capital, particularly as bridging capital is typically absent of emotional support (Granovetter, 1982). This also seems apparent through his efforts of linking social capital with MPs, with comments of Rashford 'playing politics' indicating the difference in institutional power and social stratification between the two entities.

Furthermore, the concurrent overrepresentation of black players' physical capital (in the form of speed and power) within the media and underrepresentation in senior authoritative positions reflects the assertation of Back et al. (2001, p. 5) that the 'assimilation of black people within the national imagination as sports heroes need in not any way be congruent with access to the centres of decision-making and institutional power'. Consequently, while Rashford's symbolic capital (i.e. playing renown, knowledge and experience of child poverty, and personal wealth) effectively raised funds and influenced MPs' decisions, it appears to only be recognised and commended by MPs when he performs well on the football pitch, given his inability to make policy decisions which could reduce child poverty.

Conclusion

This chapter has examined Marcus Rashford's acquisition of different forms of social capital for campaign to end child food poverty in Britain. Rashford's revered celebrity status as a professional England and Manchester United footballer

182 Keon Richardson

bestowed him with symbolic capital to bond, bridge and link social capital to reach organisations, fans and MPs through his large following on social media. This enabled him to raise £20 million for FareShare, revert the government's policy on cancelling free school meal vouchers over the holidays and draw worldwide support for his campaign. While his bridging and linking capital efforts appeared devoid of gatekeepers, his campaign was largely dependent on convincing British MPs to change their policies on child food poverty and the strengthening of Rashford's 'weak ties' with these MPs seemed to be based on support from his fans and his performance on the field.

However, the 'dark side' of Rashford's bridging and linking capital efforts included the racist abuse he received from missing the penalty in the Euro 2020 final, which suggests a rather performative relationship he has with the 'weak ties' he developed. Consequently, his ability to bridge and link social capital could be temporary and at its peak while his physical capital as a professional footballer is deemed useful serving for England and his respective (future) club. Specifically for the Black community, this could be detrimental to place professional athletes over intellectual role models as spokespersons for addressing social issues facing Black people, as athletes' capacity to generate and leverage social capital outside of their community tends to fluctuate and decrease nearer to their retirement.

From a theoretical standpoint, Putnam's (2000) social capital concept offered a critical lens into how Rashford's volunteering developed key social networks to serve disadvantaged groups through his food campaign. The distinction between bonding and bridging social capital allowed the chapter to analyse his horizontal and vertical relationships with a range of individuals, organisations and institutional agents. Putnam's idea of bridging capital, although, is limited in conceptualising how this form of social capital also has a 'dark side', which leads to negative encounters and racial tensions for Black and ethnically diverse players. Given the ongoing experiences of racism for Black and ethnically diverse players, this 'dark side' to their lived experiences in the public spotlight will thus require further theoretical and empirical analysis in future studies of this nature.

Note

1 Szymanski's (2022) report defined senior coaching roles as one of the following roles: manager, assistant manager, caretaker manager, loan player manager or academy manager. Lesser coaching was viewed as any role entailing the word 'coach'.

References

Agergaard, S. and Sørensen, J.K. (2009). The dream of social mobility: Ethnic minority players in Danish football clubs. *Soccer & Society*, 10(6), 766–780.

Back, L., Crabbe, T. and Solomos, J. (2001). *The changing face of football: Racism, identity and multiculture in the English game*. Oxford: Berg.

Baker, W.E. (2000). *Achieving success through Social Capital*. San Francisco: Jossey-Bass.

A Case Study of Marcus Rashford's Child Poverty Campaign   183

Bandyopadhyay, K (2013). *Why minorities play or don't play soccer: A global exploration.* London: Routledge.

BBC. (2019). *What is President Weah's Liberia scorecard one year on?* https://www.bbc.co.uk/news/world-africa-46947032 [Accessed 23 November 2021].

Becker, G.S. (1964). *Human capital: A theoretical and empirical analysis, with special reference to education.* New York: National Bureau of Economic Research.

Bourdieu, P. (1986). *Distinction: A social critique of the judgement of taste.* London: Routledge.

Bourdieu, P. (1991). *Language and symbolic power.* Cambridge: Polity Press.

Bourdieu, P. (1998). *Practical reason: On the theory of action.* Stanford: Stanford University Press.

Bradbury, S. (2016). The progression of black and minority ethnic footballers into coaching in professional football: A case study analysis of the COACH bursary programme. In: W. Allison, A. Abraham and A. Cole (Eds.), *Advances in coach education and development: From research to practice* (pp. 137–148). London: Routledge.

Brooke, M. (2019). *Case studies in sport Socialisation.* Champaign: Common Ground Research Networks.

Buckwell, A. and Aitchison, M. (2020). *What a result! Campaigning football star Marcus Rashford has bought five luxury homes worth more than £2 million.* https://www.dailymail.co.uk/news/article-8949391/Campaigning-football-star-Marcus Rashford-bought-five-luxury-homes-worth-2million.html [Accessed 24 November 2021].

Calvin, M. (2017). *No hunger in paradise: The players. The journey. The dream.* London: Penguin Random House UK.

Cashmore, E. (2000). *Making sense of sports.* 3rd ed. New York: Routledge.

Cashmore, E. and Cleland, J. (2011). Why aren't there more black football managers? *Ethnic and Racial Studies, 34*(9), 1594–1607.

Chaplin, K.S. (2019). Black men on the blacktop: Basketball and the politics of race. *Sociology of Sport Journal, 36*(4), 349–351.

Collins, M. (2010). From 'sport for good' to 'sport for sport's sake' – not a good move for sports development in England?. *International Journal of Sport Policy and Politics, 2*(3), 367–379.

Danes, S.M., Stafford, K., Haynes, G. and Amarapukar, S.S. (2009). Family capital of family firms: Bridging human, social, and financial capital. *Family Business Review, 22*(-3), 199–215.

FareShare (2020). *Marcus Rashford's work with FareShare.*

Field, J. (2008). *Social capital.* 2nd ed. London: Routledge.

Flood, G. (2020). *Raheem sterling: Man city and England star creating charitable foundation to help deprived youngsters.* https://www.standard.co.uk/sport/football/raheem-sterling-charitable-foundation-help-deprived-youngsters a4572878.html [Accessed 13 November 2021].

Greater London Authority (2017). *Annual London education report.* https://www.london.gov.uk/sites/default/files/final_epi_edits_design_final_gla_annual_report_2017_0.pdf [Accessed 10 November 2021].

Granovetter, M. (1982). Who gets ahead? The determinants of economic success in America. *Theory and Society, 11*(2), 257–262.

House of Commons Library. (2021). *Unemployment by ethnic background.* https://researchbriefings.files.parliament.uk/documents/SN06385/SN06385.pdf [Accessed 13 November 2021].

Kaplan, J. (2021). *MP apologises for saying Marcus Rashford should stop 'playing politics'*. https://www.gbnews.uk/news/mp-apologises-for-saying-marcus-rashford-should-stop-playing-politics/112181 [Accessed 13 November 2021].

Kelly, R. (2020). *What is Marcus Rashford's net worth and how much does the Man Utd star earn?* https://www.goal.com/en/news/what-is-marcus-rashfords-net-worth-and-how-much-does-the-man-utd- /rnkqxvcguk15lawosvtsacp6l#salary-contract-earning [Accessed 13 November 2021].

Krouwel, A., Boonstra, N., Duyvendak, J.W., and Veldboer, L. (2006). A good sport? Research into the capacity of recreational sport to integrate Dutch minorities. *International Review for the Sociology of Sport, 41*(2), 165–180.

Maguire, J.A. (1988). Race and position assignment in English soccer: A preliminary analysis of ethnicity and sport in Britain. *Sociology of Sport Journal, 5*(3), 257–269.

Miller, M. (2016). *Manchester United's Marcus Rashford gets huge new Nike deal after breakthrough season.* https://metro.co.uk/2016/07/10/manchester-uniteds-marcus-rashford-gets-huge-new-nike-deal-after-breakthrough-season-5997633/ [Accessed 13 November 2021].

Morrow, S. and Howieson, B. (2018). Learning to be a professional football manager: A Bourdieusian perspective. *Managing Sport and Leisure, 23*(1–2), 92–105.

Morse, B. (2021). *Racist abuse directed at England players after Euro 2020 final defeat is described as 'unforgivable' by manager Gareth Southgate.* https://edition.cnn.com/2021/07/12/football/england-racist-abuse-bukayo-saka-jadon sancho-marcus-rashford-euro-2020-final-spt-intl/index.html [Accessed 13 November 2021].

Nicholson, M. and Hoye, R. (2008). *Sport and social capital.* Oxon: Routledge.

Portes, A. (1998). Social capital: Its origins and applications in modern sociology. *Annual Review of Sociology, 24*(1), 1–24.

Portes, A. and Landolt, P. (2000). Social capital: Promise and pitfalls of its role in development. *Journal of Latin American Studies, 32*(02), 529–547.

Putnam, R.D. (2000). *Bowling alone. The collapse and revival of American community.* New York: Simon & Schuster.

Putnam, R.D. (1995). Bowling alone: America's declining social capital. *Journal of Democracy, 6*(1), 65–79.

Richardson, K. and Fletcher, T. (2018). Community sport development events, social capital and social mobility: A case study of Premier League Kicks and young black and minoritized ethnic males in England. *Soccer & Society, 21*(1), 79–95.

Shilling, C. (1991). Educating the body: Physical capital and the production of social inequalities. *Sociology, 25*(4), 653–672.

Siisiainen, M (2000). Social capital, power and the third sector. In M. Siisiainen, P. Kinnunen and E. Hietanen (Eds.), *The third sector in Finland* (pp. 3–25). Helsinki: STKL.

Skeggs, B. (1997). *Formations of class and gender.* London: Sage.

Spaaij, R. (2011). Beyond the playing field: Experiences of sport, social capital, and integration among Somalis in Australia. *Ethnic and Racial Studies, 35*(9), 1519–1538.

Spaaij, R. (2012). Building social and cultural capital among young people in disadvantaged communities: Lessons from a Brazilian sport-based intervention program. *Sport, Education and Society, 17*(1), 77–95.

Syal, R., Stewart, H., and Pidd, H. (2020). *Johnson makes U-turn on free school meals after Rashford campaign.* https://www.theguardian.com/politics/2020/jun/16/boris-johnson-faces-tory-rebellion-over-marcus-rashfords school-meals-call [Accessed 13 November 2021].

Szymanski, S. (2022). *Black representation in English professional football: A statistical analysis.*

Ungruhe, C. and Esson, J. (2017). A social negotiation of hope: Male West African youth, 'Waithood' and the pursuit of social becoming through football. *Boyhood Studies, 10*(1), 22–43.

Ungruhe, C. and Agergaard, S. (2020). Migrant athletes and the transformation of physical capital. Spatial and temporal dynamics in West African footballers' approaches to post-careers. *European Journal for Sport and Society, 18*(4), 1–17.

Verhagen, S. and Boonstra, N. (2014). Bridging social capital through sports: An explorative study on (improving) inter-ethnic contact at two soccer clubs in the Netherlands. *Journal of Social Intervention: Theory and Practice, 23*(4), 23–38.

Walseth, K. (2008). Bridging and bonding social capital in sport-experiences of young women with an immigrant background. *Sport, Education and Society, 13*(1), 1–17.

Whitehead, H. (2021). *Marcus Rashford tops Sunday times giving list after raising £20m to tackle food poverty.* https://www.civilsociety.co.uk/news/marcus-rashford-tops-sunday-times-giving-list.html [Accessed 23 November 2021].

Woolcock, M. (2001). The place of social capital in understanding social and economic outcomes. *Isuma the Canadian Journal of Policy Research, 2*, 1–17.

Chapter 14

'Pogba x Stormzy' and the Politics of Race and Representation

An Introduction to Stuart Hall and British Cultural Studies

Michael Hobson

Introduction

In August 2016, two things happened which served as the basis for this chapter. Firstly, French central midfielder Paul Pogba rejoined Manchester United Football Club in a world-record fee of £89m, generating a social media frenzy. Simultaneously, I started reading scholarship which applied Jamaican cultural theorist Stuart Hall's approach to decoding media representation in sport (e.g. Burdsey, 2016; Molnar and Kelly, 2013). Subsequently, this chapter synthesises the two and uses the example of the viral social media video which announced Pogba's transfer to Manchester United, featuring Pogba and British grime musician Stormzy, to explain Hall's[1] approach– a transfer labelled on Twitter by Musa Okwonga (2016a) as the 'blackest transfer ever'. In this chapter, I decode the media's representation of Pogba's Blackness and discuss the ideological meanings signified within the 'Pogba x Stormzy'[2] video. I consider affirmations of Black youth culture (Perera, 2018), commodified Blackness (Collins, 2006) and the racial politics of association football (King, 2004).

Hall's work provides a popular framework for analysing both representations of race in the media and media representation in sport. Within studies of sport and the media, his approach is applied to numerous topics such as women and femininity (Bruce, 2013), British-Pakistani boxer Amir Khan (Burdsey, 2007) and Polish nationalism in football (Jaskulowski and Majewski, 2016), to name but a few. However, it is important to note two things. Firstly, you will rarely find a subheading in a 'cultural studies' article dedicated to Hall's theories, as you do with other sociologists.[3] Procter (2004) explains this is partially due to the non-disciplinary nature of cultural studies which draws from diverse fields and academic traditions, and Hall's commitment to theorising and understanding cultural trends ('theory with a small t') as opposed to producing explanatory frameworks ('theory with a capital T'). Secondly, Hall's contribution to studying culture lasted from the 1950s through to his death in 2014. Consequently, there is not enough space in this chapter to provide a comprehensive overview of his theoretical positions.

DOI: 10.4324/9781003253990-19

An Introduction to Stuart Hall and British Cultural Studies 187

Therefore, I focus upon his approach to decoding the media, with some additional reference to his work on the media and racism.

Following Back's (2012) lead, this perspective analyses 'Pogba x Stormzy' as an important part of popular culture where the ideological terrain of race is struggled over, as opposed to being an analysis of the culture of football. It builds upon scholarship which addresses representation of celebrity in football (Cashmore and Parker, 2003) and essentialised representation of Black male sport celebrity, largely from the NBA (Andrews, 1996; Andrews and Silk, 2010). It explores the multiple meanings attributed to the video produced by Adidas (sponsors of Manchester United, Pogba and Stormzy), their attempts to market Pogba as symbol of transatlantic Black culture (Gilroy, 1993) and potential significations produced by combining football and 'grime' music – a form of music associated with counterculture derived from Black working-class youths in deprived urban areas of the UK since the mid-2000s (Fatsis, 2019a). The arguments frame a battlefield between three[4] sets of competing meanings (Hall, 2006) – football embracing Black youth culture, commodification of essentialised Black masculinity and Pogba as a threat to the imagined white traditions of football. To begin, I utilise Hall's notion of conjunctural analysis (see Grossberg, 1986) to explain the social, cultural and political forces which frame the moment, before moving on to discuss how Hall's theorising of hegemony, signs and signification, and discourse can be utilised to decode Pogba's Blackness.

Exploring the Conjuncture – Football, Politics and Race Relations in August 2016

The conjuncture football operates in reflects the political, cultural and economic terrain wider society operates in (Back, 2012). Hall (2021) refers to conjunctural analysis as a form of clustering together similar phenomena occurring in a specific cultural field and analysing how overlapping patterns related to the economy, politics and culture. Consequently, conjunctural analysis examines cultural products as part of wider cultural production, not individual objects (Gilbert, 2019). Therefore, 'Pogba x Stormzy' needs to be read as product of this specific political and cultural moment, within the context of football, anti-racist activism, grime music and politics more broadly.

The significance of this transfer cannot be underestimated for a number of reasons. Firstly, for many the years approaching 2016 were heavily influenced by the 2008 global economic crisis which lead to austerity politics within the UK. Furthermore, 2016 signalled the rise of populist politics in the UK and globally, such as the 'Leave' result in the UK's referendum on European Union membership and Donald Trump being elected as President of the USA, results which significantly impacted Black populations both in Europe (Benson and Lewis, 2019) and the USA (Andrews, 2019). Additionally, the expansion of social media increased to two billion users worldwide (Pinkney and Robinson-Edwards, 2018), which influenced rises in populist politics, anti-racist resistance and grime music, albeit in visually and sonically different ways (Charles, 2018). Therefore, it is important to note at the moment Pogba signed for Manchester United, a number of anti-racist and anti-austerity movements in both sport and grime were yet to emerge; for example, Colin Kaepernick did not kneel in solidarity with the 'Black Lives Matter' movement until September 1, 2016, and the '#grime4Corbyn' movement[5] did not emerge until 2017. Therefore, the resistance of Black male footballers and musicians as activists, and attempts to capitalise upon this by major sports clothing brands, was not as prominent as in the early 2020s (Boykoff and Carrington, 2020).

Consequently, upon seeing 'Pogba x Stormzy', I asked 'is Pogba being positioned as "The Black Beckham?"', interpreting the video through historic racialised trends in sport. Cashmore and Parker's (2003) claim celebrities' value is judged by the economic and social value of their image. They consider Beckham's image in the late 1990s and early 2000s as a point of reference, citing his ability to transcend the cultural norms of football and alternative representation of masculinity (Cashmore and Parker, 2003). Therefore, I questioned whether Pogba was commodified in the same way. Furthermore, argue Black male celebrity basketball players who appear to connect authentically to Black youth cultures are heavily commodified by major sports brands – often depicting and marketing an essentialised 'hip-hop' image associated with negative connotations of hyper-sexuality, violence and materialism (Andrews and Silk, 2010; Leonard, 2009). Therefore, my initial reading of 'Pogba x Stormzy' considered the extent to which this of these trends converged, and Adidas attempted to marketise Pogba's image as an authentic face of transatlantic Black masculinity, in the way they previously capitalised upon Beckham's metrosexuality.

When discussing this conjuncture, Boakye (2017) considers 2016–2017 the peak of grime's commercial appeal, with Stormzy's first studio album 'Gang Signs & Prayer' reaching number one in the UK album charts in February 2017. However, this was a moment before other well-known convergences of grime and football. Thus, Okwonga (2016b) considers 'Pogba x Stormzy' one of the first high-profile positive affirmations of Black youth culture and football. When decoding it, it is important to recognise this was not a whimsical marketing video based upon grime's newfound commercial popularity, but the result of a relationship between Black musical cultures in the UK and football which had lasted decades (Burdsey and Doyle, 2021).

Attempts to blend Black music and football are present as early as 1990, with ex-England and Liverpool footballer John Barnes' famous rap verse in New Order's 'World in Motion'. Grime is inspired by multiple transatlantic black music traditions – Jamaican sound system, African diasporic music, UK garage, jungle and US hip-hop – synthesising elements of these sounds with lyrics which often depict struggles of life in deprived inner-cities in Britain (Elliot-Cooper, 2020; Perera, 2018). As a genre, it emerged from east London in the early-mid 2000s, with artists such as Wiley, Kano, Skepta and JME[6] making references to football in

An Introduction to Stuart Hall and British Cultural Studies   189

lyrics as far back as 2005. Grime songs also feature heavily on Sky One's popular Saturday morning show Soccer AM during the 'Showboat' segment, a montage of clips of footballers displaying flair and skill – a combination of symbols which potentially re-enforce the negative stereotype of Black footballers as individualistic flair players who lack work ethic and intelligence (see Campbell and Bebb, 2021). During the same period, the British media routinely portrayed Black youths as criminals, and depicted grime music, and tracksuits and trainers (the associated fashion), as symbolic of gang violence (Fatsis, 2019b) – thus presenting young Black males as dangerous 'folk-devils' who threatened the morals of British society (Hall et al., 2013; Williams, 2015). Subsequently, it is important to analyse 'Pogba x Stormzy' through the sociopolitical context of 2016, the historic commodification of sporting celebrity and the relationship between Black music and football in the media.

Hegemony and Representation

If conjunctural analysis interrogates the moment when media artefacts are produced and consumed, then central to decoding media representation is understanding its power relations. Hall (1992) was concerned with understanding the hegemonic impact of media artefacts and which meanings had the most influence in society. Consequently, he proposed all media images contained multiple meanings and interpretations with varying degrees of influence over individuals' ideological beliefs. Hall built upon Gramsci's use of hegemony, explaining while multiple interpretations are awarded to media representations, ideologies become hegemonic when they exert dominance and influence over other meanings, and generate cultural domination (Molnar and Kelly, 2013). Therefore, the ideologies and beliefs associated with 'Pogba x Stormzy' and representations of Black masculinity in football become a cultural battlefield, where competing ideologies vie for dominance and have implications upon who has power and status.

By utilising hegemony, Hall does not view meanings presented in the media as being fixed ideologies imposed upon the population by a ruling class, but a space where numerous meanings are contested (Molnar and Kelly, 2013). Hereby, when individuals attributed meaning to 'Pogba x Stormzy', power over reading of the image was shaped by exposure to various competing representations of Black males, football and grime. Consequently, Burdsey and Doyle (2021) view football as a cultural battlefield bringing symbols of music, football and blackness together to generate new readings of race and football, as opposed to providing an exclusive cultural hegemony. Therefore, the attitudes and beliefs individuals held about symbols within the video (e.g. Black males; Adidas tracksuits; Pogba's dancing, jewellery and sunglasses), and how this conflicted with historical transfer unveilings in football, would impact the dominant racialised attitudes towards this. Consequently, while King (2004) argues football was historically a White domain where Black culture was oppressed, the interpretations and reaction to 'Pogba x Stormzy' both re-enforce and contest this view in 2016 – with negative reactions and responses appearing to re-enforce the racialised media narrative of Black males (Van Sterkenburg, et al., 2019), while also becoming a site of resistance and affirmation of Blackness (Burdsey and Doyle, 2021). Hall and Jefferson (1993) further argue youth subcultures often play a central part in resisting hegemonic views in society, with music (in this instance, grime) and sport both acting as sites of resistance to marginalisation of Black males (Evans et al., 2020; Fatsis, 2019a). In particular, grime musicians' embodiment of a DIY ('do it yourself') attitude and entrepreneurial spirit is viewed as form of resistance to the marginalisation Black working-class males often experience in British society (Charles, 2018; Perera, 2018).

Finally, Hall argues hegemony subordinates individuals through coercion and consent from their consumption of media and goods, instead of by force. Furthermore, Gilbert (2019) argues since the 2010s dominant social media and technology platforms where they consume culture, such as YouTube, Facebook, Google and Amazon subordinate individuals. Therefore, while internet platforms provide a space for anti-racist narratives, they also create space for racist ideologies, simultaneously monetising both ideologies and re-enforcing their cultural influence.

Upon first viewing 'Pogba x Stormzy' on my Twitter feed, I considered whether this represented what Patricia Hill Collins (2006) refers to as 'commodified Blackness', where Adidas appropriated Black cultural signifiers (a corporation whose leadership board were predominantly White) for economic gains and influence over consumer markets: marketing symbols used in the media to stereotype Black males as flashy, sexually deviant criminals such as tracksuits, trainers and hats, and re-enforcing institutional racism (White, 2020). Historically, this phenomenon was common in American sport, especially basketball, where Black athletes were both marketed on their urban 'ghetto' appeal, and subsequently demonised by the media for demonstrating traits they were marketed on (Andrews and Silk, 2010; Leonard, 2009). Therefore, hegemony occurs by accommodating selective elements of subcultures but adapting these to the nature of the dominant culture. Within the case of 'commodified Blackness', these stereotypes are then essentialised: other Black males are then stigmatised and subjected to micro-aggressions or hostility, based upon prejudiced assumptions derived from media representations of a simplistic, stereotypical view of Black masculinity (White, 2020).

From this perspective, hegemony occurs through allowing a few individuals from a subordinate group to benefit both financially, and in terms of social status from these media images, in this case potentially Pogba and Stormzy.[7] This apparent social mobility re-enforces consent from the rest of the population to support these brands and media channels, despite potentially negatively impacting the wider population. Consequently, Hall (1997a) analyses the interwoven forces of identity, production, regulation, representation and consumption to understand who benefits economically and ideologically, by using the circuit of culture decode media production. However, he recognises each of these processes are contested and can appear as a cultural battlefield for more than one meaning

An Introduction to Stuart Hall and British Cultural Studies 191

or interpretation at any one time. Therefore, this makes it possible for 'Pogba x Stormzy' to simultaneously represent: (a) a perceived threat to white traditions and cultures in football; (b) Black working-class youth resistance to hegemonic whiteness; and (c) a commodified Blackness which essentialises and stereotypes Black males.

Signs and Semiotics: Decoding Black Masculinity in 'Pogba x Stormzy'

For Hall, while hegemony explains processes which shape ideologies in society and the battleground where cultural meanings are contested, signs and semiotics construct which representations and meanings are drawn. Hall leaned heavily on Saussure's interpretation of semiotics, viewing pictures, images and symbols as generating meanings to individuals the same way words do. From this perspective, all imagery produced by the media in relation to sport evokes meaning to the person viewing it through a reading of the visual (e.g. images) and auditory signifiers (e.g. commentary and music) (Kennedy and Hills, 2009). Therefore, signs are comprised of two parts: the 'signifier' and the 'signified'. As Procter (2004: 41) explains:

> The 'signifier' is the physical aspect of the sign, for example the group of letters 'c-h-a-i-r', the spoken word 'chair' or a one-dimensional 'iconic' representation of a chair as the letter 'h'. The 'signified' is the concept the signifier refers us to: a piece of furniture with four legs, a seat and a back.

Hall (1980) built upon Saussure, arguing although each sign denotes meaning, new meanings are generated by placing it next to another sign or symbol. Thus, in the instance of 'Pogba x Stormzy', previously when footballers signed for a club they were photographed holding or wearing the teams football shirt (the signifier of the club) on the pitch of their new club (the transfer to their new club was signified). Hence, through Adidas placing Pogba in a 49-second video, where Stormzy rapped wearing a Manchester United shirt and Pogba danced wearing Adidas clothing, while historic signifiers were present, these were placed next to signs signifying forms of music, dance and fashion associated with Black youth culture.

Kennedy and Hills (2009) explain that one important function of signs is demonstrating how they differ from other signs – in this instance, signifying difference to previous world-record transfers. Consequently, this difference became a point for conversation among fans and journalists. Furthermore, ideological messages were attached through the connotative and denotative meanings of symbols. One such example is evident in Daily Mail journalist Sam Morshead's account:

> Ever the showman, traditional shirt-and-scarf pictures weren't enough for the midfielder (Paul Pogba) after putting pen to paper on a five-year contract at

Old Trafford, as he teamed up with the grime artist – real name Michael Omari – for a 45-second clip which was posted on Twitter by sponsor Adidas.

(Mail Online, 9th August 2016)

Hall borrowed Roland Barthes' notions of denotative functions to refer to the direct meanings of signs (Molnar and Kelly, 2013). From the quote above, the denotative function informs the audience of Pogba's arrival, whereas the connotative functions link signs to ideological messages; phrases such as 'shirt-and-scarf' signify traditional transfer unveilings in professional football, conveying Pogba's unveiling to conflict with traditions of football transfers. When combined with the phrases 'ever the showman' and 'weren't enough', this potentially signifies racialised stereotypes of Black footballers as flashy and overly concerned with image[8] (Campbell and Bebb, 2020; King, 2004). This is a criticism Pogba has continually faced, with tabloid newspaper The Sun declaring he's had 'almost as many haircuts as David Beckham' exemplifying one such comment (Rollings and Fairbarn, 2016). Thus, when considering the connotative functions of Pogba's Blackness, subtle connections can be made to the racialised symbol of the 'Black folk-devil' who presents a risk to cultural norms of English football (Williams, 2015). When linking to hegemony, Hall argues the dominant cultural group in society oppress others by insidiously representing them ways which have negative connotations and produce myths. However, while the layering of the images in 'Pogba x Stormzy' potentially denote these meanings to Morshead and his readers, they denote different meanings to individuals with a different cultural reading of grime music and Adidas tracksuits. For example, Pinkney and Robinson-Edwards (2018) note grime lyrics often invoke different cultural meanings to Black working-class youths living in urban areas, who see a reflection of the daily challenges they may face, contrasting sections of the tabloid media who portray it as the cause of violence.

Representation, Discourse and Meaning – The 'Blackest Transfer Ever'

Hall suggests (1997a) representation has a dual meaning when decoding media artefacts. Firstly, he argued the media reconstruct or a re-present events in society. Therefore, the media re-frames people, cultures and events which are popular with their clientele, and either consciously or subconsciously reinforce or challenge ideological positions. Secondly, he argued representation occurs in a political sense; the media representation of a person can stand in for others who share an identity, in the same way a politician represents their constituency in parliament. With every media image being created purposefully, they then serve a denotative function – e.g. to inform people Pogba signed for Manchester United – and a connotative function – to commodify the appeal of grime and Black working-class subcultures and to market Pogba as a symbol of transatlantic Blackness. This can

An Introduction to Stuart Hall and British Cultural Studies   193

capitalise upon Pogba's Franco-African heritage, and the ease at which he can signify African-American images of 'the baller' (Leonard, 2009), as was evidenced of the multiple images of him playing basketball in Adidas-branded kit in Miami weeks before signing for Manchester United in August 2016. Subsequently, images of Pogba could represent cultural forms of Blackness recognisable to both European and American audiences.

While in this piece I consider a single image, Hall argued the importance of analysing images' relations to others, and exploring the 'discourse' or language used to discuss a phenomena or moment in history. Hall utilised Foucault's understanding of discourse to explain how bodies of representation (e.g. video, photographs, newspaper articles, political speeches, social media posts) depict a particular moment in time. His concern was why some perspectives become authoritative and viewed as legitimate, while others are excluded (Procter, 2004). Thus, 'Pogba x Stormzy' could be analysed with media representations of Pogba in 2016, and videos infusing grime and sport to market clothing, such as Adidas' 'Blah, Blah, Blah' and 'First Never Follow' campaigns,[9] and Nike's 'Nothing Beats a Londoner' campaign.[10] However, perspectives which seem authoritative on one media platform, such as social media, may differ significantly to sources, such as newspapers, as in the example provided from Morshead (2016). Discussions in newspapers, focused heavily upon the power of sponsors, social media and the global markets, placing emphasis on the global football economy. In contrast, personal social media either celebrated or lambasted the video for affirming Pogba's Blackness. Hall (1997a) argued a sense of the real-world meanings people attribute to the media artefacts derive from the collective vocabulary and discussions of these cultural images. In this instance, it is not always what is said, but the daily insidious actions associated with these meanings, which present them as true.

Finally, Hall notes, the meanings produced as part of any discourse are always contested; however, the extent they are taken-for-granted represents the degree they support current power structures. He further argues unless taken-for-granted meanings are challenged this always supports current power structures (Molnar and Kelly, 2013). Returning to 'Pogba x Stormzy', it potentially represents one of the first videos to positively affirm and celebrate Black youth culture in sport on such a scale (Okwonga, 2016), omitting some of the negative historical signifiers (Andrews and Silk, 2010). Thus, some argue by celebrating his Blackness in 2016, Adidas took formative steps towards a more critical stance and challenged the hegemonic culture of football media, even if insidious racial stereotyping were still present elsewhere. The video could be viewed as part of the process of brands representing Black sportsmen in increasingly positive and less stereotypical ways (along with resistance from Colin Kaepernick, the 'Black Lives Matter' movement, Lewis Hamilton and Raheem Sterling). These forms of resistance are not without conflict and counter-resistance, exemplified by the increasing prevalence of racial abuse of footballers on social media (Kilvington and Price, 2019), underlining Hall's point meanings are not fixed and in continual conflict.

Concluding Thoughts

Though not one fixed or definitive meaning can be awarded to 'Pogba x Stormzy', I have attempted to outline a basic overview of Hall's thinking through an illustrative application of his ideas, demonstrating how his concepts of conjunctural analysis, hegemony, signs and semiotics, and representation and discourse can be used to explore the contested meanings of media artefacts in football. Ultimately, however, I return to my earlier comment that Hall's work is vast and developed significantly throughout the duration of his scholarship, and recommend readers who intend to utilise his theorising to explore his ideas further, by reading substantive overviews of his ideas such as Procter (2004) and by engaging scholarship which utilises his ideas in the analysis of media in football and sport more broadly, such as Van Sterkenburg et al. (2010). Finally, while 'Pogba x Stormzy' cannot be defined by fixed meanings, I implore you to use this example to complicate your thinking about race in the sports media, and to think carefully about how you can resist taken-for-granted stereotypical representations and promote positive affirmations of Blackness in the domain of football, sport and society.

Notes

1 Hall was a founder and, later, Director of the Birmingham University Centre for Contemporary Cultural Studies (CCCS) which is viewed as a central in shaping the Cultural Studies approaches applied in scholarship today.
2 The original Pogba x Stormzy tweet can be found here: https://twitter.com/adidasfootball/status/762794596547952640
3 Van Sterkenburg et al. (2010) is one exception to this trend.
4 Although, in line with Hall's theorising, there are likely more than three sets of competing meanings.
5 The #grime4Corbyn movement was a hashtag used on content where numerous grime artists showed their support for socialist Labour Party candidate Jeremy Corbyn during 2017.
6 Wiley, Kano, Skepta, and JME are grime musicians considered to be important in the early evolution of the genre from the early to mid-2000s.
7 It should be noted that since 2016 Stormzy has regularly used his public profile to tackle racial inequalities through his music (see, for example, his performance at Glastonbury in 2019, and appearance in fellow UK rapper Dave's video for the single 'Black') and philanthropic work (such as providing scholarships for Black Students to attend Cambridge University, and supporting Black-owned businesses), whilst Pogba has spoken out about racial abuse on social media on numerous occasions.
8 Hall (1997b) specifically referred to the attempts to signify racial differences as a "floating signifier", where attempts to signify differences among races changed over time, with society using different symbols to denote difference, and highlighting the needs for a socio-cultural understanding of race.
9 Some of the 'First Never Followed' campaign featured musician Abra Cadabra and Tottenham midfielder Dele Alli in 2017.
10 Featuring musicians such as Giggs and J Hus in 2018.

References

Andrews, D. L. (1996). The fact (s) of Michael Jordan's blackness: Excavating a floating racial signifier. *Sociology of Sport Journal, 13*(2), 125–158.

Andrews, D. (2019) *Making sport great again: The uber-sport assemblage, neoliberalism, and the Trump conjuncture.* Basingstoke: Palgrave.

Andrews, D. L., & Silk, M. L. (2010). Basketball's ghettocentric logic. *American Behavioral Scientist, 53*(11), 1626–1644.

Back, L. (2012) Review: Race, sport and politics: The sporting black diaspora. *Ethnic and Racial Studies, 35*(11), 2032–2033.

Benson, M., & Lewis, C. (2019). Brexit, British people of colour in the EU-27 and everyday racism in Britain and Europe. *Ethnic and Racial Studies, 42*(13), 2211–2228.

Boakye, J. (2017). *Hold tight: (Black masculinity, millennials and the meaning of grime).* Influx Press.

Boykoff, J., & Carrington, B. (2020). Sporting dissent: Colin Kaepernick, NFL activism, and media framing contests. *International Review for the Sociology of Sport, 55*(7), 829–849.

Burdsey, D. (2007). Role with the punches: The construction and representation of Amir Khan as a role model for multiethnic Britain. *The Sociological Review, 55*(3), 611–631.

Burdsey, D. (2016). One guy named Mo: Race, nation and the London 2012 Olympic Games. *Sociology of Sport Journal, 33*(1), 14–25.

Burdsey, D., & Doyle, J. (2021). Football and the sounds of the Black Atlantic. *European Journal of Cultural Studies, 25*(1), https://doi.org/10.1177/13675494211015332.

Bruce, T. (2013). Reflections on communication and sport: On women and femininities. *Communication & Sport, 1*(1–2), 125–137.

Campbell, P. I., & Bebb, L. (2021). 'He is like a Gazelle (when he runs)' (re)constructing race and nation in match-day commentary at the men's 2018 FIFA World Cup. *Sport in Society, 25*(1), 144–162.

Cashmore, E., & Parker, A. (2003). One David Beckham? Celebrity, masculinity, and the soccerati. *Sociology of Sport Journal, 20*(3), 214–231.

Charles, M. (2018). Grime Labour. *Soundings, 68*(68), 40–52.

Collins, P. H. (2006). New commodities, new consumers: Selling Blackness in a global marketplace. *Ethnicities, 6*(3), 297–317.

Elliott-Cooper, A. (2020). Paris-Londres: Music Migrations (1962–1989). Palais de la Porte Doree, Paris. 6 euros. Until 5 January 2020. *The London Journal, 45*(3), 340–343.

Evans, A. B., Agergaard, S., Campbell, P. I., Hylton, K., & Lenneis, V. (2020). 'Black Lives Matter:' Sport, race and ethnicity in challenging times. *European Journal for Sport and Society, 17*(4), 289–300.

Fatsis, L. (2019a). Grime: Criminal subculture or public counterculture? A critical investigation into the criminalization of Black musical subcultures in the UK. *Crime, Media, Culture, 15*(3), 447–461.

Fatsis, L. (2019b). Policing the beats: The criminalisation of UK drill and grime music by the London Metropolitan Police. *The Sociological Review, 67*(6), 1300–1316.

Gilbert, J. (2019). This Conjuncture: For Stuart Hall. *New Formations, 96*(96–97), 5–37.

Gilroy, P. (1993). *The Black Atlantic: Modernity and double consciousness.* Verso.

Grossberg, L. (1986). On postmodernism and articulation: An interview with Stuart Hall. *Journal of Communication Inquiry, 10*(2), 45–60.

Jaskulowski, K., & Majewski, P. (2016). The UEFA European Football Championship 2012 and pop nationalism in Poland: Between confirmation and contestation. *Identities, 23*(5), 555–571.

196 Michael Hobson

Hall, S. (1980). Cultural studies: Two paradigms. *Media, Culture & Society*, 2(1), 57–72.

Hall, S. (1992). Cultural studies and its theoretical legacies. In L. Grossberg, C. Nelson & P. Triechler (eds.), *Cultural studies* (pp. 277–294). Routledge.

Hall, S. (Ed.). (1997a). *Representation: Cultural representations and signifying practices* (Vol. 2). Sage.

Hall, S. (2006). Black diaspora artists in Britain: Three 'Moments' in post-war history. *History Workshop Journal*, 61(1), 1–24.

Hall, S. (2021). Nineteen race, the floating signifier: What more is there to say about "Race"? [1997b]. In P. Gilroy & R. Gilroy Wilson (eds.) *Selected writings on race and difference* (pp. 359–373). Duke University Press.

Hall, S., & Jefferson, T. (Eds.). (1993). *Resistance through rituals: Youth subcultures in post-war Britain* (Vol. 7). Psychology Press.

Hall, S., Critcher, C., Jefferson, T., Clarke, J., & Roberts, B. (2013). *Policing the crisis: Mugging, the state and law and order*. Macmillan International Higher Education.

Kennedy, E., & Hills, L. (2009). *Sport, media and society*. Berg.

Kilvington, D., & Price, J. (2019). Tackling social media abuse? Critically assessing English football's response to online racism. *Communication & Sport*, 7(1), 64–79.

King, C. (2004). Race and cultural identity: Playing the race game inside football. *Leisure Studies*, 23(1), 19–30.

Leonard, D. J. (2009). It's gotta be the body: Race, commodity, and surveillance of contemporary Black athletes. In N. K. Denzin (ed.) *Studies in symbolic interaction* (pp. 165–190). Emerald Group Publishing Limited.

Molnar, G., & Kelly, J. (2013). *Sport, exercise and social theory: An introduction*. Routledge.

Morshead, S. (2016). *Paul Pogba and Stormzy collaborate again to celebrate Frenchman's £100m move to Manchester United*, Retrieved from https://www.dailymail.co.uk/sport/football/article-3731529/Paul-Pogba-Stormzy-collaborate-celebrate-100m-Manchester-United.html

Okwonga, M. @Okwonga, (2016/10/08) "Pogba x Stormzy: The blackest football transfer ever". My new post; if of interest, please share. http://okwonga.com/pogba-x-stormzy-the-blackest-football-transfer-ever/

Okwonga, M. (2016b). *Stormzy and Paul Pogba Remind us that not only do black lives matter, they're magnificent*, Retrieved from https://www.complex.com/sports/2016/08/pogba-x-stormzy-race-grime

Perera, J. (2018). The politics of generation grime. *Race & Class*, 60(2), 82–93.

Pinkney, C., & Robinson-Edwards, S. (2018). Gangs, music and the mediatisation of crime: Expressions, violations and validations. *Safer Communities*, 17(2), 103–118.

Procter, J. (2004). *Stuart hall*. Routledge.

Rollings, G., & Fairbarn, E. (2016), *POG IDOL Mixing sport, music and social media, Pogba's extraordinary signing for Manchester United is a real game-changer*, The Sun, https://www.thesun.co.uk/sport/1583190/mixing-sport-music-and-social-media-pogbas-extraordinary-signing-for-manchester-united-is-a-real-game-changer/

Van Sterkenburg, J., Knoppers, A., & De Leeuw, S. (2010). Race, ethnicity, and content analysis of the sports media: A critical reflection. *Media, Culture & Society*, 32(5), 819–839.

Van Sterkenburg, J., Peeters, R., & Van Amsterdam, N. (2019). Everyday racism and constructions of racial/ethnic difference in and through football talk. *European Journal of Cultural Studies*, 22(2), 195–212.

White, J. (2020). *Terraformed: Young Black lives in the inner city*. Repeater.

Williams, P. (2015). Criminalising the other: Challenging the race-gang nexus. *Race & Class*, 56(3), 18–35.

Index

amateurism 4, 26–27, 29–32, 34–35, 73, 97
antisemitism 3, 15, 18–19, 22

Bourdieu, Pierre 7, 10, 94–95, 106, 176–177

coach education 4–5, 32, 39–45, 47–48, 112, 142–143, 145
coaching 4–5, 7, 8–9, 28, 30–34, 38–48, 72–75, 77–78, 93–96, 98–101, 103–106, 112–113, 115–117, 119, 137–146
commercialisation 4, 75, 77, 119, 188
commodified Blackness 10, 186, 188, 190–191
critical feminism 8, 125–127, 129–130, 132–134
critical race theory 1, 9, 167, 172
cultural studies 186–187, 189–190, 194

de-schooling 6, 66, 68–70, 78
diabetes 6, 81–86
disciplinary power 4, 27–30, 34
discourse 8, 11, 17, 26, 28, 69, 94, 98, 124–125, 143, 155, 167–168, 169, 187, 193–194
discrimination 7, 16–17, 112–115, 119, 124, 126, 129, 170, 181
docility 4, 27–29, 33–34

ecological approach 4, 27, 29–32, 35, 139
Elias, Norbert 1, 3–4, 15–22
established-outsiders 3, 16–20, 22
ethnicity 1, 17

feminism 1, 8, 124–127, 129–130, 132–134, 137, 139–141, 143–146, 155
figurational sociology 3, 15–17, 22–23
football academies 4, 26–34, 139, 142, 152
Foucault, Michel 1, 4, 7, 27–29, 94, 193
futsal 7, 39, 93–94, 96–97, 99, 102–106

gender 1–2, 7–9, 111–115, 117–120, 124–130, 132–134, 137–139, 141–146, 150, 156–157
gender inequality 7–9, 16, 126–129, 132, 143
gender stereotypes 7–8, 111, 113–114, 117–120, 127, 130
Giddens, Anthony 7, 94

Hall, Stuart 1, 10–11, 186–187, 189–194
hegemonic masculinity theory 9, 137, 141–143, 145, 149, 153–155
hegemony 11, 154, 187, 189–192, 194
homophobia 9, 142, 149–158
homosexuality 149–153, 155–156

identity 1, 3–4, 5, 6, 15–22, 54, 56, 82–84, 86–89, 134, 171, 181, 190, 192
Illich, Ivan 1, 6, 66–72, 74, 76–78
inclusive masculinity theory 9, 146, 149, 155–158

Judaism 3–4, 15–16, 18–19, 21–22

Lacan, Jacques 1, 5–6, 56–58, 60–61
lack of fit model 7, 113–119

198 Index

Maffesoli, Michael 1, 6, 82–84, 91
masculinity 8–9, 89, 115, 117–118,
 137–146, 149–152, 153–158, 187–189
McDonaldisation 1, 4–5, 38–48
media 8, 9–10, 38, 40, 46, 124–134, 152,
 156–157, 166–168, 171, 174, 181,
 186–187, 189–194
melancholy 5, 53, 55–57, 59–62

national identity 5, 20, 54, 58
nationalism 55, 58–59, 61–62, 165,
 168, 186
neo-tribes 6, 82–84, 88–89
nostalgia 53–55, 63

pedagogy 8, 34, 48, 68, 94, 96–98, 101,
 103, 106, 137, 139–141, 144–145
personal pronoun model 3, 16, 19–22
Pogba, Paul 10–11, 186–194
practice architectures 1, 7, 93–95, 101,
 103–104
professionalism 4, 26–30, 32–33, 54,
 73–74, 77–78, 112, 119, 124, 142, 177
psychoanalytic theory 5–6, 53, 56, 61–62
pundits 8, 124–125, 127–134
Putnam, Robert 10, 175–176, 177–182

race 1, 11, 16–17, 154–155, 165, 167–168,
 170, 186–187, 189, 194

racism 1, 9–11, 15, 17, 54, 59, 152,
 165–166, 168–171, 174, 181–182,
 187–188, 190
Rashford, Marcus 9–10, 165–166, 176–182
referees 7, 111–120
religion 3, 15–17, 21–22, 152
Ritzer, George 1, 4–5, 39–48, 50

Salisbury Rovers FC 6, 74–77, 79
semiotics 11, 191, 194
sexism 8, 112, 114, 116–118, 124,
 127–130, 132–134, 142, 154
sexuality 1, 141, 143, 149–156, 188
social activism 10, 11, 67, 187–188
social capital 10, 175–182
social media 8, 10, 32, 53, 84, 88–89, 125,
 127–129, 132–134, 153, 158, 165–166,
 170, 180–182, 186–187, 190, 193–194
sponsorship 119, 174–175, 187, 192–193
Starbuckisation 5, 48
stigma 6, 33, 81, 83–89, 151, 156, 190
Stormzy 10–11, 186–194
surveillance 4, 27–28

Tottenham Hotspur FC 3–4, 15–16, 18–23

whiteness 154, 165–166, 191

Žižek, Slavoj 1, 5–6, 56–59, 60–63